Kendall Hunt
publishing company

PROBLEM SOLVING
WITH
PYTHON

MARGARET BURKE

Community College of Rhode Island

www.kendallhunt.com
Send all inquiries to:
4050 Westmark Drive
Dubuque, IA 52004-1840

Contents

Acknowledgments

Thank you to the team at Kendall Hunt and specifically Brian Rowe and Rachel Guhin for this opportunity and for your frequent help and support. Thank you to my husband, James Burke, my daughters, Katherine and Maitland Burke, and my colleague Karen Allen for reading and offering constructive suggestions on how to improve portions of my initial draft. Thank you to Kevin Bryan at the University of Rhode Island for being kind enough to read and advise on the security-conscious programming chapter, and to Lisa DiPippo, Stevenson Wachira, and Bortie Teh for their suggestions.

Thank you to the faculty, colleagues, and friends who have generously shared their knowledge and contributed to my understanding of computer science and the teaching and learning of computer science. I would like to specifically thank my colleagues Mike Kelly, Kay Johnson, Tony Basilico, Jeanne Mullaney, and Donna Scattone; my professors and mentors Richard Upchurch, Kay G. Schulze, Jan Bergandy, Adam Hausknecht, Robert McCabe, Gerri August, and Adam Roth; and my friends Tom Bednarz, Rui Campos, Jim Correia, Stephen Hegedus, Kerri Hicks, Mike LeRoux, Chandra Hawley Orrill, Rich Siegel, Sandra Luzzi Sneesby, and Dennis Wilkinson for our conversations about computer science, mathematics, and education.

And finally, thank you to the people who have contributed to my love of knowledge and my joy in being an educator, and to the people who enrich my life in immeasurable ways through their love, friendship, and their unique talents, skills, and perspectives. Thank you to my parents and lifelong teachers and learners Greg and Brenda Stone, who bought encyclopedias instead of curtains when I was a child; to my dear sister Sarah Stubbs and her family Paul, Amanda, and Jeremy; to my extended families; and to my friends Bill and Sarah Bullard, Lisa Gelfand, Jim Glickman, Bob Kitchen, Julie Landry, Patti Maguire, and Brian Weissman. And again, thank you to my dearest James, Katherine, and Maitland. I would especially like to thank the students it has been my privilege to know and guide, who have shared their desire to learn, their struggles, their triumphs, and their passions. There would be no book without you.

## Chapter 1

Getting started with Python

1.1 Problem solving

During the Apollo 13 moon landing mission in April of 1970, an explosion in an oxygen tank required the crew to alter course and complete the journey in the lunar module, the craft that was designed to land on the moon. One of the life-threatening problems that arose was increasing carbon dioxide levels in the lunar module that was poisoning the astronauts, and only two accessible lithium hydroxide filters (good for 40 person-hours each) designed for the lunar module. National Aeronautics and Space Administration (NASA) engineers, within a day and a half, found a way to adapt the command module air filters to the lunar module environmental control system, using only expendable materials that could be found on board the spacecraft (Figure 1-1) (Jones & Glover, 1995).

Figure 1-1 Air filter adaptation aboard Apollo 13. Image courtesy of NASA, scan by John Fongheiser.

Many engineers cite this feat of problem-solving innovation as one of their inspirations to study engineering. It is also a problem that illustrates the components of real-world problem-solving.

Real-world problems are often problems that have not been solved before. They are poorly defined. There is usually more than one solution, each with different positive and negative effects that must be considered. Once a solution is chosen and implemented, figuring out whether it worked is sometimes a whole new problem!

In this book, you are going to solve computational problems, which are problems that can be solved by writing computer programs. Computers are ubiquitous in our lives, so knowing how to solve this class of problems means you will have the ability to impact a diverse range of fields, including social media, research, business, medical care, navigation, robotics, and cybersecurity, to list only a few. You might have your own goals which have motivated you to study computer programming.

Solving computational problems requires practicing the same set of problem-solving steps that we use to solve other kinds of problems:

- Defining the problem
- Identifying and clearly expressing solutions
- Evaluating and selecting among those solutions
- Implementing a solution
- Evaluating the result

It is not usually a linear process. In other words, you should not expect to proceed neatly from one step to the next. Sometimes you will revisit the problem-defining step during implementation and sometimes you will implement and evaluate small **prototypes**, or preliminary experimental pieces, of different solutions while you are defining the problem.

The goal of this book is to help you learn this process using the Python programming language. Solving computational problems can be enormously fun and rewarding! But you will make mistakes (generally a lot of them), and you might feel frustrated at times. That is a normal part of learning, so try not to feel discouraged when it happens. This book will help by offering strategies for when things go wrong.

1.2 Let's get started!

The best way to get good at programming is to write programs, so let's write a program!

To develop with Python, you will need to install the Python interpreter on your computer. This book uses the Python 3 programming language, which is a free development environment available at https://www.python.org/downloads. To install Python, visit the link and download and install the latest version of Python 3 that is compatible with your operating system. (You might notice there is another version of Python, called Python 2. It is different from Python 3. It will be much easier for you to learn Python if you install the same version that is used in this book.)

Your Python installation comes with a program called IDLE. IDLE is the development environment and interactive interpreter that is shown in examples in this book, and it is what you should run to

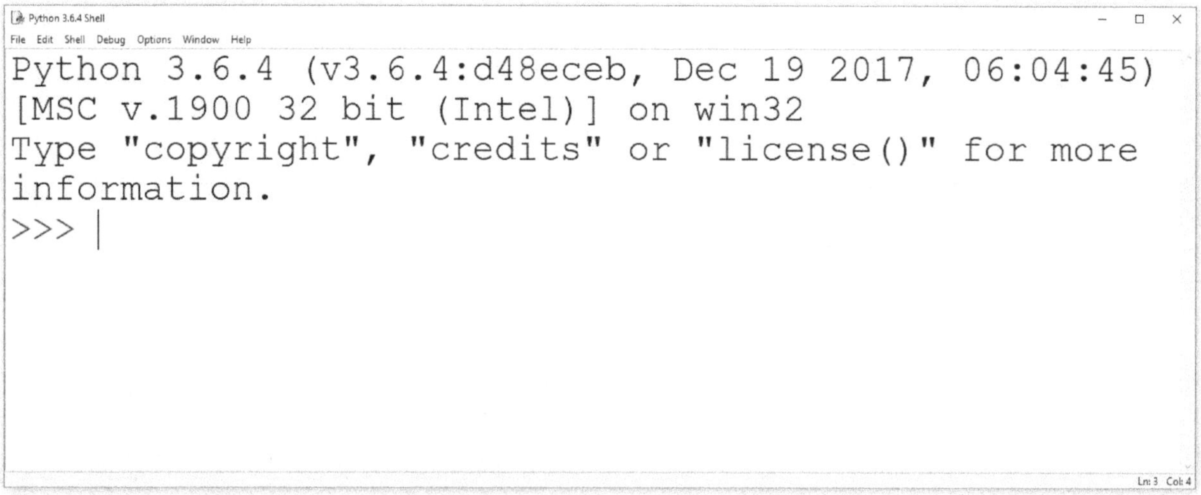
Python 3.6.4 Shell
File Edit Shell Debug Options Window Help
Python 3.6.4 (v3.6.4:d48eceb, Dec 19 2017, 06:04:45)
[MSC v.1900 32 bit (Intel)] on win32
Type "copyright", "credits" or "license()" for more
information.
>>>
Ln: 3 Col: 4

Figure 1-2 The IDLE window when it opens. Copyright © 2001-2018 Python Software Foundation; All Rights Reserved.

begin programming in Python. (There is another option called *Python (command line)* that does not have the same built-in support for programming that IDLE has.)

Figure 1-2 shows the IDLE interpreter running in the Windows operating system.

IDLE has some menus (*File, Edit, Shell, Debug, Options, Window, Help*) as well as some information about the version of Python that you are running. In this image, IDLE is running Python 3.6.4. (Make sure the message displayed in your IDLE window starts with a 3 [for Python 3] and not 2 [for Python 2].) Finally, there is a prompt, >>>, where you can type commands.

When you are reading this book, have Python open in front of you and try everything you see here. Do not take the book's word for anything—program it, change it, make it your own, break it, and have fun!

We will start by writing the canonical "Hello world!" program that many programmers write as their first program in a new language. Open IDLE and type the following and press enter (the prompt >>> will be displayed by IDLE—do not type the prompt):

```
>>> print("Hello, world!")
```

IDLE should respond with:

```
Hello, world!
```

Now you have written your first Python program!

Try this

❖ Press Alt-p (Windows) or Control-p (Mac). What happens? This is going to be very useful for experimenting in the IDLE console!
❖ What do you think each of the parts of the programming statement `print("Hello, world!")` means?
❖ What happens if you change the message that is within the quotes?
❖ What happens if you put a number (such as 5 or 3.14) inside the parentheses instead of a quoted phrase?

1.3   Meet the turtle

Python has a turtle module that allows you to draw shapes and pictures by moving a simulated turtle robot through two-dimensional space. The module is based on the Logo programming language developed by Wally Feurzeig and Seymour Papert in 1967 (Logo Foundation, 2015). The turtle module is a great way to start developing programs because the turtle's movement makes sense to us intuitively, and because the errors are often funny (and sometimes fun to look at), which can ease frustration a little bit! The turtle module is also a great way to experiment with some important programming concepts, such as flow of control.

To write a program in Python that is more than a single programming statement (as in our "Hello, world!" program, above), you will need to open an editing window in IDLE and type your program into the window.

In IDLE, choose *New File* from the *File* menu. An editing window will open. You will notice that this is different from the IDLE console window. It is called *Untitled*, rather than *Python 3.6.4 Shell*, (or whatever version of Python you have installed) and it does not have the prompt >>>. Save your program with the name `shapes_program.py` and select a directory that you will easily be able to find later. It is a good idea to make a directory for the programs you write for your programming class and save everything there.

You might be realizing now that Python has two modes: **interactive mode** and **script mode**. When you type in IDLE's console at the >>> prompt, you are interacting with Python in (you guessed it) interactive mode. It is interactive because Python immediately evaluates what you type. We will often refer to this as "the IDLE console" in this book.

When you open a new window, you are writing a script, or program. This is the way you will write most of your programs. (Remember the main difference between the two windows: when you are writing a script, you will not see the prompt >>>.) Scripts can be saved, run, edited, and run again. They can consist of many lines of code. In contrast, interactive mode is useful for testing out small bits of code—usually not more than a line or two.

Try to figure out what Listing 1.1 does:

```
1  import turtle
2  turtle.forward(100)
3  turtle.right(90)
4  turtle.forward(100)
5  turtle.right(90)
6  turtle.forward(100)
7  turtle.right(90)
8  turtle.forward(100)
9  turtle.circle(50)
```
Listing 1.1

Now type it in to your editing window, save it again, and run it (by choosing *Run Module* from the *Run* menu). Do not type the line numbers—those will be included with all program listings in this book to make it easier to talk about individual lines of code.

Were there commands that did not work exactly as you expected? What can you hypothesize about how the turtle works from watching this program execute, and what can you change in the program to challenge your hypotheses? (e.g., if you think that `turtle.forward(100)` will draw a 100-pixel line, then try using a smaller number, such as `25`, and see if the turtle draws a shorter line.) Try making some changes, such as adding, removing, or changing lines, to answer the following questions.

❖ How does the number in parentheses after the `forward` command affect what the turtle does?

❖ How does the number in parentheses after the `right` command affect what the turtle does?

❖ How does the number in parentheses after the `circle` command affect what the turtle does?

What sort of changes did you make? Did other questions come to mind as you played with it? Did you notice that each command seems to start where the last command left off? For example, the first `turtle.forward(100)` command results in Figure 1-3.

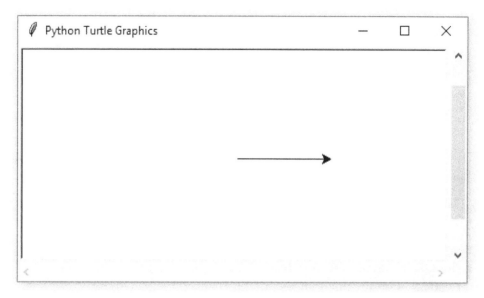

Figure 1-3 Python Turtle Graphics after the command turtle.forward(100) executes. Copyright © 2001-2018 Python Software Foundation; All Rights Reserved.

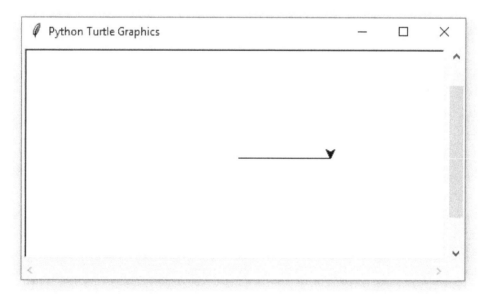

Figure 1-4 Python Turtle Graphics after moving forward 100 pixels and turning right 90 degrees. Copyright © 2001-2018 Python Software Foundation; All Rights Reserved.

This is a 100-pixel line, and the arrow at the end of the line is the turtle. So not only does the turtle draw a 100-pixel line, the turtle moves 100 pixels. When Python executes the next command, `turtle.right(90)`, the turtle remains in the same location—100 pixels from where it started—but it is now facing down, as if it turned 90 degrees to the right, as in Figure 1-4. (It did!)

The turtle is illustrating two important principles. The first is the **sequential flow of control** in this program. This means that the statements in the program execute from the top of the program file to the bottom of the file, in sequence. Figure 1-5 shows the next few steps of the program, in which the turtle moves forward another 100 pixels, turns right, and moves forward another 100 pixels, executed one at a time.

Figure 1-5   Three more steps in the square-drawing program. Copyright © 2001-2018 Python Software Foundation; All Rights Reserved

The second principle is the idea of **program state**. In this example, the program's state is the location of the turtle and the direction it is pointing (its heading). (The state also includes the fact that the turtle's pen is down, so it draws when it moves.) The turtle begins at coordinate (0, 0) on the screen, which is the middle of the Python Turtle Graphics window, facing to the right (0.0 degrees). Once we tell it to move `forward(100)`, its location changes to (100, 0), and its heading remains the same. When we tell it to turn `right(90)`, its heading changes to 270.0 degrees (picture a Cartesian coordinate system, as in Figure 1-6), and its location remains the same. Now when we tell it to move `forward(100)`, it moves from its current location (100, 0) in the direction it is currently facing (270), so it ends at (100, −100).

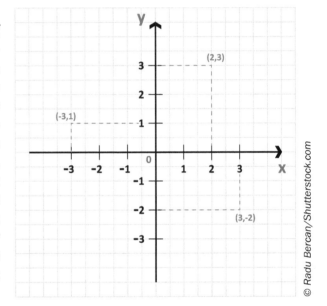

Figure 1-6   Cartesian coordinate system.

To experiment with flow of control and the turtle's state, try mixing up the order of the statements in your program. You will notice that the picture that the turtle draws is a different picture. What is the same is that the program is executing sequentially (from top to bottom in the file), and the turtle's state (its location and the direction it is pointing) is preserved from one statement to the next, so that you are always building on the last command.

Here are a few more commands that you can try with the turtle. You will replace the letters or words in parentheses with values:

❖ `turtle.left(`*angle*`)`
  Change the turtle's heading by turning left *angle* degrees. For example: `turtle.left(45)`.
❖ `turtle.penup()`
  Lift the pen up, so the turtle does not draw when it moves.
❖ `turtle.pendown()`
  Put the pen down, so the turtle draws when it moves.
❖ `turtle.setpos(`*x, y*`)`
  Move the turtle to (*x, y*). For example: `turtle.setpos(150, 150)`.
❖ `turtle.clear()`
  Clear the Python Turtle Graphics window.

There are many more commands for the turtle. You can find documentation for the turtle module here: https://docs.python.org/3.1/library/turtle.html

Try this

- ❖ Modify Listing 1.1 so the circle draws within the square.
- ❖ In Listing 1.1, the square draws on the right side of the window. Modify it so the square draws in the middle of the window.
- ❖ Draw a larger square, a smaller square, and a rectangle.
- ❖ Draw rectangles stacked on top of each other, like blocks.
- ❖ What else can you draw?

1.4   Designing solutions

An **algorithm** is a formal and specific computational description for solving a programming problem that is not written in a specific programming language. An algorithm describes how to solve a problem using the computational tools you will learn in this book. For example, if we were asked to use the turtle to draw a clock (without numbers), then we would need to describe steps that can be directly translated into code, perhaps starting with "without drawing, move the turtle to 50 pixels below the center of the clock, set the turtle's heading to 0, draw a circle of radius 100."

There are many ways to express a problem and a solution in natural language, and they usually include some ambiguity. In this example, the problem statement is very ambiguous. The algorithm started above assumes a circular-shaped 12-hour analog clock (perhaps with lines indicating 12, 3, 6, and 9), but that is not necessarily what the person asking for the program wants. There is no information about what size or color clock, where it should appear in the window, how long the lines are, and if all 12 hour lines or minute lines should also be shown. If we do not identify these assumptions and clarify the problem definition, we could program the wrong solution—a very costly mistake.

Recall the steps in solving a problem, from the first section:

- ❖ Define the problem
- ❖ Identify and clearly express solutions
- ❖ Evaluate and select among those solutions
- ❖ Implement a solution
- ❖ Evaluate the result

Before we can write an algorithm and then program that algorithm (implement a solution), we need to resolve as many ambiguities and assumptions in the problem description as possible. In this example, the way to do this is to ask questions about the problem statement until you have enough detail to begin. (We might ask questions related to the assumptions identified above, such as, do you mean a circular analog clock? What size? Where should it be drawn in the window? etc.)

Once you believe you understand the problem statement well enough to begin, you should think about different approaches to solving the problem. When drawing with the turtle, it is a good idea to use graph paper to plan out locations and headings to avoid time-consuming mistakes (see Figure 1-7).

When you are first learning to program, you may find it difficult to think of one solution, never mind several! It is worth spending time on this step, however. Think about the tools that you have learned and whether they apply to the problem you are solving. Take a moment and look over the list of turtle commands we learned and think about which ones might apply to this problem.

Moving the turtle is one example of a part of the problem that can be solved in more than one way. You can move the turtle to a location by setting its heading and using the `forward` command, but you can also move the turtle by using `setpos`.

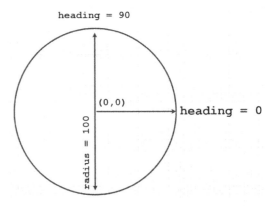

Figure 1-7 A graph paper drawing of the problem.

When you select a solution, you will consider the efficiency of your algorithm, the simplicity of your algorithm, and how easy it is to read and modify. Unless you are comparing sensible solutions with silly ones, there are probably no efficiency concerns with drawing the clock. It will be a constant number of drawing steps that is not outrageously large (unless you are thinking of a silly solution). So you should probably choose the solution that is simplest and that is easiest to read.

Once you have chosen a solution, you should write up the algorithm (again, use that graph paper!), and then program the solution. Finally, you can evaluate the result by comparing the clock drawn by the program with the problem statement. If the program does not draw the clock that was specified in the problem statement, then you will need to find where your algorithm went wrong. The following program is the beginning of one possible solution to the problem.

```
1   import turtle
2   turtle.penup()
3   turtle.setpos(0, -50)
4   turtle.pendown()
5   turtle.circle(100)
6   turtle.left(90)
7   turtle.forward(25)
8   turtle.penup()
9   turtle.forward(150)
10  turtle.pendown()
11  turtle.forward(25)
```
Listing 1.2

Try this

❖ Finish the program in Listing 1.2 so it draws the clock with lines at 3, 6, 9, and 12.
❖ Add an hour hand and minute hand to the clock.
❖ Implement the clock drawing program in a different way.

1.5   When things go wrong

Your program can produce the wrong results (or no results) in a frustratingly large variety of ways. Programmers generally classify these errors, or bugs, into three different categories:

* ❖ Syntax errors
* ❖ Run-time errors
* ❖ Semantic errors

Syntax errors occur when you have put the programming language tokens together in a way that Python does not understand. **Tokens** are the individual units of a program, such as values, punctuation, and commands, that can be combined in only a limited number of meaningful ways. Compilers and interpreters can only understand programming statements that are constructed in exactly the right way. For example, in our first program we had the statement:

```
>>> print("Hello, world!")
```

Python can understand this statement only if we have the word `print` followed by an open parenthesis `(`, followed by an argument to be printed (in this case, a phrase, which must be enclosed in quotes), followed by a close parenthesis `)`. Any other order of these tokens will result in a syntax error. For example:

```
>>> print)"Hello world!("
SyntaxError: invalid syntax
```

Unfortunately, as you can see, the error message is not always helpful. What is a little helpful is that Python will put a red highlight around the first token it did not understand. This tells you that the error occurred just at or before the highlighted token. (Never after.) Think of Python as stumbling on the incorrect syntax and falling where the red token is. When you are debugging, you must find where it stumbled. The bad news about syntax errors is that you will probably have a lot of them when you are first learning Python. The good news is that they will happen a lot less often the more you practice, and you will learn to fix them very quickly when you have them.

Run-time errors are errors that occur once your program starts executing, but that cause it to crash (abruptly stop executing) with an error message. We will see examples of run-time errors in Chapter 2.

Semantic errors occur when your program executes from beginning to end but does not produce the correct result. For example, if we intend to draw a square with the turtle, but instead we draw a crooked line, we would have a semantic error (or error in meaning). At some point in developing the algorithm, we made an incorrect assumption about the program's internal state and wrote a statement that proceeded from that incorrect assumption. For example, perhaps we assumed the turtle had a heading of 270.0, when it actually had a heading of 90.0. To debug a semantic error, you must find the incorrect assumption and change the code to match reality.

Try this

* ❖ The programmer who wrote Listing 1.1 intended to draw a square and circle. What assumptions does the programmer make about the state of the turtle at the beginning of the program?

❖ What is the state of the turtle (location, heading, pen status) after line 4 in Listing 1.1?

❖ Insert code after line 4 in Listing 1.1 to draw a line from (0, 0) to (100, 75).

❖ Select a line of code in your program and choose *Comment Out Region* from the *Format* menu. Run your program. What effect did that have? (You can select the line again and choose *Uncomment Region.*)

❖ Do you see any debugging value in being able to comment out code? (Could it help you find errors in your code?) How could it help?

1.6   Challenge accepted!

1. Write out the rules of tic-tac-toe (or another children's game that you have played). Once you have written out the rules, imagine that you are showing them to a very mischievous, clever, loophole-loving friend (who somehow does not know how to play tic-tac-toe). What assumptions did you make that your friend can exploit? Can you write a more complete set of rules?

2. Write an algorithm for selecting a square in which to place your marker in tic-tac-toe. (It does not have to be an algorithm for drawing with the turtle; simply an algorithm for a human to follow.)

3. If you were asked to draw a flower with the turtle, what questions would you ask to define the problem?

4. We wrote the "Hello, world!" program in the IDLE console (interactive mode). Create a script program (by choosing *New File* from the *File* menu) and write the "Hello, world!" program in a script.

5. Write a program (like "Hello, world!") to print a top five list, with each item on its own line. (Choose a topic you like.)

6. Write a program to draw a tic-tac-toe board with the turtle.

7. Write a program to draw a chessboard with the turtle. (A chessboard is an eight by eight grid of squares.) Find the repetition in the problem and in your solution. (We will learn how to use the repetition in Chapters 4 and 5 to make the code much shorter.)

8. Write a program to print the lyrics of a favorite song in Python using several print statements. Run your program. Now change the order of some of the print statements, predict the results, and run the program again. Was your prediction correct?

9. In the IDLE console, write the "Hello, world!" program, paying close attention to the syntax of the statement. Now write some variations of the program—some that are syntactically correct and some that are syntactically incorrect. Note the different responses that you get from IDLE for the variations. It will help you to debug in the future if you know what bugs and error messages go together. For example, you might try:

```
>>> print
>>> print(Hello, world!)
>>> print("Hello, wrlod!")
```

What else can you think of?

10. The `turtle.color()` command allows you to set the pen and fill color when you are drawing with the turtle. You can place a color name in quotes inside the parentheses. For example:

```
turtle.color("red")
```

The `turtle.begin_fill()` and `turtle.end_fill()` mark the beginning and ending, respectively, of a series of drawing commands that will be filled with the turtle's color.

You can further research the `turtle.color()` and fill commands here:

https://docs.python.org/3.6/library/turtle.html#turtle.color
https://docs.python.org/3.6/library/turtle.html#turtle.begin_fill

Use these commands to write a program to draw a filled square.

11. Explain each statement in Listing 1.2. In your explanation, describe the turtle's location (x, y), heading (degrees), and pen position (up or down), and then how the command alters the turtle's state (location, heading, and pen position) and what, if anything, is drawn to the turtle graphics window.

12. Ask a friend to write a turtle graphics program of five to 15 lines and figure out what it does without running it. (Hint: Use graph paper and the process described in question 11.)

13. Write a program that will draw a scene with the turtle. As the program is drawing, have it display messages to the console (using the `print` command) that describe what parts of the drawing it is currently working on. Do not write "draw a line," or "draw a square," but instead explain what part of the scene is being drawn. For example, "draw the bridge," or "draw the hero (no cape)."

Chapter 2

Input, processing, output programs

2.1   Your programming tool kit

For the moment, we are going to set aside the turtle and look at programs that interact with a user to obtain some input, process it, and produce output. The following Python program solves a specific computational problem—calculating the weight of some components that are being shipped. Here is the program:

```
1  """Compute the weight of some components."""

2  # Set weight and number of components.
3  weight = .245
4  num_components = 3

5  # Calculate the total weight.
6  total_weight = weight * num_components

7  # Display the total weight amount to the user.
8  print("Total weight of", num_components, "is", total_weight, ".")
```
Listing 2.1

When this program executes (by choosing *Run Module* from the *Run* menu), it produces this output:

```
Total weight of 3 is 0.735 .
```

If you think the output is ugly, it is! There are techniques for making the output look the way you want. We will cover those later in the chapter.

This program contains expressions, operators and operands, variables, literal values, print and assignment statements, and comments. These, plus your knowledge of sequential flow of control and program state, will become the first tools in your programming tool kit. We will go over each of these new tools in some detail in the following sections.

2.2   Literals and data types

Programming is a process of manipulating data using an algorithm to produce a result, so it is important, first, to understand what that data might be and how it is represented.

A **literal value** (or simply "literal") is a single syntactical element in your program that means literally what is typed. This might seem like a very strange sort of definition, but once we talk about variables, you will understand why we distinguish literals in this way. The literals we can see in Listing 2.1 are .245, 3, "Total weight of", "is", and "." If you open the IDLE interpreter and type each of these values in, one at a time, you will see that IDLE responds with the exact same value. Literal values are evaluated by Python as what is typed.

```
>>> .245
0.245
>>> "is"
'is'
```

Each of these literals has a **type**, which relates not only to the sort of data they are representing, but also to what can be done to them and the way in which Python represents them when it stores (or "remembers") them in memory. The three data types that we can see in our program are **float** (.245), **int** (3), and **string** ("is" and the other values enclosed in quotation marks).

The two numeric data types, int and float, are used to represent integer and real values, respectively. Integers are whole numbers (including zero and negative whole numbers), and real numbers are numbers that have a decimal part. They are called "float" because of the "floating" decimal point, as when you represent a number in scientific notation; 0.245, in scientific notation, would be represented as 2.45×10^{-1}. (This is similar to the way a floating-point value is represented by Python when Python stores and calculates with it.)

Python has a built-in function, or command, called type, that you can use to discover (or confirm) the type of a literal value.

```
>>> type(.245)
<class 'float'>
>>> type(2.45E-1)
<class 'float'>
>>> 2.45E-1
0.245
>>> type(3)
<class 'int'>
```

When we pass a number such as .245 to the type function, Python tells us it is of the class (or type) float, which is, of course, what we expect. The literal 3 is of the type int. In this console session, you can also see a way to write floating-point numbers using scientific notation. The E in the number 2.45E-1 stands in for "times ten raised to the," where −1 (the value after the E) is the exponent. Therefore, 2.45E-1 is a way to write 2.45×10^{-1}.

```
>>> type("is")
<class 'str'>
```

In this console session, Python tells us that the type of "is" is str, which is the type name for string data in Python (it is an abbreviation of the word string). A string is a sequence of characters, which includes letters, numbers, spaces, punctuation, and many other symbols. The entire string must be enclosed in quotes, so that Python knows where the string begins and ends.

```
>>> type('A string can be enclosed in single quotes')
<class 'str'>
>>> type("or double quotes")
<class 'str'>
>>> type("""or three double quotes""")
<class 'str'>
>>> type('''or three single quotes''')
<class 'str'>
>>> type("but you cannot mix the quotes''')

SyntaxError: EOL while scanning string literal
```

From the console session above, you can see that you can use single, double, three single, or three double quotes (with no space between them) to enclose a string literal, but you must start and finish your string with the same kind of quotes. If you want to include a single quote within a string, you can use double quotes to enclose your string. And, not surprisingly, if you want to include a double quote within a string, you can use single quotes to enclose your string. Since we rarely see three single or double quotes in our text, you can use these to safely enclose either single or double quotes. (There is a way to include a single quote in a single-quoted string, or a double quote in a double-quoted string, called an escape sequence, which we will cover later in the book.) Triple-quoted strings can be spread across many lines, but single and double-quoted strings cannot.

Try this

❖ Triple-quoted strings can span multiple lines (whereas strings enclosed in single or double quotes cannot). Try typing the following triple-quoted string in the IDLE console. What do you think the \n in Python's response means?

```
>>> '''Here
is a
triple quoted
string!'''
```

❖ Type a string enclosed in single or double quotes and include \n within the string. What do you expect Python's response to be? Is it what you expected? Now enclose that in a print statement (as in line 8 of Listing 2.1). What happens?

❖ What data type is each of the following literals? Answer without using IDLE, and then use the type function in the console to confirm your answers:

```
3.14159      "3.14159"              3
-3           0                      0.1
-0.1         "Hello, world!"
```

(Continued)

(Continued)

❖ Type each of the following into the console and note how IDLE color codes your tokens (syntactical elements) and how Python responds:

```
print("Hello world)
print('Top o' the morning, world!')
print(Hello world)
```

Even if you do not completely understand what is right and wrong in each of these lines of code, you can make note of Python's color-coding and response to help you learn correct syntax. What do you note about the color-coding and the responses? What syntax does it seem to relate to? How does correct syntax look different from incorrect syntax?

2.3   Variables

Variables allow us to ask Python to remember information while a program is running. A variable has a name, so if we need to use the information, we refer to the variable name. For input–processing–output programs (such as the weight calculating program in Listing 2.1), we use variables to store input values, temporary results, and output values. In Listing 2.1, there are three variables: `weight`, `num_components`, and `total_weight`.

We use the **assignment statement** to tell Python the names of variables and the values that should be associated with them. In Listing 2.1, there are assignment statements on lines 3, 4, and 6 of the program. We will look first at lines 3 and 4, which assign a literal to a variable.

```
3  weight = .245
4  num_components = 3
```

Here, first, the floating-point value `.245` is assigned to the variable named `weight`. Line 4 assigns the integer `3` to the variable name `num_components`. Here we are assigning a `float` and an `int` to two different variables, but we can also assign a string to a variable.

The **assignment operator**, `=`, looks like an equals sign, but it is not used like the equals sign in math. It is used to associate a value with a name, so Python will remember the value for later use. (The equals sign is the assignment operator in many programming languages, including C, Java, JavaScript, and C++.)

When we need to use these values, as in the calculation of the total weight on line 6, we refer to the variables by name, and Python substitutes the value that is associated with the variable where the variable appears in the expression. Notice how this differs from literals. When we ask Python to evaluate a literal, such as `.245`, Python responds with `.245`. This console session shows how Python evaluates a variable:

```
>>> num_components = 3
>>> num_components
3
```

Python does not evaluate `num_components` as `num_components`, it evaluates it as the value associated with `num_components`, which is 3.

Just as Python will tell us the type of a literal, it will also tell us the type of a variable, which is the type of the value associated with the variable. For example:

```
>>> student_age = 18
>>> type(student_age)
<class 'int'>
>>> name = "Luis"
>>> type(name)
<class 'str'>
>>> pi = 3.14159
>>> type(pi)
<class 'float'>
```

Try this

❖ Write an assignment statement assigning your age to the variable `my_age`. Have Python evaluate the variable. Pass the variable to the `type` function. What type is it?
❖ Write an assignment statement assigning your name to the variable `my_name`. Have Python evaluate the variable. Pass the variable to the `type` function. What type is it?

2.4   Variable names and keywords

Programmers choose the names for variables in their programs. In Listing 2.1, we chose the name `weight` for the weight of the individual components, and `total_weight` to store the total weight of all components.

There are some rules for what Python can and cannot understand as a **variable name**:

❖ Variable names can be as long as you need them to be.
❖ Variable names can be made up of letters, numbers, and the underscore (_), and nothing else. (e.g., no spaces.)
❖ Variable names cannot begin with a number.
❖ Variable names cannot be one of Python's keywords (there is a list below).
❖ Variable names are **case sensitive**, meaning that uppercase and lowercase letters are treated differently. For example, `highest_mpg` and `highest_MPG` are two different variable names.

If you break one of these rules, Python will respond with a syntax error. See if you can identify which rule is broken for each of these names:

```
>>> my name = "Haneen"
SyntaxError: invalid syntax
>>> big$money = 1000000000
SyntaxError: invalid syntax
>>> 20percent = .20
SyntaxError: invalid syntax
>>> user_level = 1
```

```
>>> user_Level
Traceback (most recent call last):
  File "<pyshell#23>", line 1, in <module>
    user_Level
NameError: name 'user_Level' is not defined
```

Did you find the broken rule in each example? The first two, my name and big$money, each have an illegal character in them. (Remember that a space is an illegal character.) 20percent is illegal because it begins with a number. user_level does not break any rules and is assigned the value 1. But user_Level, with an uppercase L, is a different variable. When we ask Python to evaluate user_Level, it responds that the variable is not defined—Python has never heard of it, because variable names in Python are case sensitive.

Using Python keywords as variable names is also illegal. Here is a list of Python keywords. You can find a current list in the Python documentation:

https://docs.python.org/3/reference/lexical_analysis.html#keywords

```
False    class      finally    is         return
None     continue   for        lambda     try
True     def        from       nonlocal   while
and      del        global     not        with
as       elif       if         or         yield
assert   else       import     pass
break    except     in         raise
```

Notice that if we try to use one of the keywords as a variable, not only does it result in a syntax error, but IDLE highlights the word for us in a new color. If you learn to pay attention to IDLE's syntax highlighting, it can prevent a lot of errors.

```
>>> lambda = 5
SyntaxError: invalid syntax
```

Besides these variable naming rules, there are also variable naming **conventions**. Conventions are practices that good programmers follow so that their code meets software engineering standards. When you follow variable naming conventions, your program will be more readable to experienced programmers, and you will not unintentionally say something untrue about your program with your variable names. (e.g., a hashtag is a convention used to identify a theme of content on social media. If a person used a hashtag in a different way, such as enclosing their entire post or a link within hashtags, it would be confusing.)

This book will (mostly) use the Python conventions that are found in the document PEP 8—Style Guide for Python Code, found here: https://www.python.org/dev/peps/pep-0008/ In a very few cases we will not use the conventions where they will make the code more difficult to read in a textbook format. You should follow the conventions in the Python style guide unless your professor or organization uses different conventions. The purpose of following the conventions is to produce code that is readable to the people who will be reading it.

Here are some Python variable naming conventions based on the style guide:

❖ Variable names use all lowercase letters and should never begin with an uppercase letter or an underscore.

❖ Variable names should be made up of complete words and not abbreviations, unless the abbreviations are commonly used and will not be ambiguous.
❖ In variable names that are made up of multiple words (like `total_weight`), the words should be separated by an underscore. (Do not use **camelCase** (connected words with each new word capitalized), which you may have seen used in other languages such as Java.)
❖ Variable names are meaningful to the human reader of the program and relate to the problem that is being solved.

It is very important that your variable names are meaningful. Compare line 6 from Listing 2.1 with a functionally equivalent line of code (6') that uses obscure variable names:

```
6   total_weight = weight * num_components
6'  a = b * c
```

Would you have any way of knowing that line 6' is computing the weight of a shipment of components, based on the variable names? No, because a, b, and c do not relate the code to the problem of computing a weight. Giving your variables meaningful names makes it much easier to understand what the code is doing. Code is read much more than it is written, so writing readable code is a standard in software engineering.

Try this

❖ Identify the variable names that follow Python's variable naming rules. Confirm your answers using the console:

```
name          5th_input      email@domain
dog age       dog_name       raise
pass          edition        num_pens
```

❖ Select a good variable name (one that follows both rules and conventions) to reference the following values. What data types would they be?
The temperature outside
The area of a floor (e.g., measured in square feet)
The number of people who can safely occupy a building
The gravity on Mars
The name of a dog
The number of planets

2.5   Constants

Literals should be used sparingly in programs. Consider the following situations:

❖ You are using a numeric literal, such as a light bulb wattage of 60, in calculations in a program.
❖ You are repeatedly using a literal, such as the menu item name "View source."
❖ You are using the same literal with more than one meaning in the program, such as 60 meaning both wattage and the number of minutes in an hour.

Because numeric literals are ambiguous, it is better to use a name in place of a number. Compare this calculation:

```
cost = 13 * 12 * 60 * 9.515
```

to this calculation:

```
cost = hours * num_bulbs * wattage * cost_cents
```

It is much clearer that an energy cost calculation is being performed in the second computation, because the quantities are all named.

If there is a quantity (or string) in your program that you will be using repeatedly and that will not change, then you should define it as a constant.

To define a constant in Python, you use an assignment statement. In Python, constants are no different from variables, except that the convention is to name them with all uppercase letters. Therefore, for the calculation above, if the wattage were going to remain constant in our program, we might declare:

```
WATTAGE = 60
```

If, in the future, a more energy-efficient bulb is being used, then you would not have to search for every instance of 60 in your program (and confirm it referred to wattage and not something else, like minutes) and change it to the new wattage—you would only have to change the value assigned to WATTAGE.

By convention, constants are placed at the top of the program, which makes them easy to find.

Constants improve program readability and make programs easier to modify and less prone to errors.

2.6   Evaluating expressions

To **evaluate an expression** means to resolve it to a value. We have seen that literals, such as the integer 20 and the string "Hello, world!" evaluate to literally what is typed, and variables evaluate to the value associated with the variable. These are simple expressions.

Expressions can be more complex; however, such as on line 6 of Listing 2.1:

```
6  total_weight = weight * num_components
```

What happens here? Remember that the assignment statement is not like the equals sign in math. We are not expressing an equality. Assignment statements work in a particular way: the expression on the right side of the assignment operator (weight * num_components) is evaluated (resolved to a value), and then that value is associated with the variable on the left (total_weight).

To evaluate the expression on the right, the values associated with weight and num_components are evaluated and the results are substituted in, giving us .245 * 3. Python computes that result, getting .735. That value is then associated, via the assignment operator, to the variable total_weight.

Remember that programs follow a sequential flow of control, with each step building on the last. If we assign one value to a variable, such as 5, and then in a later statement assign a new value to the variable, such as 6, then the variable will evaluate to the new value after that. For example, look at this console session:

```
>>> level = 5
>>> level
5
>>> level = level + 1
>>> level
6
>>> level = level + 1
>>> level
7
```

This is a very common statement in programming, called an increment. After the first assignment statement, the value 5 is associated with the variable `level`. In the next assignment statement, the right side is evaluated first. The variable `level` evaluates to 5, and the literal 1 evaluates to 1. They are then added together, so the expression evaluates to 6, and 6 is stored in the variable on the left, which happens to be `level`. The result is that we have added 1 to the variable `level`. We do it again in the next assignment statement, adding 1 to `level` on the right side. This time `level` has the value 6 (because each statement builds on the last, and the state of `level` is preserved from one statement to the next), so the expression evaluates to 7, and that is stored back in `level` (Figure 2-1).

```
>>> level = 5
>>> level
5             5 + 1
>>> level = level + 1
>>> level
6             6 + 1
>>> level = level + 1
>>> level
7
```

Figure 2-1   The variables on the right side are evaluated first.

Just as you can ask Python the type of a literal value or variable, which are simple expressions, you can ask Python the type of a more complex expression. The type of an expression is the type of the result after it is evaluated. Here are three expressions with three different types:

```
>>> type(5 * 20)
<class 'int'>
>>> type(1.4142 * 3)
<class 'float'>
>>> type("Hello " + "world!")
<class 'str'>
```

Python must be able to evaluate the type of an expression so that it can determine how to store the result. There will be more about storage of different data types in Chapter 3.

Try this

❖   Write an assignment statement assigning 3.14159 * 2 to the variable tau. Have Python evaluate the variable.

(Continued)

(Continued)

❖ Type in this console session:

```
>>> age = 5
>>> age
5
>>> age = age + 1
>>> age
6
>>> age = age + 1
>>> age
7
```

Predict what will happen if you write age = age + 1, then test in the console to confirm your prediction. Predict what will happen if you write age = age - 1 and confirm your prediction.

2.7   Operators and operands

Python understands many of the arithmetic operators you are familiar with from math, including + for addition, − for subtraction, and * for multiplication. (The last one might be a little unfamiliar. In most programming languages, you must use * for multiplication.) They work essentially as you would expect. In this console session, you can see addition and subtraction operations on both literals and variables:

```
>>> 10 + 5
15
>>> 10.0 + 5
15.0
>>> 10 - 5
5
>>> a = 10
>>> a * 5
50
```

There should not be anything in this console session that is too surprising, although you might have noticed that when both addition operands (the values being added) are integers, the result is an integer. When one (or both) operands are floats, the result is a float. This is so no information is lost in the computation.

Python also has an exponentiation operator, which is **. That is two asterisks, with no space between them. The operand to the left of ** is the base, and the operand to the right is the exponent. Therefore, 5 ** 2 is five squared (25), but 2 ** 5 is two raised to the fifth power (32). This console session illustrates the exponentiation operator being used with two variables and two literals:

```
>>> a = 4
>>> b = 3
```

```
>>> a ** 2 + b ** 2
25
```

Here Python evaluated a as 4 and b as 3 before each was squared (raised to the second power), giving 16 and 9, and the results added, giving the result 25.

Division in Python requires a little bit of explanation. There are three operations in Python (and other programing languages) related to division. They are integer or **flooring division**, floating-point division, and **modulo**.

If you want to perform the sort of division that you are accustomed to from math, and that you would compute on your calculator, then you want to perform a floating-point division. In Python 3.0, you simply use the / operator. While this may seem straightforward, it is not actually typical. In many languages, even Python 2.0, the division operator works differently.

An interesting example that illustrates the three different division operators is a school bus packing problem. Imagine that you have 300 students who will be going on a school trip, and you need to figure out how many school buses you will need. Each school bus can hold 72 students.

```
>>> students = 300
>>> buses = students / 72
>>> buses
4.166666666666667
```

A traditional floating-point division, computed above with the / operator, tells us we need 4.16 (repeating) buses. And we are clever enough to know that this means we will need five buses, because we cannot hire .16 (repeating) of a bus. But suppose we need more information, such as the number of full buses, and the number of students who will be on the partially filled fifth bus?

You would need to perform an integer or flooring division to find the number of full buses, and then a modulo, or mod, to learn the remainder (the number of students on the fifth bus).

The flooring division operation in Python uses the operator //. That is two division operators with no space between them. The mod operator is %. Many students have not seen mod before and mistakenly think that the % operator computes a percent. (It does not!) Fortunately, this operator is used in many programming languages, so it is worthwhile to commit this very useful operator to memory.

We will compute how many full buses we will have and find out how many students are left over:

```
>>> students = 300
>>> full_buses = students // 72
>>> students_left = students % 72
>>> full_buses
4
>>> students_left
12
```

Notice that when we use the mod operator, the operands are in the same order as for the flooring division. The mod operator is going to give us whatever is left from students after we have taken out as many *whole* 72's as we can.

A drawing such as Figure 2-2 can help us understand the operation:

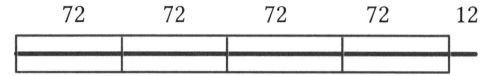

Figure 2-2   300 partitioned into four blocks of 72 with 12 left over.

This image shows a line of length 300 (representing our students), boxed up into four lines of length 72 (each box representing a full bus), with a line of length 12 left over. The result of 300 // 72 is 4, because the expression evaluates to the number of whole 72's that are in 300. The result of 300 % 72 is 12, because the expression evaluates to the number that is left of the 300 after we have taken out as many whole 72's as we can.

Modulus is a very useful operation, so it is worth practicing with it until it is as familiar as the other arithmetic operations that you have known since you were in elementary school. You will see additional uses for it in Chapters 3, 5, and 9.

Both flooring division and mod work in ways you might not expect when one or the other of the operands is negative. Flooring division always moves to the left on the number line (if you think of it as rounding, it always rounds down, to the smaller value). Once you know the flooring division result, multiply the flooring result by the divisor and add the mod result to yield the original dividend.

Try this

❖ Predict the results of these division operations and then test your answers in the Python console:

```
5 / 4          5 // 4          5 % 4
10 / 3         10 // 3         10 % 3
4 / 5          4 // 5          4 % 5
```

❖ What pattern do you notice when you mod sequential numbers by 2?

```
1 % 2          2 % 2          3 % 2
4 % 2          5 % 2          6 % 2
7 % 2          8 % 2          9 % 2
```

❖ Try using a number other than 2 as the divisor, such as 3, 4, or 5. What general patterns do you notice?

2.8   Order of operations

In school, you probably learned a mnemonic (a memory aid) to remember order of operations—PEMDAS—which stands for Parentheses, Exponentiation, Multiplication and Division, Addition and Subtraction. The order of operations is the order in which different arithmetic operations are evaluated in an expression with multiple operations.

In Python, this order of operations is also followed. It is important to follow a standardized order of operations so that, when we write expressions, they are evaluated in the way we expect. For example, in the expression 5 + 2 * 3, if addition had a higher precedence than multiplication (it does not!), then the addition would be evaluated first, giving us 7 * 3, and the result would be 21. But because multiplication has the higher precedence, the multiplication is carried out first, giving us 5 + 6, which is 11. Without an agreed-upon order of operations, we would not be able to write unambiguous expressions with multiple operations.

To review the order of operations, expressions enclosed in parentheses are evaluated first. This allows you to force parts of an expression to be evaluated earlier than others by enclosing those parts in parentheses.

Exponentiation is evaluated next. Remember that Python has an exponentiation operator, which is **.

After all parentheses and exponentiations are evaluated, multiplication, division, and modulus operations are evaluated from left to right in the expression. (This is where the mnemonic can sometimes confuse people. PEMDAS seems to imply that multiplication has a higher precedence than division, but it does not. Multiplication, division, and modulus have the same level of precedence.)

Finally, addition and subtraction have the same precedence, and are evaluated left to right in an expression. For now, they have the lowest precedence, but in Chapter 3 you will be introduced to operators with lower precedence.

We will look at one example, written with the Python symbols:

```
200 / 5 ** 2 * 4 + (20 - 15)
```

Before you look at the step-by-step evaluation below, determine the order in which the operations will take place. There is a division, an exponentiation, a multiplication, an addition, a subtraction, and parentheses. You can determine the order using PEMDAS and the position of the operators in the expression (for operators with the same level of precedence).

Of all the operators, the parentheses have the highest precedence, and the subtraction is within the parentheses. Therefore, that is computed first, giving us:

```
200 / 5 ** 2 * 4 + 5
```

Now we are left with division, exponentiation, multiplication, and addition. The highest precedence here? Exponentiation. After that is computed, we have:

```
200 / 25 * 4 + 5
```

This leaves division, multiplication, and addition. Because multiplication and division have the same level of precedence and the division occurs first in the expression, the division is computed first, giving us:

```
8.0 * 4 + 5
```

Now we have only multiplication and addition. Multiplication has a higher precedence; therefore, we have:

```
32.0 + 5
```

And finally, we perform the addition to achieve a result of 37.0.

One way you can communicate operator precedence in your code is to put white space around the lowest-priority operator. For example, instead of writing 5 + 2 * 3, write 5 + 2*3, with more white space around the + than the *. (Never use more than one space on each side of an operator, though.)

Try this

❖ Evaluate the following expressions, one step at a time, according to order of operations:

```
3**2 * 4**3
27 - 256 / 4**3
9 * (5 + 3)**2 - 144
21//2 + 21%2
```

2.9   Math functions and mathematical expressions in Python

Now that we have seen some familiar (and perhaps unfamiliar) arithmetic operations in Python and reviewed operator precedence, we will translate some mathematical formulae to Python.

In math, we can write expressions over other expressions, under radicals, and with superscripts—none of which we can do in Python. When writing a mathematical expression in Python, we are confined to what we can type in a straight line, using the characters found on a standard keyboard. This means that understanding and preserving the order of operations is critically important to achieving a correct result.

We will look at a common formula, the slope of a line: $\dfrac{y2 - y1}{x2 - x1}$

That is y2 - y1 over x2 - x1. The division bar acts as a grouping operator in mathematics, grouping the numerator and the denominator separately. When converting an equation with a division bar to a programming equation, we must group the numerator and denominator explicitly, with parentheses. We therefore enclose the numerator and denominator of a fraction or rate in parentheses to ensure that they are computed before the division takes place.

If we do not use parentheses, then we might write: y2 - y1 / x2 - x1. (This is wrong! Do you see why?) In this expression, the division y1 / x2 will take place before the two subtractions, which is incorrect. We should write this expression with parentheses around the numerator, and parentheses around the denominator: (y2 - y1) / (x2 - x1). This forces y2 - y1 and x2 - x1 to be calculated before the first result is divided by the second. You will not always need to enclose the numerator and denominator in parentheses in order to achieve a correct result, but it is a good idea to do so because it reinforces the meaning of the division bar as a grouping operator.

Another rule is that you must always use the asterisk * when you are multiplying two expressions. This can be illustrated with the slope-intercept equation of a line, which contains the expression $mx + b$.

In our previous equation, y1, y2, x1, and x2 each represented individual quantities, which were variable names in our Python expression. Here, m and x are separate quantities being multiplied together, so we will have separate variables m and x.

In algebra, we will sometimes see quantities appended together (like mx) or appended to a quantity in parentheses (like m(x)), or we will see a multiplication sign or a dot used to represent multiplication (like m × x, or m · x). In Python, you must use an asterisk (*) between any two expressions that you wish to multiply (literals, variables, more complex expressions, or functions, as we will soon see). Therefore, this expression in Python would be m * x + b. Many beginning programmers (especially those who do a lot of math) forget the asterisk, resulting in a syntax error. Here are a couple of errors you might trigger if you forget this rule:

```
>>> mx + b
Traceback (most recent call last):
 File "<pyshell#7>", line 1, in <module>
  mx + b
NameError: name 'mx' is not defined
>>> m(x) + b
Traceback (most recent call last):
 File "<pyshell#8>", line 1, in <module>
  m(x) + b
TypeError: 'int' object is not callable
```

For many mathematical operations, such as square root, absolute value, and log, there is no symbol in Python for performing the operation. Some of these operations have built-in functions in Python. For example, if we want the absolute value of a number, we can use abs:

```
>>> abs(-5)
5
>>> abs(5)
5
```

Similarly, we can round a number using round, which has an optional second argument which is the number of digits to round the value to:

```
>>> round(3.14159)
3
>>> round(3.14159, 2)
3.14
```

In Python, round has a somewhat odd functionality of rounding .5 to the nearest even number, which rounds up roughly half of the time and rounds down the other half, in a predictable way.

```
>>> round(1.5)
2
>>> round(2.5)
2
```

Other functions, such as log and square root, require the math library. To use functions in the math library, you will need to import the library at the top of your program with the statement import math, and then prepend the functions you wish to use with math. Here is an example of a program that uses three functions from the math library, log, pow, and sqrt:

```
1 import math
```

```
2  # Get and print the log base 2 of 512.
3  log_512 = math.log(512, 2)
4  print("The log base 2 of 512 is", log_512)

5  # Now raise two back to that power and print.
6  raise2 = math.pow(2, log_512)
7  print("Two raised to the", log_512, "is", raise2)

8  # Take a square root of a perfect square and print.
9  root25 = math.sqrt(25)
10  print("The square root of 25 is", root25)
```
Listing 2.2

And here is the program's output:

```
The log base 2 of 512 is 9.0
Two raised to the 9.0 is 512.0
The square root of 25 is 5.0
```

It is a silly program, but you can see the `import math` statement on line 1. On line 3, the expression `math.log(512, 2)` evaluates to the logarithm base 2 of 512, which is `9.0`. This value is assigned to the variable `log_512`. On line 6, the expression `math.pow(2, log_512)` raises 2 to the `9.0` power, which evaluates to `512.0`, and an assignment statement associates the result with the variable `raise2`.

The `pow` function, short for "power," raises the first operand to the second. This is very similar to the `**` operator, except it converts its operands to the `float` data type (and the result, therefore, is a `float`). Many languages do not have an exponentiation operator like `**`, but they do have a `pow` function in their `math` libraries.

Finally, on line 9, the expression `math.sqrt(25)` evaluates to `5.0`, and that result is assigned to the variable `root25`.

We will convert one more mathematical expression to Python. This time we will convert an expression that contains a square root: $2\sqrt{a^2 + b^2}$

This, the formula for the length of the hypotenuse of a right triangle, is the square root of a squared plus b squared. In this case we are multiplying by the value 2, to make the expression a little more interesting. We have learned three different operations that we can use to compute the squares: we can use the exponentiation operator `**`, we can use the `pow` function, and we can simply multiply the quantity by itself using `*`.

Here are three solutions that use these different squaring strategies:

```
>>> import math
>>> a = 3
>>> b = 4
>>> c = 2 * math.sqrt(a**2 + b**2)
>>> c
10.0
>>>
>>> c = 2 * math.sqrt(math.pow(a, 2) + math.pow(b, 2))
```

```
>>> c
10.0
>>> c = 2 * math.sqrt(a*a + b*b)
>>> c
10.0
```

The way these expressions are structured might seem a little confusing, so we will unpack them. Function calls have a very high precedence in Python, so the function calls above (`math.sqrt` and `math.pow`) have a higher precedence than the multiplication (`2 * math.sqrt`). But the operands to the function (e.g., `a ** 2 + b ** 2`) have a higher precedence. They must be computed first so Python has a value to pass in to the function call. So within each function call, the arguments are evaluated first, and then passed into the function. In the first expression, the exponentiations take place first, from left to right, followed by the addition, and then the function is called, followed by the multiplication, and finally the assignment:

```
c = 2 * math.sqrt(a**2 + b**2)
c = 2 * math.sqrt(9 + b**2)
c = 2 * math.sqrt(9 + 16)
c = 2 * math.sqrt(25)
c = 2 * 5.0
c = 10.0
```

See if you can figure out the order for the other two expressions.

2.10   Input and type conversion functions

The weight shipment program (Listing 2.1) is not an input–processing–output program because it does not obtain input from the user. We can make the weight shipment program much more general and useful by obtaining input from the user with Python's built-in input function.

```
1   """Compute the weight of some components."""

2   # Obtain the weight and number of components
3   # from the user.
4   weight = float(input("What is the component weight? "))
5   num_components = int(input("How many components? "))

6   # Calculate the total weight.
7   total_weight = weight * num_components

8   # Display the total weight amount to the user.
9   print("Total weight of", num_components, "is", total_weight,".")
```
Listing 2.3

Running the program yields two prompts. The user types a value at each prompt and presses enter. Once the user has entered the values (in this case the same values as we used before, but the user could type any values of the correct types), the program computes and displays the result. This program is more general than the program in Listing 2.1, because it will now compute the total weight for any number of components entered for any weight entered. (It is also now vulnerable to bad input from the user. There will be more on that in future chapters.)

```
What is the component weight? .245
How many components? 3
Total weight of 3 is 0.735 .
```

There are input statements on lines 4 and 5 in Listing 2.3. The input statement is the Python keyword input, followed by a prompt enclosed in parentheses. The prompt itself is a string, so if you are using a string literal, that will be enclosed in quotes.

When the program runs, the input statement displays the prompt to the console and waits for the user's response. Once the user has typed a response and pressed the enter key, the input statement evaluates to the user's response, just as expressions evaluate to a value. The type of an input statement is always str. Because of this, if we want to convert the user's response to a different type (such as float or int, as above), then we must convert the response to the appropriate type.

In this console session, you can see that the result of an input statement is a str. How can you tell?

```
>>> input("What is the component weight? ")
What is the component weight? .245
'.245'
```

In a program, you will almost always put the input statement on the right side of an assignment statement, because you will want Python to remember what the user typed for later use. In our program, the input statement on line 4 is converted to a float data type and stored in the variable weight. The input statement on line 5 is converted to an int data type and stored in the variable num_components. Those values can then be used in the calculation of the total shipment weight. If they are not stored in variables, they cannot be used.

The two type converter (sometimes called **type casting**) functions in the program, int and float, will try to convert the expression within parentheses into values of types int and float, respectively. This will work only if the values are already numeric types (in other words, an int can be converted to a float, and a float can be converted to an int), or if the value is a string that is a character version of an int or a float. This console session shows a few conversions that work and one that does not:

```
>>> int(3.14159)
3
>>> float(3)
3.0
>>> int("3")
3
>>> int("3.14159")
Traceback (most recent call last):
  File "<pyshell#3>", line 1, in <module>
    int("3.14159")
ValueError: invalid literal for int() with base 10: '3.14159'
>>> float("3.14159")
3.14159
```

We will sometimes want to convert a numeric type to a string. (You will see why this is useful in the next section.) This console session shows the str function being used to convert int and float data to the string type:

```
>>> str(3.14159)
'3.14159'
>>> str(5)
'5'
```

Try this

❖ Would the type converter functions be able to convert a number with commas to an int or a float? What about a number with a + or – sign in front of it? What about a word, such as "two"? Experiment in the IDLE console to find out.

❖ Can you think of other ways users might express numbers? Experiment to learn what variations can be converted with int and float.

❖ Type int (at the IDLE console and wait for the tip to come up. What do you think it means? Can you use int in a different way?

2.11   Formatting output

You might recall from our program in Listing 2.1 and 2.3 that the output looked pretty bad:

```
Total weight of 3 is 0.735 .
```

This output is the result of the following print statement:

```
print("Total weight of", num_components, "is", total_weight,".")
```

The print statement is the statement we will use to display output to the console in IDLE. You will notice that it is composed of the keyword print, followed by a list of arguments enclosed in parentheses. The arguments are separated by commas, and each argument can be a literal, a variable, or a more complicated expression.

This is sufficient for very simple messages and for temporary print statements to confirm that your program is functioning properly. But because Python inserts a space between each argument in the output (such as between the value of the weight and the period), and because it does not do any work to format floating-point values, it will not usually be sufficient. If you want to create something a little neater, such as a table of output with floating-point values displayed to a particular precision, it absolutely will not do.

The first tool that we can use to improve the output is **string concatenation**. This will allow us to control the spacing and construct a string from literal values, variables, and more complex expressions. String concatenation uses the + operator to join strings together, inserting no space between them. Here is a first attempt at an improved version of our output string using string concatenation. Note that, to do this, we must use the str function to convert the two floating-point variables to strings:

```
print("Total weight of" + str(num_components) + "is" + \
      str(total_weight) + ".")
```

And here is the output:

```
Total weight of3is0.735.
```

What happened? It turns out that in several places (between the numeric values and the words "of" and "is") we were relying on the spaces between arguments automatically inserted by the print command. We can fix it by adding the space within the string, exactly where we want it to appear in the output:

```
print("Total weight of " + str(num_components) + " is " + \
      str(total_weight) + ".")
```

Note the space within the strings "Total weight of " and " is ". This yields the following output:

```
Total weight of 3 is 0.735.
```

(You might have also noticed that the last two print statements were each split over two lines using the line continuation token \. You can use the line continuation token to make long statements easier to read. In this book, it will be used to split long lines on the page in a way that preserves Python's syntax.)

That is much better! But we have no control over the number of decimal places in our floating-point number, and there are many situations in which it will be important to display floating-point data to a certain number of positions. String concatenation will sometimes give us the control we need, and it is easy to use once you have practiced a bit. But there is a more sophisticated way of formatting output that will give us many more options, and that is the format function.

The format function has its own mini language for specifying how a string should be formatted. Here, we will look at a few examples that will give you a sense of how it works and enough tools to handle several different situations. If you are interested in learning more, you can read the Python documentation on string formatting, here: https://docs.python.org/3.4/library/string.html#format-string-syntax

Here is our print statement with the output formatted using the format function, with the floating-point value displayed to two decimal places:

```
print("Total weight of {:d} is {:.2f}."\
      .format(num_components, total_weight))
```

The format string is a little intimidating to look at, but the output is exactly what we want:

```
Total weight of 3 is 0.73.
```

We can examine the parts of that by first looking at a simpler version. We format a string by writing the string, then a period, and then the word format followed by arguments within parentheses. The arguments are inserted into the string within the curly braces { } in order. So, the first set of curly braces receives the first argument (num_components), and the second set of curly braces receives the second argument (total_weight).

Here is a simpler version of the print and format functions without any special commands within the curly braces:

```
print("Total weight of {} is {}.".format(num_components, total_weight))
```

And here is the output:

```
Total weight of 3 is 0.735.
```

You can see we are back to the same output we could achieve with string concatenation. The curly braces act as a placeholder for the values to be inserted into the string.

If we want the values to be displayed in a particular way, then we must use **format specifiers** within the curly braces. Format specifiers describe how each argument should be formatted, like : . 2f, which you may have guessed from the output specifies a floating-point value (f for float) with two decimal places (. 2). The format specifier :d (of course?) specifies an integer is being formatted.

The following paragraphs show some examples of other specifiers that you might use. The order of specifiers within the curly braces is important, so for example, if you want to specify alignment, field width, commas, and precision, they must appear in that order.

Although you cannot insert commas into numeric values in a Python program, you can format numbers with commas for display. This example shows a floating-point value displayed with commas and a precision of two decimal places. It is the same as the first example, but with a comma between the colon (:) and the .2f.

```
print("{:,.2f}".format(1000000000.5))
```

Here is the result:

```
1,000,000,000.50
```

You can also include **escape characters** in your strings, which are used to specify nonprinting and other special characters. One of the most useful is the newline. You can insert a newline into your output using the \n escape character, as in this example:

```
print("{}\n{}\n{}".format("line 1", "line 2", "line 3"))
```

This yields the following result:

```
line 1
line 2
line 3
```

There are other escape characters that you can experiment with, such as \t, which inserts a tab in your output, and \' and \", which allow you to escape a single or double quote so you can include it in a string that is delimited with the same kind of quote. For example, you will receive a syntax error if you write "She said "Hello" when I saw her." But you can write "She said \"Hello\" when I saw her." The backslash in the escape character tells Python that the next character is special: either it should not be treated as a literal, but should be interpreted according to its special meaning, as with p and t, or it should be treated as a literal, and should not be interpreted according to its special meaning, as with the same sort of quote that is enclosing the string. Because of its special meaning, if you want to include a literal backslash in your string, you must escape it with another backslash!

Field width and alignment specifiers allow you to create tables of data. Here is a very simple table containing two rows of two columns each, with the first column containing strings and having a field width of 8, and the second column containing floats and having a field width of 6. The data in both columns is left aligned, specified by the less-than sign (<):

```
print("{:<8s}{:<6.2f}\n{:<8s}{:<6.2f}" \
        .format("GPA 1", 3.682, "GPA 2", 3.775))
```

Here is the result:

```
GPA 1 3.68
GPA 2 3.77
```

The field width of 8 in the first and third format specifiers tell Python to display those values ("GPA 1" and "GPA 2") in eight characters, even if the value itself is less than eight characters. Any extra width will be filled with white space on one side or the other, depending on the alignment. (So what is printed is "GPA 1   " and "GPA 2   ".) This causes the second and fourth values to line up at the ninth character, which is how we produce a table with columns that are the same width. The less than sign < tells Python to left-align the value in the field. (Try changing the example to use the greater-than sign >. What do you expect the result to be?) The s after the field width means that the value will be a string value.

The second and fourth specifiers are slightly more complex. Can you pull them apart and explain each piece? The less than sign < means the data will be left aligned, the 6 means a field width of six characters, the .2 means Python should display two positions to the right of the decimal, and the f signifies that the data will be floating point.

Try this

❖ Store your name and age in two separate variables, then use a `print` statement with a `format` specifier to display your name and age. (Hint: use this string: `"{}{}"`.)
❖ Modify the previous statement to give your name a field width of 25.
❖ Modify the previous statement to left align your name.
❖ Remove the field width and alignment from the message, but add text, so if the value stored in name were `Amelia`, and the value stored in age were `19`, the output would be, `"Hello, Amelia, you are 19 years old."`
❖ Experiment with the different escape characters \n, \t, \', \" and \\. What happens if you try to format a table using tabs with variable-length data in the columns?
❖ If you plan your format specifiers carefully, the syntax will not be intimidating. Produce a three-column table of a header and at least three rows of data. You can include whatever you like in your table, but if you do not have any data in mind, you can reproduce this table. The field widths of each column are 20, and they are left aligned.

```
Plant group         SoilpH              Average growth
1                   6.0                 12.6
2                   6.2                 23.0
3                   6.4                 45.8
```

2.12   Comments

We have not discussed lines 1, 2, 3, 6, and 8 in Listing 2.3:

```
1   """Compute the weight of some components."""
```

```
2  # Obtain the weight and number of components
3  # from the user.
4  weight = float(input("What is the component weight? "))
5  num_components = int(input("How many components? "))

6  # Calculate the total weight.
7  total_weight = weight * num_components

8  # Display the total weight amount to the user.
9  print("Total weight of", num_components, "is", total_weight, ".")
```
Listing 2.3

These lines are **comments**. Comments are notes in your code for you and other programmers to read. They are ignored by Python. There are two kinds of comments shown here. On line 1 we have a **docstring comment**. Docstring comments are strings, as the name suggests. You begin a docstring comment with three double quotes, and you end it with three double quotes. As with all triple-quoted strings, it can extend across multiple lines. The wording of a docstring comment should be a command and not a description (as in "compute the weight," not "computes the weight"), and it should end in a period. There are specific times that docstring comments are appropriate. For now, the only time to use a docstring comment is at the top of your program, to describe what the program does. It should be the first line of your file.

The other comments are Python comments. They begin with a # and they extend to the end of the line. They should be complete sentences and should follow standard capitalization and punctuation rules.

Well-written comments will make your code easier to read. Here is our program if we take out everything but the Python comments:

```
2  # Obtain the weight and number of components
3  # from the user.
6  # Calculate the total weight.
8  # Display the total weight amount to the user.
```

The comments are an outline of the solution to the component shipping calculation problem. Under each comment, you can find the code that solves the part of the problem described by the comment. For example, under the comment on lines 2 and 3, we have all the code that obtains the weight and number of components from the user. Under the comment on line 5, we have the code that calculates the total weight, and under the comment on line 7, we have the code that displays the total weight to the user. Compare those comments to the following comments:

```
2  # Get inputs.
6  # Calculate.
8  # Display result.
```

While accurate, these comments do not describe how the code is solving the component shipping calculation problem. In fact, these comments could apply to almost any input–processing–output program! When you write your comments, be sure to use them to link the code to the problem being solved. This relates to our software engineering standard of writing readable code, because code is read more than it is written.

2.13 Using your tool kit

We have learned about sequential flow of control, program state, variables, expressions, input statements, assignment statements, print statements, and function calls in the context of a few examples, but we have not talked about how to use them to solve a programming problem.

So we will now solve a programming problem step by step. This is the sort of problem that you might see in the back of a chapter introducing input–processing–output programs, or one you might pose to yourself as you weigh how much time to devote to studying for a final exam:

The final exam in an introductory programming course is worth 25% of the final grade. Write a program that prompts the user for their average before the final, and then produces a table displaying their final grade if they earn a 100, 90, 80, and 70 on the final exam.

The program should look like this running:

```
Please enter your average: 92
Final Exam  Final Grade
100            94.0
90             91.5
80             89.0
70             86.5
```

We will use the problem-solving steps from Chapter 1:

- ❖ Define the problem
- ❖ Identify and clearly express solutions
- ❖ Evaluate and select among those solutions
- ❖ Implement a solution
- ❖ Evaluate the result

2.13.1 Define the problem

Programming problems are often incomplete and have unstated assumptions. Before you open your programming tool kit, you must clarify the requirements. Problem descriptions often describe or show inputs that are an average case, and leave out unusual inputs (like negatives, zero, or very high or low values) or leave the nature of the inputs ambiguous (e.g., it might show whole numbers when reals are acceptable).

One way to clarify the requirements is to imagine the program running on different inputs. (Sometimes a sample run or two is provided with a problem definition, but they rarely cover all the situations that your solution must be programmed to handle.)

Do we understand how the input in the sample run that is provided, 92, produces the output table? (If not, that is a question we should ask.) Whether we ask or figure it out on our own, the current average (in this case, 92) is 75% of the total grade, and the projected final exam grade (100, 90, etc.) is 25% of the total grade. So, the formula for each line in the table is:

```
Final Exam  Final Grade
100            (100*.25) + (92*.75)
90             (90*.25) + (92*.75)
80             (80*.25) + (92*.75)
70             (70*.25) + (92*.75)
```

To fully understand the problem, we should think of the different possible input values the user might enter and clarify what assumptions we might reasonably make. Then we should compute the output for those values and confirm that our understanding of the system is correct.

When you start computing examples, if they are varied enough, you will start generating questions about the problem. For example, can the user enter a floating-point value for their average? What precision should we use in displaying the result?

Are we assuming the user will enter a number? Are we assuming grades between 0 and 100? What happens if they[1] enter a value outside of that range?

You might think of other questions. You can discuss the questions with your professor (or client), but sometimes you must make the decisions yourself. In that case, it is a good idea to reason through the answers and explicitly state your assumptions. Here are the assumptions and reasoning for the questions above:

- ❖ The user might enter nonnumeric data, but there is nothing we can do about it (with our current tool kit) and the program will crash. Therefore, we will assume the user will enter numeric data.
- ❖ It is reasonable for the user to enter a floating-point value for their average, as grade averages are almost never integers.
- ❖ This program does assume grades on the 0–100 scale, so if the user enters a value outside of that range, the output will not make sense. (You have probably heard the phrase "garbage in garbage out.")
- ❖ We will display the final grade to one decimal place, to give a little more information than if we rounded it to a whole number.

To summarize, we have identified the following strategies for defining the problem:

- ❖ Imagine the programming running on different inputs, and especially consider edge cases, including special values like zero and negatives, and different kinds of data.
- ❖ Confirm, through computations by hand, that you know how the output is produced from the input.
- ❖ Pay attention to questions that arise as you compute with sample data (and answer them).

This might seem like a lot of time spent thinking about a pretty small problem. But there is enormous value in taking this time. First, you will not end up solving the wrong problem! Second, you will find situations (such as the floating-point input) that you might not have expected and might change the way you program the solution, which avoids potentially costly mistakes. Third, it gives you the opportunity to solve a number of example problems, which will help you develop your algorithm (the steps in the solution), and later, will help you test your solution.

2.13.2   Identify and clearly express solutions

Now that we understand the problem better, we will think about the tools we have, and what parts of this problem we might be able to solve with them. Think about how you would program parts of the solution (or all of it) before you look at the table below.

---

1   This text uses *they* as a gender-neutral singular pronoun throughout.

Problem	Tool
Prompt the user for their average before the final	`input` statement
	assignment statement
	variable, floating point, to store the average
The final exam is worth 25%	variable, floating point, to store the final grade
The user's average before the final is worth 75%	assignment statement
	multiplication * and addition +
	floating-point and literal arguments
Produce a table	`print` statement
	String formatting

You might not know how to solve every part of a problem right away. Do not worry about that! Programs should be written incrementally: write a small piece, test it thoroughly, and then add another small piece. Before you know it, you will have your solution! Remember that you can also use interactive mode (the IDLE console) to test out pieces of code as you are working.

With the tools listed above, we can start to define an algorithm, which is how we clearly express a programming solution:

1. Obtain the current average from the user.
2. Calculate the final grades for exam grades of 100, 90, 80, and 70.
3. Display a table of results.

It is important that our algorithm is numbered, because a program executes sequentially. We must have the current average before we can perform the calculations on it, and we must know the final grades before we can display them in a table.

We could also solve the problem in a slightly different order:

1. Obtain the current average from the user.
2. Calculate the final grade for the exam grade of 100 and display.
3. Calculate the final grade for the exam grade of 90 and display.
4. Calculate the final grade for the exam grade of 80 and display.
5. Calculate the final grade for the exam grade of 70 and display.

2.13.3   Evaluate and select among those solutions

Both solutions will work. Once we have ideas for solutions, we should use the standards and principles that we know to select among them. For example, our solution should solve the problem that was posed. If it does not, then we should throw it out. Our solution should be as simple and easy to read as possible, because code is read more than it is written, and simple code is less likely to have bugs.

We are going to use our software engineering standard of readability to choose between the two solutions. We will choose the first solution, because it will be easier to read the computation code if it is together, and it will be easier to read the table code if it is together. It will also be easier to change all the rows of the table (e.g., to change the precision or adjust the column width) if they are all located in one place in the program.

2.13.4   Implement a solution

We can take our algorithm and turn it into comments in our program. Here is a first version of the program, which is nothing but comments!

```
"""Produce a table of final grades, given current average."""
# Obtain the current average from the user.
# Calculate the final grades for exam grades of 100, 90, 80, & 70.
# Display a table of results.
```

(We will add line numbers when the program is complete, to avoid confusion.)

Are there pieces that you could write? You do not have to write the program from the top to the bottom, although it might be easier at first.

We will develop this program incrementally (one small piece at a time), so that it is easier to find and fix bugs as we go. We will start by getting the input from the user, computing one of the grades, and printing it out. We can compare that to the output that we have calculated in the first step, to make sure we are on the right track.

Do you see where we need a variable? Remember that variables are used for inputs, temporary results, and outputs. Here is the first line of the sample run, provided with the programming problem, and the table we computed earlier. The user's input is underlined.

```
Please enter your average: 92
Final Exam    Final Grade
100           (100*.25) + (92*.75)
90            (90*.25) + (92*.75)
80            80*.25) + (92*.75)
70            (70*.25) + (92*.75)
```

The user's input is going to be stored in a variable, and then multiplied by .75 in our computations of the final grades.

```
"""Produce a table of final grades, given current average."""
# Obtain the current average from the user.
average = input("Please enter your average: ")

# Calculate the final grades for exam grades of 100, 90, 80, & 70.
final_100_grade = 100*.25 + average*.75

# Display a table of results.
print(final_100_grade)
```

And here is what the output looks like:

```
>>>
 RESTART: D:/grades.py
Please enter your average: 92
Traceback (most recent call last):
  File "D:/listing2-4.py ", line 6, in <module>
    final_100_grade = 100*.25 + average*.75
TypeError: can't multiply sequence by non-int of type 'float'
>>>
```

Oh, no! That looks like a bug. What happened? Perhaps you can spot the error in the program, or perhaps you can figure it out from the error message. This is a run-time error, because the program started to run (therefore, not a syntax error), but then it halted abruptly with an error message.

Debugging is a problem-solving process that also must begin with defining the problem. It can be tempting to change the code without understanding what caused the error in the first place. When we do this, we often change working code, leave the buggy code, and even add new bugs!

In this case, we can see that the error occurred at the computation, and the problem is a "TypeError," in which we asked Python to "multiply sequence by non-int of type 'float.'"

If that is not helpful enough, then we can try a debugging strategy. Debugging strategies help us see program state, which is the values of variables during program execution. We could try printing out the input value before the computation, to make sure it was read in correctly. If we did that, we would notice the quotation marks around the number, meaning that we forgot to convert the user's input to a float. Python threw a run-time error when we then tried to multiply a string by .75.

If we fix that bug and continue in the implementation process, adding small pieces and testing (and fixing bugs) as we go, we will eventually complete our program. Listing 2.4 is the finished program.

```
1   """Produce a table of final grades, given current average."""
2   # Obtain the current average from the user.
3   average = float(input("Please enter your average: "))

4   # Calculate the final grades for exam grades of 100, 90, 80, & 70.
5   average_75_percent = average * .75
6   final_100_grade = 100*.25 + average_75_percent
7   final_90_grade = 90*.25 + average_75_percent
8   final_80_grade = 80*.25 + average_75_percent
9   final_70_grade = 70*.25 + average_75_percent

10  # Display a table of results.
11  print("{:<15}{:<15}".format("Final Exam", "Final Grade"))
12  print("{:<15d}{:<15.1f}".format(100, final_100_grade))
13  print("{:<15d}{:<15.1f}".format(90, final_90_grade))
14  print("{:<15d}{:<15.1f}".format(80, final_80_grade))
15  print("{:<15d}{:<15.1f}".format(70, final_70_grade))
```
Listing 2.4

Rather than repeat the computation `average * .75` four times, it is computed once and placed in a variable on line 5, and then the variable is used in the next four computations on lines 6–9.

Here is an example of the program running:

```
Please enter your average: 82.6
Final Exam    Final Grade
100           86.9
90            84.4
80            81.9
70            79.4
```

2.13.5 Evaluate the result

Are we done yet? No! The program now needs to be tested. If we tested each piece as we developed it, then a lot of our testing work is done. But how should we test your program? It can be quite difficult to test your own programs, for a couple of reasons. First, it is difficult to identify your own assumptions. There could be assumptions that you have made that you are not aware of. If you are not aware of them, you might not come up with test cases that challenge them. Second, you want your program to work. So, testing it can be painful, because finding a bug means more work fixing it. You might not test as thoroughly as you should, in order to avoid that work. You also might not have left yourself enough time to test, and you might think, since your program produces some output, it is good enough. (It is not.)

We will first test the program by simply comparing it to the specifications, which is the brief problem description we worked from. Does it do everything it was required to do in the way it was required to do it? It does obtain an average from the user, and then computes and displays the final grade for exam grades of 100, 90, 80, and 70, worth 25% of the final grade. We explicitly stated and justified some assumptions as additional specifications, such as that the program would function properly only with numeric input, it would accept floating-point input, and values out of the range 0–100 would produce meaningless results.

We will then test this program by designing test cases that are within expected parameters, but at the limits. We will not test inputs that do not match our assumptions, such as inputs that are not numeric, or inputs outside the 0–100 range.

When you write a test case, you list the input or inputs, and then you compute the expected output. You must list the expected output, and then compare it to what your program actually produces.

Here is a table of test cases for this program:

Description	Input	Expected outputs (calculated on a TI-83 Plus)
Test bottom of range	0	25, 22.5, 20, 17.5
Test top of range	100	100, 97.5, 95, 92.5
Test a very small value*	1	25.75, 23.25, 20.75, 18.25

(Continued)

(Continued)

Description	Input	Expected outputs (calculated on a TI-83 Plus)
Test a value so small it does not show up in the results	.01	25.0075, 22.5075, 20.0075, 17.5075
Test a value so large it does not show up in the results	99.99999	99.9999925, 97.4999925, 94.9999925, 92.4999925

*The results when you run the program are different from the results you might expect if you round the values shown here because of Python's unusual way of rounding values.

After we have created our test cases, we run the program and compare the program's output to the results that we computed. If the program's output does not match our computations, then we will need to find and correct the error, and then test again.

Once we have thoroughly tested this program and repaired any errors that we found during testing, we can be reasonably confident that our program solves the original problem. Now test your own skills on some of the Challenge accepted! problems at the end of this chapter!

2.14 Challenge accepted!

1. Write a program that accepts a weight in pounds, converts the weight to kilograms, and displays the result with two positions to the right of the decimal. The formula for converting pounds to kilograms is kg = lbs ÷ 2.205.
2. Write a program that accepts a mass in kilograms, then calculates and displays the weight on Mars with two positions to the right of the decimal. The formula for converting mass to weight on mars is weight = kg × 0.38.
3. Write a program that accepts a weight on Earth in pounds and converts that weight to kilograms, and then calculates the weight on Mars. Use the formulae from questions 1 and 2 above.
4. The formula for computing the area of a cylinder is $2\pi r^2 + h(2\pi r)$. Write a program to obtain the radius (r) and height (h) of a cylinder from the user, compute the area, and display the result. What assumptions should you make about the inputs (radius and height) to this problem?
5. You might remember the formula for the quadratic equation, $\frac{-b \pm \sqrt{b^2 - 4ac}}{2a}$. Write a program to obtain the values for a, b, and c from the user, compute both solutions, and display the results.
6. Write a program to display a table of five URLs, usernames, and passwords. The first line should be headings. Each column should have a width of 40.
7. Write a program to obtain the following information for five videos: name, the number of views, the number of likes, and the number of dislikes. Compute the percentage of likes and dislikes for each video (out of the total likes + dislikes) and display a table of the results with columns for name, percentage of likes, and percentage of dislikes. Use a consistent column width for each column and display one decimal place for the percentages. The first row should contain meaningful headers.

8. Write a program that accepts a number of seconds from the user and uses the flooring division //
and mod % operators to display the value as hours, minutes, and seconds. (Hint: Follow the
problem-solving process and solve several different examples by hand first, including seconds
less than a minute, less than an hour, more than several hours, and options with no remainder
and with remainders, so that you fully understand the problem before you solve it. You can also
start with a smaller problem, such as accepting a number of seconds and displaying it as minutes and seconds.)

9. Write a program to obtain a width and height from the user and draw five stacked rectangles
using turtle graphics that exactly fill the space.

10. Write a program to obtain the size of a square side and the diameter of a circle, and draw the
square and the circle, both centered around (0, 0), using turtle graphics.

11. Write a program that obtains appointments from the user for one week (Monday to Sunday). It
should then display a calendar for the week, with a column for the day on the left and a column
for the appointment on the right.

12. Create a quiz or flash card program that asks the user a question, obtains their answer, and then
displays both their answer and the correct answer. Have the program ask the user three questions. For example, one question might look like this:

```
What symbol do you use to write a comment in Python? #
You wrote #. The correct answer is #.
```

13. Create a turtle graphics program to draw a fractal composed of 15 circles. Begin with one large
circle in the center of the screen. Then draw a circle half the diameter of the large circle on each
side of the circle. Then repeat that for the next set of circles, and for one more set. The final
drawing should look like this:

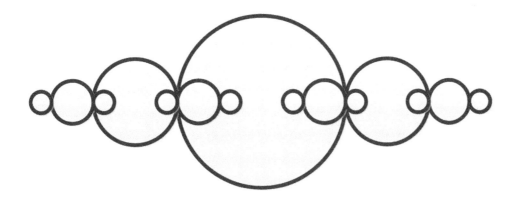

14. Write a program that inserts user input into a story or song lyric. Prompt the user for different
categories of words (such as parts of speech, cities, and names of famous people), and then use
string formatting to insert them into a lyric or story that you print for the user.

15. Write a program that will scale a small recipe based on the number of servings that the user
wants to cook and display the scaled recipe for the user. For example, if the recipe is for mac and
cheese and one serving is 2 ounces of macaroni, ¼ cup of cheddar cheese, ⅛ cup of parmesan
cheese, ¾ cups of milk, and ¼ of a stick of butter, and the user wants to make three servings,
display the amount of each ingredient needed in table form for the user. (The left column should
be the measurement; the right column should be the ingredient.)

16. Create a turtle graphics program that draws a simple map of a city, public transportation system, or game that you would like to model. Use color in your map.

17. Create a turtle graphics program that draws a (scaled) unit circle of radius 100 with lines every 30 degrees and every 45 degrees. (So at 0, 30, 45, 60, 90, etc.) See the image to the right for an example.

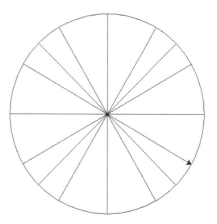

18. Obtain five temperatures from the user representing the average temperature for each of 5 days. You may assume the temperatures will be between 50 and 80 degrees. Display the data in two ways: both as a table and as a graph drawn with turtle graphics. You can use turtle.dot() to place a dot on the graph for each temperature. An example of a graph is shown below for the temperatures 60, 68, 75, 52, and 72. The horizontal lines represent the temperatures 50, 60, 70, and 80, and the vertical lines separate the 5 days.

## Chapter 3

Logic and conditional statements

3.1   Changing the flow

The tools we have learned so far allow us to write programs that proceed sequentially, obtaining input, performing computations, and displaying results for the user. With these tools, we can solve a very large number of computational problems, but there is no way to make decisions based on the given or computed values. Our programs, so far, can do only one thing. To write more complex programs that are responsive to different conditions, we need Boolean logic and conditional statements.

We will solve an input–processing–output problem that requires a decision: converting Global Positioning System (GPS) longitudinal coordinates from degrees minutes seconds (DMS) format to decimal degrees (DD) format.

Any location on the globe can be identified by its longitude and latitude, which is a grid system that you can imagine covers the earth. Longitude lines are the grid's vertical lines, which run from pole to pole. The prime meridian is the line at longitude zero, and all other longitude lines are measured in degrees that increase from the prime meridian to the east or to the west. Each degree of longitude is further divided into 60 minutes, and each longitudinal minute is further divided into 60 seconds. The DMS coordinates format displays the longitude as separate degrees, minutes, and seconds values, with E or W to indicate whether the location is to the east or the west of the prime meridian, respectively (Figure 3-1). (Latitude measurements are similar but use N or S to indicate whether the location is to the north or south of the equator, which is latitude zero.)

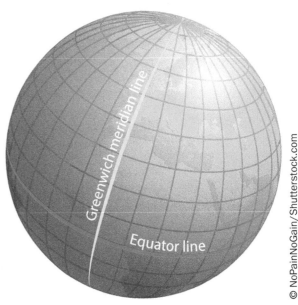

Figure 3-1   Longitude lines to the east and west of the prime meridian.

The longitude coordinate of the Community College of Rhode Island (CCRI) campus in Warwick, Rhode Island, USA, in DMS format is 71° 28′ 48.551″ W. To convert that to DD format, we use the following formula:

$$\text{decimal degrees} = \text{degrees} + \text{minutes} / 60 + \text{seconds} / 3600$$

If the longitude is to the west of the prime meridian, we must then multiply the result by −1. Therefore, the longitude of CCRI Warwick in DD format is 71 + (28 / 60) + (48.551 / 3600), which is 71.480153. We must then multiply that by −1, because Warwick is to the west of the prime meridian, giving us −71.480153.

In this problem, we multiply by −1 only under certain conditions, so we must do something new in our code. We must use conditional execution, or conditional flow of control. Listing 3.1 solves this problem.

```
1    """ Convert a longitude from DMS to DD format."""

2    # Obtain longitude values from the user.
3    degrees = int(input("Please enter the degrees: "))
4    minutes = int(input("Please enter the minutes: "))
5    seconds = float(input("Please enter the seconds: "))

6    direction = input("Enter E or W: ")
7    # Convert to DD format (absolute distance).
8    longitude_dd = degrees + minutes/60 + seconds/3600

9    # If west of the prime meridian, multiply by -1.
10   if direction == "W":
11       longitude_dd = longitude_dd * -1

12   # Display the DD longitude to the user.
13   print("The longitude in decimal degrees format is {:.6f}." \
             .format(longitude_dd))
```

Listing 3.1

Here is the program executing with the CCRI Warwick coordinates as input:

```
Please enter the degrees: 71
Please enter the minutes: 28
Please enter the seconds: 48.551
Enter E or W: W
The longitude in decimal degrees format is -71.480153.
```

If we execute the program on coordinates to the East of the prime meridian, our result is positive:

```
Please enter the degrees: 6
Please enter the minutes: 4
Please enter the seconds: 15.56
Enter E or W: E
The longitude in decimal degrees format is 6.070989.
```

You probably noticed the new keyword, operator, and indented code on lines 10 and 11:

```
10   if direction == "W":
11       longitude_dd = longitude_dd * -1
```

This is the code responsible for making the decision about whether to multiply by negative one or not and performing the multiplication under the appropriate conditions. This is a **conditional statement**, sometimes called an if statement, because it begins with the keyword `if`. The syntax for the conditional statement is:

```
if expression:
    conditionally executed code
```

It is the keyword `if`, followed by an expression of a new kind: a Boolean expression. The Boolean expression will evaluate to either `True` or `False`. (More on those in a moment.) Following the expression is a colon (`:`), and then code that will be executed only if the expression evaluates to `True`, which is indented four spaces.

You may have as many conditional (indented) lines as you need, so if you must execute one line, two lines, or several pages of code if the condition evaluates to `True`, then they will all be indented four spaces. If the condition evaluates to `False`, then execution skips the indented lines and continues with the first line of code that has the same level of indentation as the keyword `if`. In our program, that is the `print` statement on line 13.

This listing shows only executable lines of code, with the lines that execute if the condition evaluates to `True` highlighted in yellow:

```
3    degrees = int(input("Please enter the degrees: "))
4    minutes = int(input("Please enter the minutes: "))
5    seconds = float(input("Please enter the seconds: "))
6    direction = input("Enter E or W: ")
8    longitude_dd = degrees + minutes/60 + seconds/3600
10   if direction == "W":
11       longitude_dd = longitude_dd * -1
13   print("The longitude in decimal degrees format is {:.6f}." \
            .format(longitude_dd))
```

Here is the same listing with the lines that execute if the condition evaluates to `False` highlighted in yellow:

```
3    degrees = int(input("Please enter the degrees: "))
4    minutes = int(input("Please enter the minutes: "))
5    seconds = float(input("Please enter the seconds: "))
6    direction = input("Enter E or W: ")
8        longitude_dd = degrees + minutes/60 + seconds/3600
10   if direction == "W":
11       longitude_dd = longitude_dd * -1
13   print("The longitude in decimal degrees format is {:.6f}." \
            .format(longitude_dd))
```

Note that the test always executes, because it is reached sequentially after line 8 executes. But when the condition evaluates to `False`, the conditional, indented code on line 11 is skipped.

3.2   Relational operators and Boolean expressions

We will now focus on writing conditional expressions, such as `direction == "W"` in Listing 3.1.

Conditional expressions evaluate to a new data type, the Boolean data type (or `bool`, in Python). To review, the data types that we have discussed so far are `float`, `int`, and `str`. While there are, in theory, an infinite number of floating-point literals, integers, and strings, there are only two Boolean literals: `True` and `False`. These are written exactly as you see them here, and they are literal values, just as `5`, `3.14`, and `"Hello, world!"` are literal values. Try evaluating `True` and `False` in the IDLE console:

```
>>> True
True
>>> False
False
```

As with all literals, Python responds with the same value. `True` evaluates to `True`, and `False` evaluates to `False`. Note that they begin with uppercase letters, which is the standard for built-in constants in Python.

Boolean expressions are used to test the values in variables (or to test the values in more complicated expressions). This allows a program to respond to different conditions in different ways while a program is running. In Listing 3.1, the program responds one way if the value in the variable `direction` is `"W"`, and a different way if the value is not `"W"`.

We can test for more than a variable being equal to a specific value. We can test for whether values are less than, equal to, or greater than each other, plus the opposite conditions (called **complementary conditions**), using the relational operators. This table shows the relational operators.

Operator name	Operator symbol
Equal to	==
Not equal to	!=
Less than	<
Less than or equal to	<=
Greater than	>
Greater than or equal to	>=

In programming, we use these operators to test for specific conditions occurring in the state of the program while it is running. We test for conditions if we want to change the way the program will respond based on the outcome of the test. In the longitude format conversion program in Listing 3.1, we test for the value stored in `direction` to be equal to `"W"`, because if it is, we will multiply our result by negative one.

We will consider some examples of problems in which we need to test for conditions to direct the program's behavior:

Operator name	Operator symbol
| If the value in `state` is equal to Rhode Island, we will suggest coffee milk. | ```python
if state == "Rhode Island":
    print("How about some coffee milk?")
``` |
| If the value in `power_saver` is not equal to `"Y"`, we will set sleep to 60. | ```python
if power_saver != "Y":
    sleep = 60
``` |
| If the value in `pieces` is less than `minimum`, we will set it equal to `minimum`. | ```python
if pieces < minimum:
    pieces = minimum
``` |
| If the value in `age` is 12 or less, we will show the junior menu. | ```python
if age <= 12:
    print("For smaller appetites: ")
    print("Small baked chicken")
    print("3 oz. steak")
    print("Junior pasta")
``` |
| If the value in `grade` is greater than 93, set the value of `letter` to `"A"` | ```python
if grade > 93:
    letter = "A"
``` |
| If the value in `age` is greater than or equal to `18`, we will display a message that the user is eligible to vote. | ```python
if age >= 18:
    print("You are old enough to vote!")
``` |

You might have noticed that some of these operators are made up of more than one character. The test for equality (==) is two equals signs, the test for inequality (!=) is an exclamation point followed by an equals sign, the test "less than or equal to" (<=) is a less-than sign followed by an equals sign, and the test "greater than or equal to" (>=) is the greater-than sign followed by an equals sign. When an operator is made up of two symbols, there is no space between the symbols, and they must be typed in the order shown here. (Notice that they are typed in the order that they are spoken if you read them the way they are written here, and if you pronounce the exclamation point as "not.") These operators are used in many programming languages, so it is a good idea to memorize them and become accustomed to using them.

You should also take care to distinguish between the assignment operator = and the test for equality ==. The first associates a value with a variable, and the second performs a test that evaluates to `True` or `False`.

These expressions are tests that will evaluate to `True` or `False`, just as the expression 8 * 2 evaluates to 16. The test 15 <= 12 is not stating that 15 is less than or equal to 12, it is asking Python to evaluate 15 <= 12 to either `True` or `False`. If the test is the condition of an `if` statement and the test evaluates to `True` (if 15 is either less than 12 or equal to 12), then the indented code that follows the test will execute. If the test evaluates to `False`, then the indented code will be skipped. In the example age <= 12 in the table, there are four indented lines of code after the test, so either all four will execute if the test is `True`, or all four will be skipped if the test is `False`.

It can sometimes be helpful to draw a number line when reading or writing an expression written with a relational operator. If we are interested in executing some conditional code for all values of temperature less than and including 10, for example, we might represent that on a number line by drawing a filled circle over 10 and a line extending to the left as in Figure 3-2.

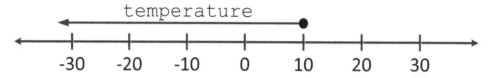

Figure 3-2   A number line representing a value less than or equal to 10.

In this drawing, our line represents all values for which the expression `temperature <= 10` should evaluate to `True`. If `temperature` is associated with a value that is not on the line (such as 10.1, 11, 100, or any other number over 10), then the expression will evaluate to `False`.

Try this

- ❖ What code executes if the user enters a value other than `"E"` or `"W"` when prompted for a direction in the program in Listing 3.1 (such as `"N"` or `"yes"`)? Predict the answer and run the program to test your prediction.
- ❖ For what values of `age` is the test `age <= 12` True? For what values is it `False`?
- ❖ For what values of `state` is the test `if state == "Rhode Island"` True? For what values is it `False`?
- ❖ For what values of `power_saver` will the test `power_saver != "Y"` be True? For what values is it `False`? In the code in the table, for what values of `power_saver` does `sleep` take the value 60?
- ❖ In the table above, for what values of `age` is the junior menu displayed?
- ❖ Modify this code so that `letter` is assigned the value `"A"` for all grades 93 and above:

```
if grade > 93:
    letter = "A"
```

- ❖ Write some code to obtain a temperature from the user, and print `"It's a nice day"` if the temperature is greater than 70.

3.3   Boolean operators and short-circuiting

3.3.1   Boolean operators

We sometimes want to test more complex conditions than can be written with a simple relational expression. The Boolean operators `and` and `or` allow us to write expressions that connect expressions written with relational operators.

For example, if we will allow a library customer to place a hold on a book only if their card status is active and they have less than $5 in charges on their account, then we might write:

```
if card_status == "active" and charges < 5:
    hold = account_name
```

In this example, we have two complete relational expressions as operands to the `and` operator: `card_status == "active"`, and `charges < 5`. Each of these expressions will evaluate to either `True` or `False`. There are therefore only four combinations of operands for an `and` operator, and we can list them in a truth table:

Operand 1	Operand 2	Operand 1 and Operand 2
True	True	True
True	False	False
False	True	False
False	False	False

You can see that the only way an `and` expression evaluates to `True` is if both operands are `True`. Does that work for the library card example? We want to allow the customer to place a hold only if the card status is active and they have less than $5 in charges on their account. If the `card_status` is equal to `"active"` then the expression on the left evaluates to `True`, and the top two rows of the table apply. If the value in `charges` is less than 5, then the expression on the right evaluates to `True`, and so we have the two `True` operands to our `and`, which is the top row in our table, and the entire expression evaluates to `True`. Our library patron will be allowed to put a hold on the book. If either of the expressions evaluated to `False` (or if both did), then we would have one of the other three rows in the table, the conditional code would not execute, and the patron would not be allowed to put a hold on the book.

Consider a situation in which only one of two conditions needs to be true in order for us to proceed with some action. For example, imagine you are going to eat 20% more protein in a day if you have either run at least 10 miles or lifted weights for at least 60 minutes. Because either condition will result in the protein increase, we use an `or` operator:

```
if miles >= 10 or weights >= 60:
    protein = protein * 1.2
```

This example is like the example with the `and` operation, because we have two complete relational expressions as operands to the `or` operator: `miles >= 10`, and `weight >= 60`. Each of these expressions will evaluate to either `True` or `False`. As with the `and` operator, there are only four combinations of operands for an `or` operator, and we can list them in a truth table:

Operand 1	Operand 2	Operand 1 or Operand 2
True	True	True
True	False	True
False	True	True
False	False	False

The only way an `or` expression evaluates to `False` is if both operands are `False`. In our example, the protein will be increased if either of the conditions evaluates to `True` (the first three lines of the table), which is what we want.

3.3.2   Short-circuiting

If you look at the truth tables for the `and` and `or` operators, you might notice that the first operand is sometimes predictive of the outcome of the expression. In an `and` operation, if the first operand is `False`, the entire expression will be `False`:

Operand 1	Operand 2	Operand 1 and Operand 2
True	True	True
True	False	False
False	True	False
False	False	False

In an `or` operation, if the first operand evaluates to `True`, then the entire expression will evaluate to `True`:

Operand 1	Operand 2	Operand 1 or Operand 2
True	True	True
True	False	True
False	True	True
False	False	False

Python (and many other languages) will skip evaluating the second operand if the value of the first operand is sufficient to determine the outcome of the entire expression. This is called **short-circuiting**. Therefore, if the first operand to an `and` expression is `False`, then the second operand is not evaluated. If the first operand to an `or` is `True`, then the second operand is not evaluated.

You will sometimes read code in which programmers have taken advantage of short-circuit evaluation. For example, a programmer might test, in the first operand, whether a resource exists before accessing it in the second operand. Or the programmer might test to see if a value is zero before dividing by it in the second expression, to avoid a divide-by-zero error.

There are equivalent ways to write a short-circuited expression without relying on short-circuiting. (e.g., splitting the test into multiple expressions.) Because there are many different approaches to how short-circuiting works in different languages, you cannot always port code easily to a new language if it relies on short-circuiting. When you write your own code, you must decide what is most readable and most robust (least prone to error). But when you are reading (or debugging) code, it is important to understand how short-circuiting works, as it is commonly used by many programmers.

3.3.3   The `not` operator

There is another Boolean operator, the `not` operator, which takes a single Boolean operand and complements it (evaluates to the opposite value). Here is the truth table for `not`, which is quite simple:

Operand 1	not Operand 1
True	False
False	True

This operator is placed in front of an expression to change its value to the opposite of its evaluated value. For example, if we wish to offer coffee-flavored ice cream to somebody whose state is not Rhode Island (so they can discover what they have been missing), we might write:

```
if not state == "Rhode Island":
    print("Wouldn't you like to try some coffee ice cream?")
```

This operator should be used sparingly, as it can be confusing to read logical expressions with negation in them. (Do you immediately know when the following expression evaluates to `True` and when it evaluates to `False`? `not age != 18`)

A little later, we will go over better ways to complement Boolean expressions. The `not` operator is best used for complementing Boolean variables, which we will also cover in a later section.

3.3.4   Order of operations

We have now learned nine new operators: `<, <=, >, >=, ==, !=, and, or, not`

We have not discussed where they fall in the operator precedence table. This is something that is not consistent across programming languages, so remember to check when you are learning a new language and remember that you can always force the order of evaluation by using parentheses (including with Boolean expressions).

In Python, the operator precedence for the arithmetic, relational, and Boolean operators is, from highest to lowest:

```
()
function calls
**
* / // %
+ -
< <= > >= == !=
not
and
or
```

We will evaluate the following expression to illustrate operator precedence:

```
not x + y > z and m % 2 == 0
```

We will give the value 10 to x, y, z, and m. Look over the expression, compare it to the operator precedence table, and determine the order of evaluation before you read the solution here.

First, substituting in the value 10 for each of the variables yields:

```
not 10 + 10 > 10 and 10 % 2 == 0
```

Arithmetic is still performed first, with the mod operator having a higher precedence than addition. So the mod will be computed first, and then the addition, yielding:

```
not 10 + 10 > 10 and 0 == 0
not 20 > 10 and 0 == 0
```

Relational operators have a higher precedence than logical operators, and relational operators all have the same precedence. They are therefore evaluated left to right in the expression:

```
not True and 0 == 0
not True and True
```

The logical operators all have a different precedence. not has the highest precedence, followed by and. Therefore, the not is evaluated first, giving:

```
False and True
```

This expression would be short-circuited, because it is an and statement with False as the first operand, so it cannot evaluate to True. The entire expression evaluates to False.

Try this

- Write Boolean expressions to test for the following conditions:
  The variable temperature is at least 75 and the variable cloud_cover is less than 20.0
  The variable age is at least 7 and the variable height is at least 42
  The variable length is less than 120 and the variable cost is less than 10
- Evaluate the following Boolean expressions. Assume max has the value 1024, num has the value 5, min has the value −10, x has the value 3, and y has the value .5. Is short-circuiting evaluation used for any of these expressions? Explain your answer.

```
not y < 0 and max < num
1024 >= max and num < 5
num - 1 < min and x + y >= 3.5
-10 != min or y > x
```

3.4   Checking ranges

It would be a good idea to add some **input validation** to the longitude coordinate program in Listing 3.1. Input validation is the process of checking data that comes from a source outside the program to determine if it falls within expected parameters. Input validation is critically important to writing secure software. The first step in validating input is specifying the allowed type, size, and range of values for the input data. This relates to the first step in the problem-solving process: defining the problem.

In the longitude coordinate program, we accept four inputs, on lines 3–6:

```
2  # Obtain longitude values from the user.
3  degrees = int(input("Please enter the degrees: "))
4  minutes = int(input("Please enter the minutes: "))
5  seconds = float(input("Please enter the seconds: "))
6  direction = input("Enter E or W: ")
```

From the casting operators, you can see that we are accepting two integers, a float, and a string. We do not yet know how to check that the user enters data of the correct type, or that they do not enter so much data at a prompt that it causes our system to crash, but these are considerations for the future.

What we can do is check that the data is within the correct numeric range, so that we are not trying to convert data that does not make sense.

The value for `degrees` entered by the user must be between 0 and 180. We will focus here on validating the value for `degrees`, because it raises the interesting question of how to check that a value falls within a range. In this example, the value of the variable `degrees` must be between 0 and 180, inclusive (including the end points). For this discussion, we will not concern ourselves with the values that are in `minutes` and `seconds`.

The number line in Figure 3-3 illustrates the values for `degrees` that should yield a `True` result in our range check:

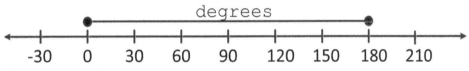

Figure 3-3   Valid longitudinal degrees.

The value for `degrees` has to be greater than or equal to 0, and also less than or equal to 180. Numbers that are less than 0 or greater than 180 should result in our test evaluating to `False`, but numbers that are both greater than or equal to 0 and less than or equal to 180 should result in our test evaluating to `True`. Therefore, we will use an `and`, testing for both ends of the range:

```
0 <= degrees and degrees <= 180
```

There are other ways you can write this expression, as long as the same relationships between `degrees`, 0, and 180 are preserved, and as long as you use an `and`. For example, you could write `degrees >= 0` for the first operand, and you could write `180 >= degrees` for the second operand.

If you test the expression on values within (such as `10`, `30`, and `170`), without (such as `-5`, `200`, `250`), and on the threshold (`0`, `180`) of the valid range, you will see that this expression correctly evaluates to `True` when `degrees` is between 0 and 180, inclusive.

Testing for values outside of a range also requires a compound expression. Suppose we want our expression to evaluate to `True` when `degrees` is outside of the valid range, so when `degrees` is less than 0, exclusive (not including 0), or greater than 180, exclusive? To be outside of the range, degrees can either have a value that is less than 0, such as -11, -10, or -45, or it can have a value that is greater than 180, such as 181, 190, or 230. (But it could never be both at the same time!) Therefore, we write expressions that will be True for those two conditions, and join them with an or, because the value in degrees cannot simultaneously be lower than 0 and greater than 180. It will be one or the other.

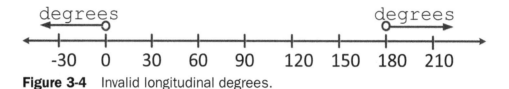

Figure 3-4   Invalid longitudinal degrees.

This expression tests for degrees outside of the range, and evaluates to True if degrees is either less than 0 or greater than 180:

```
degrees < 0 or 180 < degrees
```

As with the within-range test, there are other ways to express the same relationship between degrees, 0, and 180. Writing 0 > degrees for the first operand or degrees > 180 for the second operand, or changing the order of the operands, would also yield the same truth value.

Try this

❖ Write Boolean expressions to test for values falling within the following ranges:
The variable age falling between 20 (inclusive) and 25 (exclusive)
The variable temperature falling between 160 and 170, inclusive
The variable amount falling between 500 (inclusive) and 1000 (exclusive)

❖ Write Boolean expressions to test for values falling outside the following ranges:
The variable temperature being less than 50 or greater than 80, exclusive
The variable voltage being less than 120 or greater than 130, exclusive
The variable time being less than 10 (inclusive) or greater than 20 (exclusive)

❖ In our within-range test for longitudinal degrees, what would happen if we had used an or instead of an and? Test values within, without, and on the threshold of the valid range and explain why we must use an and rather than an or. Draw the expression on a number line.

❖ In our outside-range test for longitudinal degrees, what would happen if we had used an and instead of an or? Test values within, without, and on the threshold of the valid range and explain why we must use an or rather than an and.

❖ Can you think of a way, using the mod operator, to accept values greater than 180 for the longitude degrees and convert them to a meaningful value between 0 and 180?

❖ What values are acceptable for the input variables minutes and seconds? What is the highest possible set of values of degrees, minutes, and seconds that our program should accept? What is the lowest possible set of values?

3.5   Boolean variables

Just as you can create variables that reference values of type `int`, `float`, and `str`, you can create variables that reference the Boolean values `True` and `False`. This kind of variable is sometimes called a **flag**, because it is used to mark a state within your program that could change your program's execution. For example, you might use a Boolean variable to note whether input is valid or invalid.

Boolean variables are usually named in a way that reflects their dual nature. A Boolean variable is going to evaluate to either `True` or `False`. So, for example, a Boolean variable might have a name such as `isValid`, or `keepPlaying`, or `addTax`. Imagine these holding values of `True` or `False` and being used in a test, such as:

```
if addTax:
    bill = bill + tax
```

To assign a value to a Boolean variable, you use an assignment statement with the variable to the left of the assignment operator =, and an expression that evaluates to a Boolean result to the right. Here are some examples:

```
addTax = True
isValid = 0 <= degrees and degrees <= 180
userAnswer = input("Do you want to continue? Y or N: ")
keepPlaying = userAnswer == "Y"
```

The first example has a simple expression on the right, the literal Boolean value `True`. The first assignment statement assigned the value `True` to `addTax`.

The second example is more complex. You might recognize the expression on the right as our test for `degrees` evaluating to a value within the range of 0 to 180, inclusive. If `degrees` is within that range, then the expression on the right of the assignment operator will evaluate to `True`, and `isValid` will then be assigned the value `True`. If `degrees` is outside the range, then the expression on the right will evaluate to `False`, and `isValid` will be assigned the value `False`.

The third example first obtains input from the user. The prompt asks for the user to enter "Y" or "N", but the user could enter anything. If the user enters "Y", then the expression `userAnswer == "Y"` will evaluate to `True`, and `keepPlaying` will be assigned the value `True`. If the user enters anything else, then the expression will evaluate to `False`, and `keepPlaying` will be assigned the value `False`.

We will return to the input validation problem in Listing 3.1. We could use a Boolean flag to keep track of the validity of the input. We can initialize the flag to `True`, and if any of the inputs are invalid, set it to `False`. We can then confirm that the flag is still `True` before proceeding with the computation.

We start by setting the flag to `True`:

```
# Initialize flag to keep track of the validity of the input.
inputValid = True
```

We then read the degrees from the user, and set the flag to `False` if degrees is not within the valid range:

```
# Obtain longitude values from the user and validate
degrees = int(input("Please enter the degrees: "))
if degrees < 0 or degrees > 180:
    inputValid = False
```

We can do the same with all inputs, and then test the flag before proceeding with the calculations. Using a flag makes this code readable and easy to modify. If we wrote one Boolean expression that tested the range of all input values it would be very complex, difficult to read and debug, and difficult to modify if we added or removed input values.

```
# Perform conversion to DD format (absolute distance) if input valid.
if inputValid:
    longitude_dd = degrees + minutes/60 + seconds/3600

    # If west of the prime meridian, multiply by -1.
    if direction == "W":
        longitude_dd = longitude_dd * -1

    # Display the DD longitude to the user.
    print("The longitude in decimal degrees format is {:.6f}." \
        .format(longitude_dd))
```

Our program is actually a little more complicated, because it is the degrees, minutes, and seconds together that must be within the range of 0 and 180. However, this is a good example of how a flag can be set in multiple places within a program, simplifying a later test.

Try this

❖ Listing 2-3 obtains two values from the user: weight and number of components. Write input validation for these two values that checks that the weight is greater than or equal to 0, and the number of components is between 1 and 10. Use a Boolean variable `inputValid` and check the `inputValid` variable before computing the total weight and displaying the result.

❖ Obtain an age from the user in years, months, and days. Validate that each of these values falls within an appropriate range, using a Boolean variable to store the result. Display either `"Input is valid"` or `"Input is not valid"` based on the value in the variable.

3.6   What else?

Conditional statements give us a powerful tool for executing code only when the state of the program requires it. There are some common, efficient variations on the `if` statement. The first is the `else` clause. An `else` clause is matched with an `if`. The code in the `else` clause will execute when the condition in the statement is `False`.

Suppose we want to display a message for the user if the value they entered for degrees is out of range, but we will proceed with obtaining input if it is within range. We might write the following code:

```
if degrees < 0 or 180 < degrees:
    print("The value for degrees must be between 0 and 180.")
else:
    minutes = int(input("Please enter the minutes: "))
    # etc.
```

The else statement is appropriate to use when we have two mutually exclusive states. In other words, if there are two program states that cannot both exist at the same time. In this example, if degrees is within range, then it cannot be outside of the range. If degrees is outside of the range, then it cannot be within range. This is an appropriate use of an else clause. The else clause executes when the if condition is False.

The else keyword is at the same level of indentation as its matching if and is followed by a colon. The code that is indented after the else keyword will execute when the condition is False. The test will always execute, but only one or the other of the conditional blocks will execute. The if block executes if the test evaluates to True, and the else block executes if the test evaluates to False. After one of the blocks has executed, execution begins at the first line after the indented else block.

3.7   Complementing logical expressions

It is important to be able to state exactly when the code in an else block executes, because misunderstanding when an else block is entered is a common source of programming errors. The else block, as you know, executes when the if condition is False. But when exactly is a condition False?

A condition is False when the **complement** of the condition (the opposite condition) is True. If we write a complement for the if condition, then we will be writing the condition that is True for an else block.

For example, imagine we have the following condition:

```
age > 18
```

You can probably state a number of values for the variable age for which this condition is True (19, 20, 65, etc.). But exactly when is this condition False? People who are learning Boolean logic are often inclined to say, "when age is less than 18," but that is not strictly correct. There is one value for age that is not accounted for, and that is 18 itself. When age is 18, the condition age > 18 is not True. Therefore, age equal to 18 must be part of the complementary expression.

If a relational operator excludes a value, then the complementary operator must include it. If a relational operator includes a value, then the complementary operator must exclude it. This table lists the complements of the relational operators (you can read the table in both directions):

Operator	Complement
==	!=
<	>=
>	<=

The logical operators and and or are complemented using a technique called DeMorgan's theorem. Recall the truth tables for and and or. Here there is a new column, which is the complement of the outcome.

Operand 1	Operand 2	Operand 1 and Operand 2	Complement
True	True	True	False
True	False	False	True
False	True	False	True
False	False	False	True

Operand 1	Operand 2	Operand 1 or Operand 2	Complement
True	True	True	False
True	False	True	False
False	True	True	False
False	False	False	True

To achieve this outcome, you will complement each operand, and change the and to an or, or the or to an and. We will use prime (′) to denote a complement.

The complement of operand1 and operand2 is operand1′ or operand2′

The complement of operand1 or operand2 is operand1′ and operand2′

You can confirm this for yourself by completing a truth table with the complements of each operand. A good way to visualize this is with ranges. When we tested the value degrees, we drew the following number line (Figure 3-3):

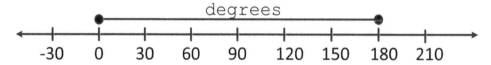

This number line represents the test:

```
0 <= degrees and degrees <= 180
```

The complement of this condition is represented by the test for degrees falling outside the range, depicted on the number line in Figure 3-4:

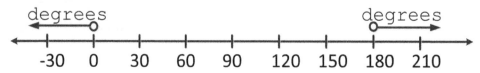

And representing this test:

```
0 > degrees or degrees > 180
```

You can see that the first operand in the within-range test, `0 <= degrees`, is complemented to `0 > degrees` in the outside-range test. The second operand in the within-range test, `degrees <= 180`, is complemented to `degrees > 180` in the outside-range test. And finally, the `and` in the within-range test is changed to an `or` in the outside-range test.

It is also visually clear from the number lines that every value for degrees that will result in a `True` within-range test will result in a `False` outside-range test, and every value for degrees that will result in a `True` outside-range test will result in a `False` inside-range test. These are complementary conditions.

Complementing a condition written with a `not` is comparatively easy! Simply remove the `not`. Therefore, if we have:

```
not validInput
```

the complementary condition is:

```
validInput
```

Try this

❖ Confirm DeMorgan's theorem by drawing out truth tables for the Boolean operators. The truth table for the complement of `and` is started for you:

Op 1	Op 2	Op 1 and Op 2	Op 1'	Op 2'	Op 1' or Op 2'
True	True	True	False	False	False
True	False	False	False	True	True
False	True	False	True		
False	False	False	True		

❖ Complement (do not evaluate) the following relational expressions:

```
.5 <= y
x == y
max >= y ** 2
max != 1000
```

❖ Complement (do not evaluate) the following logical expressions:

```
finished or num < max
10 < max and 1.5 < z
finished and num < max
1024 >= max or num < 5
```

3.8 Testing assumptions with assert statements

Many languages, including Python, include an `assert` statement that allows you to error-check assumptions within your program. The syntax of an `assert` statement is the keyword `assert`, followed by a Boolean expression. This allows the programmer to encode assumptions about the program state that Python will check. If the assumption is correct (if the Boolean condition in the `assert` statement evaluates to `True`), then the program will proceed as usual from the `assert` statement. However, if the Boolean condition evaluates to `False`, then Python will throw a run-time exception, and you know that you have made an incorrect assumption about the state of the program at that point in your code.

Listing 3.2 is a program that computes the current of a very specific circuit after asking the user to enter the battery type. It computes the current using different values for the two different possible battery types, so it uses an `if` statement to select the appropriate computation. However, the program makes an incorrect assumption. See if you can spot it:

```
1   """Compute the current across a circuit with a 350 ohm resistor
2   and a battery."""

3   # Set a constant for the resistor.
4   RESISTANCE = 350
5   # Obtain the type of the battery.
6   battery = input("Please enter N for a 9V battery and T for 12V: ")

7   # Compute the current.
8   if battery == "N":
9       current = 9 / RESISTANCE
10  else:
11      assert battery == "T"
12      current = 12 / RESISTANCE

13  # Display the current.
14  print("The amperage of the circuit is {:.3f}.".format(current))
```
Listing 3.2

A couple of test runs of the program look good, and you might think the program is functioning perfectly:

```
====== RESTART: D:/ current.py ======
Please enter N for a 9V battery and T for 12V: N
The amperage of the circuit is 0.026.
>>>
====== RESTART: D:/ current.py ======
Please enter N for a 9V battery and T for 12V: T
The amperage of the circuit is 0.034.
```

Did you spot the bad assumption, and can you determine what input will cause Python to crash on the `assert` statement?

```
====== RESTART: D:/ current.py ======
Please enter N for a 9V battery and T for 12V: n
Traceback (most recent call last):
  File "D:/ current.py", line 14, in <module>
    assert battery == "T"
AssertionError
```

We assumed that the user would enter only "N" or "T" at the prompt, but that is an incorrect assumption. The user might enter "n", "t", or any other string (such as "9V"). If the user does not enter "N" at the prompt, the program (without the `assert` statement) will simply compute the amperage as if the user had indicated a 12 V battery. It might not be obvious that the computation is wrong. The `assert` statement formalizes the assumption, and Python throws an assertion error when the incorrect assumption is asserted. This allows us to find an error that might not show up in testing.

The `assert` statement does not do anything in the way other statements, such as `if`, `print`, `input`, and assignment statements, do something. It does not change the value in a variable, interact with the user, or change the program's flow of control. What it does is error-check the programmer's assumptions, and help the programmer find potential bugs based on incorrect assumptions.

Try this

❖ Add an assert statement to the following else clause:

```
if age >= 18:
    print("You are old enough to vote!")
else:
    print("You are not old enough to vote!")
```

❖ Add an assert statement to the following else clause:

```
if degrees < 0 or 180 < degrees:
    print("The value for degrees must be between 0 and 180.")
else:
    minutes = int(input("Please enter the minutes: "))
```

❖ For what input or inputs will the following `assert` statement throw an error?

```
if temperature < 0 or temperature > 90:
    print("You might want to stay indoors.")
else:
    assert temperature > 0 and temperature < 90
    print("It is safe to go outside!")
```

3.9　Series if statements

The `if-else` statement is an efficient programming tool if we have two mutually exclusive options that should result in different problem-solving steps, and therefore different paths of execution in our program. However, we sometimes have more than two mutually exclusive options. For example, suppose we want to modify the program from Listing 3.2 to allow for battery voltages of 12, 9, and 1.5. The battery can have only one voltage, so there are three mutually exclusive possibilities. We might write the program using an `if-elif-else` statement:

```
 1   """Compute the current across a circuit with a 350 ohm resistor
 2   and a battery."""

 3   # Set a constant for the resistor.
 4   RESISTANCE = 350

 5   # Obtain the type of the battery.
 6   battery = input("Enter battery type (N for 9V, T for 12V, " + \
                     "O for 1.5V): ")

 7   # Compute the current.
 8   if battery == "N":
 9       current = 9 / RESISTANCE
10   elif battery == "O":
11       current = 1.5 / RESISTANCE
12   else:
13       current = 12 / RESISTANCE

14   # Display the current.
15   print("The amperage of the circuit is {:.3f}.".format(current))
```
Listing 3.3

The `elif` keyword is short for "else if." The syntax is the keyword `elif`, followed by a condition and a colon, and then indented code that is executed if the `elif` condition evaluates to `True`. The `elif` condition is evaluated only if the `if` condition is `False`.

This program begins with a sequential flow of control, which is the default flow of control. Line 4 executes, assigning the value 350 to the constant variable `RESISTANCE`. Line 6 then executes, obtaining a value from the user and storing it in the variable `battery`. We will assume the user enters `"N"`. Execution then reaches line 8. Line 8 will always execute, because it is reached sequentially. It is a test. Because the user entered `"N"`, the test on line 8 evaluates to `True`, line 9 will execute, and the rest of the `if` statement (the `elif-else` portion) will be skipped. Execution will resume on the first line after the `if` block, on line 15.

This listing shows only the executable lines of code, with the lines that execute if the user enters `"N"` highlighted in yellow.

```
4     RESISTANCE = 350
6     battery = input("Enter battery type (N for 9V, T for 12V, " + \
                      "O for 1.5V): ")
8     if battery == "N":
9         current = 9 / RESISTANCE
10    elif battery == "O":
11        current = 1.5 / RESISTANCE
12    else:
13        current = 12 / RESISTANCE
15    print("The amperage of the circuit is {:.3f}.".format(current))
```

Assume the user enters "O". Then, on line 8, the test evaluates to False, and the test on line 10 will execute. That test will be True, and so line 11 will execute, the rest of the if block (the else portion) will be skipped, and execution will resume on the first line after the if block, on line 15.

This listing shows only the executable lines of code, with the lines that execute if the user enters "O" highlighted in yellow.

```
4     RESISTANCE = 350
6     battery = input("Enter battery type (N for 9V, T for 12V, " + \
                      "O for 1.5V): ")
8     if battery == "N":
9         current = 9 / RESISTANCE
10    elif battery == "O":
11        current = 1.5 / RESISTANCE
12    else:
13        current = 12 / RESISTANCE
15    print("The amperage of the circuit is {:.3f}.".format(current))
```

Assume the user does not enter "N" or "O". The test on line 8 will evaluate to False and the test on line 10 will evaluate to False, the else block will execute (lines 12 and 13), and execution will resume on the first line after the if block, on line 15.

This listing shows only the executable lines of code, with the lines that execute if the user enters anything other than "N" or "O" highlighted in yellow.

```
4     RESISTANCE = 350
6     battery = input("Enter battery type (N for 9V, T for 12V, " + \
                      "O for 1.5V): ")
8     if battery == "N":
9         current = 9 / RESISTANCE
10    elif battery == "O":
11        current = 1.5 / RESISTANCE
12    else:
13        current = 12 / RESISTANCE
15    print("The amperage of the circuit is {:.3f}.".format(current))
```

In an `if-elif-else` block, you can see that fewer statements execute if the first test evaluates to `True`. If you know which condition is most likely to execute, you can improve the efficiency of your program by listing that condition first. (It will result in a very modest improvement in efficiency.)

You can write as many `elif` conditions as you need to solve your problem. The `elif` blocks must always follow the `if` condition. If there is an `else` block, it must follow the `if` and all `elif` blocks (if any). The next two listings obtain text from the user and place HTML tags around the text based on user choice. Listing 3.4 shows an `elif` block with three tests:

```
1    """Style some text with HTML tags."""

2    # Obtain the text to be styled.
3    text = input("Please enter the text: ")

4    # Obtain the desired styling.
5    print("Please choose (S)trong, (E)mphasized, or (C)ode.")
6    styling = input("What is your choice? ")

7    # Style the text.
8    if styling == "S":
9        text = "<p><strong>" + text + "</strong></p>"
10   elif styling == "E":
11       text = "<p><em>" + text + "</em></p>"
12   elif styling == "C":
13       text = "<p><code>" + text + "</code></p>"
14   else:
15       text = "<p>" + text + "</p>"

16   # Display the new text string.
17   print("{}".format(text))
```
Listing 3.4

Listing 3.5 shows an `if` block with an `elif` but no `else`.

```
1    """Style some text with HTML tags."""

2    # Obtain the text to be styled.
3    text = input("Please enter the text: ")

4    # Obtain the desired styling.
5    styling = input("Do you want strong (S) or emphasized (E) text?: ")
6    # Style the text.
7    if styling == "S":
8        text = "<strong>" + text + "</strong>"
9    elif styling == "E":
10       text = "<em>" + text + "</em>"
```

```
11   # Display the new text string.
12   print("{}".format(text))
```
Listing 3.5

Try this

❖ List the lines of code that execute in Listing 3.4 if the user enters "S", "E", "C", or something else.

❖ List the lines of code that execute in Listing 3.5 if the user enters "S", "E", or something else.

3.10   Nested if statements

Python, like other programming languages, allows you to test conditional statements within conditional statements. If you are solving a problem in which there are decisions that need to be made in a sort of tree structure (one decision leads to additional decisions), then you might need a nested if to solve the problem.

For example, imagine that you are writing a program to calculate the cost of shipping an item. You might first ask the type of package—standard envelope or box. If the package is a box, you might ask the dimensions (or allow preset dimensions, such as small, medium, and large). Code to solve the box portion of this problem might look like Listing 3.6:

```
1    """Calculate the cost of shipping a box."""

2    # Obtain the type of package.
3    package_type = input("Is the package a (B)ox or (E)nvelope? ")

4    # Calculate the cost for a package.
5    if package_type == "B":
6        # Set a valid input flag.
7        valid_input = True
8        # Obtain the size.
9        size = input("Is the package (S)mall, (M)edium, " +\
                      "or (L)arge? ")
10       # Assign the cost based on size.
11       if size == "S":
12           cost = 8.15
13       elif size == "M":
14           cost = 15.50
15       elif size == "L":
16           cost = 21.25
17       else:
18           assert size != "S" and size != "M" and size != "L"
```

```
19              valid_input = False
20          # Display the cost.
21          if valid_input:
22              print("The cost for your box is ${:.2f}.".format(cost))
23          else:
24              print("That is not a valid package size.")
```
Listing 3.6

This program first asks the user for the type of package. What is shown here is the code that handles a user input of "B" for box. If the package type is a box, then the program asks the user the size of the box. The prompt, "Is the package (S)mall, (M)edium, or (L)arge?" is displayed only if the user has first entered "B" for box. Otherwise, the code that asks for the box size, calculates the cost, and displays the cost is never executed.

Python's requirement that conditional code be indented makes it easy to tell which if, elif, and else statements belong together as a single block. An if block that is nested within another if block will be indented with the other conditional code. That is how you know that it executes only if the outer if condition is True.

On line 5 in Listing 3.6, we have the initial if statement. Lines 6–24 are indented, as they will execute only if the condition on line 5 is True.

On line 11 is a nested if statement, and at the same level of indentation, on lines 13, 15, and 17, are elif and else statements that are part of that nested if block. The conditional code for each of those statements (the code that executes if the condition is True) are further indented (lines 12, 14, 16, 18, and 19).

If the user enters "B" for box, and then "S" for small, lines 3, 5, 7, 9, 11, 12, 21, and 22 execute, highlighted below:

```
3    package_type = input("Is the package a (B)ox or (E)nvelope? ")
5    if package_type == "B":
7        valid_input = True
9        size = input("Is the package (S)mall, (M)edium, " +\
                      "or (L)arge? ")
11       if size == "S":
12           cost = 8.15
13       elif size == "M":
14           cost = 15.50
15       elif size == "L":
16           cost = 21.25
17       else:
18           assert size != "S" and size != "M" and size != "L"
19           valid_input = False
21       if valid_input:
22           print("The cost for your box is ${:.2f}.".format(cost))
23       else:
24           print("That is not a valid package size.")
```

Try this

❖ Which lines in Listing 3.6 execute if the user enters "B" and then "L"?
❖ Which lines in Listing 3.6 execute if the user enters "B" and then "T"?
❖ Which lines in Listing 3.6 execute if the user enters "E"?

3.11   Desk checking and debugging conditional statements

3.11.1   Desk checking

Writing conditional code means that there are many possible execution paths through your program. For example, there is one execution path, in Listing 3.6, that is followed if the user enters the proper inputs to calculate the cost for a small box. That execution path is different (different lines of code execute) if the user correctly enters the code for calculating the cost for an envelope, or the cost for a large box, or if they type in an unexpected character, such as "X".

When a program has many execution paths, it becomes more difficult to understand, more prone to error, and more challenging to debug when something goes wrong.

One technique for checking your code as you write it, or after you have written it, is called **desk checking**. Desk checking involves writing down the program state (the values in the variables) and the lines of code that execute for a given set of inputs.

We will desk check Listing 3.6 when the user enters "B" and then "M".

To do this, we create a desk-checking table. The rows in the table represent the program state after each line executes. We will have columns in the table for the number of the line that is executing, for each variable in the program, and for input and output (if any). With conditional code, it is sometimes helpful to also have columns for the conditions, so we can record if they are True or False. (And you can include other columns if they will help you step through, or desk check, your code.)

On line 3, the program obtains the package type from the user, and the user enters "B".

```
3 package_type = input("Is the package a (B)ox or (E)nvelope? ")
```

Line #	package_type	valid_input	size	cost	package_type == "B"	size == "S"	size == "M"	size == "L"	Input	Output
3	"B"								B	

After line 3 executes, line 5 is reached sequentially. Line 5 is the test package_type == "B". The test evaluates to True, so the conditional code will be entered. The flag valid_input is set and the user is prompted for the size of the box. (New lines in the desk-checking table will be highlighted in yellow.)

```
 5    if package_type == "B":
 7        valid_input = True
 9        size = input("Is the package (S)mall, (M)edium, " +\
                         "or (L)arge? ")
```

Line #	package_type	valid_input	size	cost	package_type == "B"	size == "S"	size == "M"	size == "L"	Input	Output
3	"B"									B
5	"B"				True					
7	"B"	True								
9	"B"	True	"M"							M

Line 11 is now reached sequentially. Line 11 is the test `size == "S"`. This test evaluates to `False`, and so the conditional code on line 12 is skipped and the next `elif` is executed on line 13. The `elif` condition is `size == "M"`, which evaluates to `True`, so the conditional code on line 14 will execute.

```
11    if size == "S":
12        cost = 8.15
13    elif size == "M":
14        cost = 15.50
```

Line #	package_type	valid_input	size	cost	package_type == "B"	size == "S"	size == "M"	size == "L"	Input	Output
3	"B"									B
5	"B"				True					
7	"B"	True								
9	"B"	True	"M"							M
11	"B"	True	"M"			False				
13	"B"	True	"M"				True			
14	"B"	True	"M"	15.5						

Because a test evaluated to `True` in the `if` block, the rest of the block (lines 15–19) is skipped. Control moves sequentially to line 21, which is the test `valid_input`. This test, which is the evaluation of a Boolean variable, evaluates to `True`, and the conditional (indented) code on line 22 executes. The rest of the conditional statement (lines 23 and 24) is skipped, and the program is finished executing.

```
21    if valid_input:
22        print("The cost for your box is ${:.2f}.".format(cost))
```

```
23   else:
24       print("That is not a valid package size.")
```

Line #	package_ type	valid_ input	size	cost	package_ type == "B"	size == "S"	size == "M"	size == "L"	Input	Output
3	"B"								B	
5	"B"				True					
7	"B"	True								
9	"B"	True	"M"							
11	"B"	True	"M"			False				
13	"B"	True	"M"				True			
14	"B"	True	"M"	15.5						
21	"B"	True	"M"	15.5						
22	"B"	True	"M"	15.5						*

*The cost for your box is $15.50.

You must be careful, when desk-checking code, to play the role of Python interpreter, and perform the exact computation that is written into the code. It is very tempting to assume the code does what you want it to do. Taking a methodical, step-by-step approach will often uncover assumptions and other errors.

Try this

❖ Construct a desk-checking table and desk check Listing 3.6 for input values of "B" and then "S".
❖ Construct a desk-checking table and desk check Listing 3.6 for input values of "B" and then "L".
❖ Construct a desk-checking table and desk check Listing 3.6 for an input value of "E".
❖ Desk check Listing 3.3, entering an invalid battery type.
❖ Desk check Listing 3.4 and enter "C" at the prompt.

3.11.2 Debugging

Many integrated development environments, like IDLE, have a built-in tool called a **debugger** that allow you to step through your code line by line and examine the program state. Debuggers show you the values associated with the variables and which lines of code are executing (and which are not).

To debug a program in IDLE, choose *Debugger* from the *Debug* menu in the IDLE console, then run your program. When you do, you will see a message in the console indicating that the debugger is on:

```
>>>
[DEBUG ON]
>>>
```

And the *Debug Control* window will appear (see Figure 3-5). The Debug Control window has three sections. At the top, you can see controls: *Go, Step, Over, Out,* and *Quit.* You will use these controls to step through your code.

In the middle, you can see the line of code that is currently executing.

At the bottom, you can see the values in your variables. There are a lot of environment variables (they begin and end with two underscores __) that will be unfamiliar to you. You do not need to worry about those. To step through the lines of code, you should use the *Over* button.

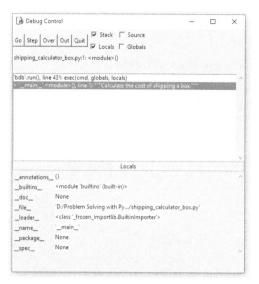

Figure 3-5 The IDLE Debug Control window.

You might set your screen up so that you can see all three windows at the same time, as in Figure 3-6. Here you can see the code on the left, and the debugger and console windows on the right.

Figure 3-6 Setting up Python for debugging.

If we press the *Over* button two more times, Python is executing the input statement, and we are shown the prompt in the IDLE console, as in Figure 3-6.

If we type a "B", the debugger window shows us that it is executing line 7, `if package_type == "B"`. (Note that Python does not distinguish between blank lines and lines with text, so line 7 is the seventh line in the program file.) In the variables area at the bottom, we can see our variable `package_type` and the value `'B'` next to it, as in Figure 3-7. This is what we expect.

If we press the *Over* button again, then we enter the conditional code because the condition was `True`.

We can proceed this way through the program, confirming that the values associated with the variables and the lines of code that execute are what we expect. If there is a bug in the program, we will eventually see a value in a variable or a line of code execute (or not execute) that does not match our expectations. Then we need to figure out why!

When you are debugging, you usually have an idea about where your program is going wrong. For example, if I am typing "B", but my program is not producing the correct output, then I would really like to examine the values in

Figure 3-7   The Debug Control window after a few lines have executed.

variables after I type "B" but before the output is computed. In a large program, it would be convenient to be able to jump to a location near the faulty code. (Or near what you believe is the faulty code.)

Debuggers allow you to do this by setting a **break point**. A break point is a line of code that you can tag. You then press the *Go* button in the *Debug Control* window, and the program will execute up to the break point and then stop. At that point, you can examine the values in variables and proceed with the *Over* button, or you can press *Quit* if examining the variables shows you your bug.

To set a break point, right-click within the line in your program that you want to stop on and choose *Set Breakpoint* from the contextual menu that appears. When you are finished debugging, you can right-click again and choose *Clear Breakpoint*. The default appearance for a line on which you have set a breakpoint is a yellow highlight.

Try this

- ❖ Run Listing 3.6 in the debugger. Use the *Over* button to step through the code, one line at a time. Type in input values of "B" and then "S".
- ❖ Run Listing 3.6 in the debugger. Use the *Over* button to step through the code, one line at a time. Type in input values of "B" and then "L".
- ❖ Run Listing 3.6 in the debugger. Use the *Over* button to step through the code, one line at a time. Type in an input value of "E".
- ❖ Set a break point in Listing 3.6 at the test `if valid_input:`, and run your program in the debugger. Instead of using the *Over* button, use the *Go* button. Type in input values of "B" and then "S".
- ❖ Debug Listing 3.4 with the value "C" as input. Confirm your desk check from the last section while debugging.

3.11.3 Debugging with print statements

One other debugging technique that programmers use is inserting temporary print statements in strategic locations within a program to display the values in variables to the console, or to confirm that certain conditional blocks are entered (or not).

For example, if you are not certain if the correct cost is being set when the user chooses a medium box size, you might put a print statement inside the conditional block, and print the values in size and cost:

```python
if size == "S":
    cost = 8.15
elif size == "M":
    cost = 15.50
    print("Inside M size elif, cost = {}.".format(cost))
    print("Size = {}.".format(size))
elif size == "L":
    cost = 21.25
else:
    assert size != "S" and size != "M" and size != "L"
    valid_input = False
```

Here is what happens when you run the program and type "M" at the package size prompt:

```
Is the package a (B)ox or (E)nvelope? B
Is the package (S)mall, (M)edium, or (L)arge? M
Inside M size elif, cost = 15.5.
Size = M.
The cost for your box is $15.50.
```

Programmers sometimes leave this debugging code inside their program, and simply place a comment in front of it when it is no longer needed. If they need the debugging code again, they can remove the comment tokens. In IDLE, you can select lines of code and choose *Comment Out Region* from the *Format* menu, and it will comment the selected code.

```python
elif size == "M":
    cost = 15.50
##    print("Inside M size elif, cost = {}.".format(cost))
##    print("Size = {}.".format(size))
```

Try this

❖ Add some print statements to Listing 3.3 in the final else. Print the values of battery and current.

❖ Select your print statements and choose *Comment Out Region* from the *Format* menu. Select them again and choose *Uncomment Region*.

3.11.4 Debugging is problem-solving

Quite often when new programmers encounter a bug, they will try making changes to their code without first investigating what the problem is. This generally leads to:

❖ Not finding the problem that was causing the bug
❖ Introducing new bugs as the new programmer transforms working code into broken code

When your program is not functioning correctly, the most successful approach will be to follow the problem-solving steps outlined earlier.

❖ Define the problem
❖ Identify and clearly express solutions
❖ Evaluate and select among those solutions
❖ Implement a solution
❖ Evaluate the result

If you also keep an engineering journal of your debugging, then you can easily undo any "fix" that did not solve your problem. (It is a good idea to keep an engineering journal that documents all of your design and programming decisions. It is an excellent reference if you are asked why certain decisions were made, what inputs you tested, and it can help you if you need to solve a similar problem in the future.)

Suppose we have written a program that will ask the user if they prefer fruit or chocolate for dessert. If they answer chocolate, then the program will ask if they prefer milk or dark. The program will suggest a fruit salad, a dark truffle, or a milk chocolate bar depending on the user's answers. The program is shown in Listing 3.7:

```
1    """Program to suggest a dessert."""

2    # Get the user's preference.
3    preference = input("Chocolate or fruit for dessert? ")

4    # Get more information.
5    if preference == "chocolate":
6        kind_of_chocolate = input("Do you prefer dark or milk? ")

7    # Suggest a dessert.
8    print("You should try a fruit salad.")
9    if kind_of_chocolate == "dark":
10       print("You should try a dark chocolate truffle.")
11   else:
12       print("You should try a milk chocolate bar.")
```
Listing 3.7

The first step is defining the problem. The more clearly you define the problem, the easier it will be to identify and clearly express solutions, and the easier it will be to evaluate if your solution, once implemented, solved the problem.

To define this problem, we must test the buggy code thoroughly so that we have a complete description of what it is doing right and what it is doing wrong. We can clearly define the expected behavior of this program in a table, and then test the program and compare our results to the expected behavior:

Input at first prompt	Input at second prompt	Expected output	Actual output

`fruit`	`N/A`	`You should try a fruit salad.`	`Chocolate or fruit for dessert? fruit`
			
			`You should try a fruit salad.`
			
			`Traceback (most recent call last):`
			
			`    File "D:/ buggy.py", line 12, in <module>`
			
			`        if kind_of_chocolate == "dark":`
			
			`NameError: name 'kind_of_chocolate' is not defined`

`chocolate`	`dark`	`You should try a dark truffle.`	`Chocolate or fruit for dessert? chocolate`
			
			`Do you prefer dark or milk? dark`
			
			`You should try a fruit salad.`
			
			`You should try a dark chocolate truffle.`

`chocolate`	`milk`	`You should try a milk chocolate bar.`	`Chocolate or fruit for dessert? chocolate`
			
			`Do you prefer dark or milk? milk`
			
			`You should try a fruit salad.`
			
			`You should try a milk chocolate bar.`

By thoroughly testing the program, we begin to understand what sorts of errors we are encountering. The program almost works if we first choose chocolate, but it suggests fruit salad before suggesting a kind of chocolate dessert. If we choose fruit, then the program suggests fruit salad followed by a run-time error with the text `"name 'kind_of_chocolate' is not defined"`. It will be helpful to understand exactly which lines of code are executing to fully understand how the program is producing this output.

We know three techniques for examining the internal state and execution path of our program as it runs: desk checking, debugging, and adding print statements. We can choose among them to further define the problem that we are having with the code. We want to know which lines are executing, and what the state of the program is as it executes.

If we choose to debug, we might place a breakpoint after the program obtains the user's preference. Perhaps we will start with the input `"fruit"`, as that seems to be the worst bug (because it causes a run-time error) or because it is first in the table. When we step through the code, we will discover that after the program suggests a fruit salad to the user, it then tests the value in the variable `kind_of_chocolate`. But this variable has no value, as it is only assigned a value if the user enters `"chocolate"` at the first prompt. That causes the run-time error.

It might be tempting now to make a change, but we have not yet fully defined the problem. So we debug the program for the two cases in which the user enters `"chocolate"` at the first prompt, and we discover that the program is always displaying the fruit salad message, regardless of what the user has entered.

We have now fully defined the problem: we have thoroughly tested the program, and we have run our test cases in the debugger to see which lines of code are executing and how they are causing the incorrect behavior.

The next problem-solving steps are to identify and clearly express solutions, then select and implement a solution, and evaluate the results.

We will leave these steps as an exercise for you! Remember to think of all the tools that you know and evaluate whether those tools will help you to write the correct behavior. We need the program to display the fruit salad message only if the user has chosen fruit at the first prompt, and we need the program to test the value in the `kind_of_chocolate` variable only if the user has chosen chocolate at the first prompt. Finally, once you have chosen and implemented the solution, you must thoroughly test it again to evaluate it. Good luck!

3.12   Data representation

3.12.1   Representing continuous data in a digital world

The underlying representation of data in a computer system is digital. Everything that is stored, including videos, sound, images, text, and computer programs, are ultimately stored as a series of bits, each representing one of two states. We think of those two states as being the binary numbers 0 and 1. On a physical storage medium, those two states might be represented by magnetic bits, a pitted or reflective surface, or a component holding an electric charge.

In high-level programming languages like Python, we do not often have to think about that underlying representation. But there are occasions when the limits of the representation, because it is physical and because it is binary, can cause problems with our programs. If we understand something about the representation, then we can avoid some of those problems.

Many of the solutions to the difficult problem of representing continuous data on a digital system are encoded in standards. Standards represent well-designed solutions that allow for the sharing of data across systems. Examples of standards include the American Standard Code for Information Interchange (ASCII) and Unicode standards for representing character data, and the IEEE 754 standard for representing floating-point numbers.

3.12.2 Numeric types

In mathematics, numbers are an abstraction. If we use the number 3.5, for example, it could represent interest computed on an account in euros, the length of the hypotenuse of a triangle, or the number of inches between balusters supporting a railing. Although we use a real number to represent those quantities, are there details of the underlying digital representation that mean we should choose different data types for them?

A physical representation of data will naturally have limitations. (Such as the number of bits available on the storage medium.) Even though we are not usually directly manipulating the bits that represent our numbers, our computations are still vulnerable to errors introduced by the representation. It is therefore important to understand how the different data types are represented in the underlying hardware.

An integer representation is relatively simple. In most programming languages, integers are stored in a fixed number of bits (e.g., 32). Because bits have only two states, the number that is stored is a binary representation of the integer. In a 32-bit representation, one bit indicates the sign of the number (1 for negative, 0 for positive), and the other 31 are available for representing the value of the integer. In a 32-bit representation, then, you can represent integer values from -2^{31} through $-2^{31} - 1$, or $-2,147,483,648$ through $2,147,483,648$. There are details that are not included here, but this is roughly how integers are represented.

Limitations of integer representation in most languages are related to the size of the integer we can represent. In most languages, if you need to represent integers larger than roughly two billion (or smaller than roughly negative two billion), you will not be able to use an integer (Figure 3-8).

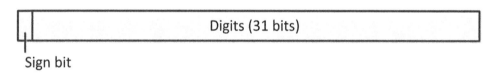

Sign bit

Figure 3-8 Representation of a 32-bit integer.

Python is unusual in that there is not a fixed number of bits allocated for an integer. In Python, the size of an integer is constrained only by the amount of available memory. If the data that you are representing is inherently countable, you should be able to represent it with an integer in Python, even if it might have a very large or small magnitude.

Booleans are a special subset of integers, with 0 representing `False` and 1 representing `True`.

Floating-point values are represented in a format like scientific notation. (Again, very specific details of the representation will not be discussed here.) Numbers are stored in three parts: the sign, the significand (significant digits), and the exponent. The IEEE 754 standard (2008) defines a double-precision number as using 64 bits: one for the sign, 11 for the exponent, and 52 for the significant digits (Figure 3-9).

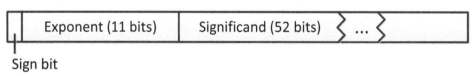

Sign bit

Figure 3-9 Representation of a 64-bit float.

We will discuss two limitations to the representation of double-precision floating-point numbers that might affect your decision to use a float or to perform computations with a float. The first is precision, and the second is the difference between binary and decimal math.

Although a floating-point number can, theoretically, have any number of digits after the decimal point, we are limited in the number of digits we can store. We have only a fixed number of discrete bits for storage. We can store numbers with a very large magnitude because there are a lot of digits for the exponent. The largest magnitude integer we can represent in 32 bits is −2,147,483,648, and we will store every single digit of that number. The largest magnitude float we can represent in Python is $1.7976931348623157 \times 10^{308}$ (that is 2^{1024}), but most of that large number will be zeroes, because only 17 significant digits can be stored. This is a consideration if you are solving a problem in which you need more precision than the float can provide, or if you are performing arithmetic on numbers that are so different in size that when they are normalized to the same power of 10, one number is lost. For example, Python loses the smaller number in the second computation:

```
>>> 1.0e+15 + 1.0
1000000000000001.0
>>> 1.0e+16 + 1.0
1e+16
```

The other source of potential problems is the difference between binary and decimal representation. The value 1/3, in decimal, is a repeating decimal. If we perform the division, we get .3 (repeating), or an infinite number of threes to the right of the decimal. If asked, we could not write the whole solution—we would be writing forever. (Maybe we should just stick to fractions!) In the binary number system, there are different repeating decimals. So while we might expect the result of 1/3 to be infinite, we might be surprised to find that 1/10, for example, is a repeating decimal in the binary number system. Computations that we expect to be straightforward are not going to be precise. For example, look at this console session:

```
>>> .1 + .1 + .1 + .1 + .1 + .1 + .1 + .1
0.7999999999999999
```

For now, you should be aware of these problems. For example, if you wrote a test to compare .1 * 7 to .7, the test would evaluate to `False` and you might be very confused if you did not remember the representational disadvantages of floats.

When you are designing software in the future, you might look for special number types in the language that you are using or in libraries. For example, there is a module available for Python called numPy which can be used for scientific computing applications, and many languages have a decimal number representation that you can use to avoid differences between binary and decimal math. There are trade-offs with every number representation, so you must choose what is best for the problem you are solving.

3.12.3 Strings

Strings are a collection of characters, with each character represented by a numeric code. Python supports several different Unicode encodings, but considering an ASCII representation (which is a predecessor of Unicode) will be sufficient for this discussion.

The following piece of the ASCII table shows the binary, decimal, and hexadecimal representation for some commonly used characters:

Binary	Decimal	Hex	Character	Binary	Decimal	Hex	Character
0100000	32	20	space	1010100	84	54	T
0100001	33	21	!	1010101	85	55	U
0100010	34	22	"	1010110	86	56	V
0100011	35	23	#	1010111	87	57	W
0100100	36	24	$	1011000	88	58	X
0100101	37	25	%	1011001	89	59	Y
0100110	38	26	&	1011010	90	5A	Z
0100111	39	27	'	1011011	91	5B	[
0101000	40	28	(	1011100	92	5C	\
0101001	41	29	)	1011101	93	5D	]
0101010	42	2A	*	1011110	94	5E	^
0101011	43	2B	+	1011111	95	5F	_
0101100	44	2C	,	1100000	96	60	`
0101101	45	2D	-	1100001	97	61	a
0101110	46	2E	.	1100010	98	62	b
0101111	47	2F	/	1100011	99	63	c
0110000	48	30	0	1100100	100	64	d
0110001	49	31	1	1100101	101	65	e
0110010	50	32	2	1100110	102	66	f
0110011	51	33	3	1100111	103	67	g
0110100	52	34	4	1101000	104	68	h
0110101	53	35	5	1101001	105	69	i
0110110	54	36	6	1101010	106	6A	j
0110111	55	37	7	1101011	107	6B	k
0111000	56	38	8	1101100	108	6C	l
0111001	57	39	9	1101101	109	6D	m
0111010	58	3A	:	1101110	110	6E	n
0111011	59	3B	;	1101111	111	6F	o

(Continued)

(Continued)

Binary	Decimal	Hex	Character	Binary	Decimal	Hex	Character
0111100	60	3C	<	1110000	112	70	p
0111101	61	3D	=	1110001	113	71	q
0111110	62	3E	>	1110010	114	72	r
0111111	63	3F	?	1110011	115	73	s
1000000	64	40	@	1110100	116	74	t
1000001	65	41	A	1110101	117	75	u
1000010	66	42	B	1110110	118	76	v
1000011	67	43	C	1110111	119	77	w
1000100	68	44	D	1111000	120	78	x
1000101	69	45	E	1111001	121	79	y
1000110	70	46	F	1111010	122	7A	z
1000111	71	47	G	1111011	123	7B	{
1001000	72	48	H	1111100	124	7C		
1001001	73	49	I	1111101	125	7D	}
1001010	74	4A	J				
1001011	75	4B	K				
1001100	76	4C	L				
1001101	77	4D	M				
1001110	78	4E	N				
1001111	79	4F	O				
1010000	80	50	P				
1010001	81	51	Q				
1010010	82	52	R				
1010011	83	53	S				

You can ask Python for the decimal value of a single-character string with the `ord` function:

```
>>> ord("A")
65
```

Because characters have a numeric value, they can be compared in a meaningful way with the relational operators. Just as you can compare 65 and 66, you can compare "A" and "B". You might notice that the character representations of the digits zero through nine, the uppercase letters, and the lowercase letters are all in numeric or alphabetic order. Therefore, "0" < "1", "A" < "B", and "a" < "b" will all evaluate to True in Python. But you must be careful, because "Z" < "a" will also evaluate to True, as the uppercase letters have smaller numeric values than the lowercase letters.

You can compare strings of characters using the relational operators; not just individual characters. The rules for comparison are called **lexicographic ordering**. They should be familiar, as they are how we alphabetize words and compare nonnegative integers. The rules are as follows:

❖ Python compares the first character of each string. If one character is larger, then that is the larger string. For example, "Turing" > "Pascal" because "T" is represented by a larger value than "P".

❖ If the first characters are the same, Python continues with the second character, then the third, continuing along each string comparing characters in the same position until it finds characters that are different. The first characters that Python finds that are different determine the ordering of the string. For example, "application" > "apple" because "i" > "e", and these are the first same-position characters in the strings that are different.

❖ If two strings are the same to the end of one string, but the other string is longer, then the longer string is larger. For example, "smithereens" > "smith" because they are the same for all five letters of "smith", but then "smithereens" continues. It is therefore larger.

❖ If two strings are the same length and contain exactly the same characters in the same order, then the strings are the same. For example, "python" == "python".

Try this

❖ At the IDLE prompt, type: int(True)
❖ At the IDLE prompt, type:

```
if 5:
    print("5 isn't a Boolean!")
if 0:
    print("Is 0 a Boolean??")
```

What is IDLE's response to each? What does that tell you about the underlying representation of Booleans?

❖ Find another computation (like adding very small and very large floats) that does not work the way you expect because of the underlying number representation.

❖ Can you find another unexpected repeating decimal resulting from a binary division?

❖ Determine which of the following pairs of strings is greater (or if they are the same). Check your answers in the Python interpreter.

```
"art", "arthur"        "Art", "arthur"     "Python", "C++"
"alphabet", "zebra"    "@-@", "$$$"        "!!", "!!"
```

3.13　The random library

Python has a library that will generate pseudorandom numbers. This can be useful for many applications, including games and encryption (although there is a separate library in Python for generating random numbers for encryption). Listing 3.8 is a simple program that simulates the roll of two six-sided dice and reports the sum of the dice to the user:

```
1    """Simulate the roll of two d6, sum, and display the result."""

2    import random

3    # Simulate the rolls.
4    die1 = random.randint(1,6)
5    die2 = random.randint(1,6)

6    # Sum the rolls.
7    sum_dice = die1 + die2

8    # Display the result.
9    print("You rolled {}.".format(sum_dice))
```
Listing 3.8

To generate a random number, you will first import the random library at the top of your program with the statement `import random`, as on line 2 of Listing 3.8.

To generate a random integer, you will then use the `random.randint` function. You pass the start and end of the range you want (a, b) as arguments, and Python will generate a random integer between a and b (inclusive). You will need to do something with the generated value, such as store it in a variable. On lines 4 and 5 in Listing 3.8, random integers in the range 1, 6 are generated and associated with the variable names `die1` and `die2`.

The random library has other functions that you can read about in the documentation at:

https://docs.python.org/3/library/random.html

Try this

❖ Modify Listing 3.8 by asking the user for the number of sides of the dice (instead of using 6). Randomly generate a value between 1 and the number of sides for each simulated die roll.

❖ Randomly generate a number between 1 and 100 and print the number.

❖ Prompt the user for a low and high value, and randomly generate a number between those values.

3.14   Challenge accepted!

1. Design a program that converts a longitude coordinate from DD format to DMS format. The DMS degrees value will be the integer value for the DD degrees, but without the sign. Remember that a negative DD value for degrees is to the West of the prime meridian, and a positive value is to the East. Take the value to the right of the decimal and multiply by 60. The integer portion of that will be the minutes. Take the value to the right of the decimal and multiply by 60 again, and that is the seconds. For example, −73.9874 DD is 73° 59′ 14.64″ W.

2. Modify Listing 3.1 to include input validation for all four inputs.

3. Write a program that randomly generates a value between 1 and 4, representing a card suit (spades, clubs, hearts, and diamonds) and displays the suit to the user.

4. Write a guess-the-number program that randomly generates an integer between 1 and 10 and gives the user three guesses. Tell the user if each guess is too high, too low, or correct.

5. Write a program that asks the user if they would like to know their weight on Mercury, Venus, or Mars. Ask them for their weight on Earth. Convert their weight to mass using the formula kg = lbs ÷ 2.205 and then calculate their weight on the planet they have chosen and display the result. (The conversion equation for Mercury is kg ∗ .38, for Venus is kg ∗ .91, and for Mars is kg ∗ .38)

6. Write a program that asks the user the year of their birth. It should then tell them the name of their generation. Use the following ranges and names:

   ✦ 1902–1926 GI Generation
   ✦ 1927–1945 Silent Generation
   ✦ 1946–1964 Baby Boomers
   ✦ 1965–1980 Gen X
   ✦ 1981–2000 Millennials
   ✦ 2001–Present Generation Inclusive

7. Create a quiz or flash card program that asks the user a question, obtains their answer, and then tells them if their answer is right or wrong. If their answer is wrong, tell them the correct answer. Have the program ask the user three questions. For example, one question might look like this:

   ```
   What symbol do you use to write a comment in Python? //
   No, that's wrong. The correct answer is #.
   ```

8. Write a program that allows the user to choose where to dig for treasure. Your program should generate a "map" with quadrants. This could be as simple as a 20 × 20 square split into four equal pieces. Randomly generate an (x, y) coordinate within the map to be the location of the treasure and give your user one to three chances to dig for the treasure (depending on how many quadrants you have). Let them know if they find the quadrant with the treasure. You could further enhance the program by drawing the map for the user with turtle graphics. Once the user has used up all of their guesses, draw the x to show them the location of the treasure.

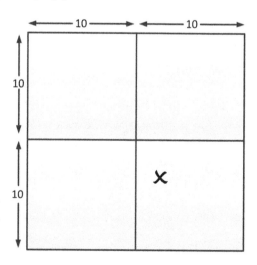

9. A company sells promotional flash drives for $7.75 each for orders up to 50 flash drives. For orders of 50 up to 100, they cost $7.00 each, and for orders of 100 or more, they cost $6.50 each. Write a program that asks the user how many promotional flash drives they are ordering and displays the total cost.

10. Write a program that requests three scores as input and displays the average of the two highest scores. The output should show two positions to the right of the decimal point.

11. On a beach walk, you have recorded observations of scallop shells. The observations include the length of each shell. You would like to find the average length of all shells that were 2 inches long or more. Write a program that allows the user to input the lengths of five scallop shells, and then find the average length of only those shells that have a length of at least 2 inches. (So, e.g., if the lengths were 1.78, 2.14, 2.3, 1.92, and 2.44, you would average 2.14, 2.3, and 2.44, giving you 2.29.) Display the result with two positions to the right of the decimal. Hint: You will have to keep both a running total and a running count of shells two inches or longer.

12. Write a program that will tell the user if a year is a leap year. The rules are as follows: every year divisible by four is a leap year, but years divisible by 100 are not, unless they are divisible by 400. For example, the years 1996 (divisible by 4, but not divisible by 100 or 400) and 2000 (divisible by 4, 100, and 400) were leap years, but 1900 (divisible by 4 and 100 but not 400) was not. Write a program that requests a year as input and states whether it is a leap year.

13. In the classic game of Planks and Bones (okay, we just made it up, but we think it should be a classic), each player is given three dice. In the first round, they roll all three dice. In the second round, they may reroll one die, two dice, or all three dice, and they may do the same in the third. The goal is to achieve three of a kind (e.g., three fives) or three in a row (e.g., 2, 3, 4). At the end of the three rounds, the game is scored as follows: add the values on the dice. Multiply by two if the user rolled three of a kind or three in a row. The player with the higher score wins. (The rounds can be repeated for as long as the players like, with the scores accumulating between rounds.) Write a program that will allow one player to play the game alone for one set of three rounds and simplify the game by allowing only three of a kind (no three in a row). The program should start by simulating the roll of the three dice using the `random` library and reporting the rolls to the user. It should then ask the user which dice (if any) they would like to reroll, and it should reroll those dice only. It should do that again for the third round, and then total the dice, multiply by two if it was three of a kind and tell the user their score. (For a more challenging project, add the three in a row goal back into the game.) For example, a round of the game might look like this:

```
You rolled: 2, 5, 6
Would you like to re-roll the 2? (Y or N) Y
Would you like to re-roll the 5? (Y or N) Y
Would you like to re-roll the 6? (Y or N) N
You rolled: 3, 6, 6
Would you like to re-roll the 3? (Y or N) Y
Would you like to re-roll the 6? (Y or N) N
Would you like to re-roll the 6? (Y or N) N
You rolled: 1, 6, 6
Your score is 13.
```

14. You are going to write a quick app to help you decide the best Buy-One-Get-One (BOGO) deal. In the BOGO deal, the higher-priced item is full price, but the lower-priced item is 50% of its

original price. Write a program that prompts the user for the two prices and reports what the final cost will be. (The program must determine which is the higher-priced item.)

15. Write a program that will calculate an area for the user. The program should begin by presenting the user with a menu of different shapes. (e.g., it could present square, circle, rectangle, and triangle.) It should prompt the user to make a selection from the menu. Depending on the choice, it will then prompt the user for the dimensions needed to compute the area, it will compute the area, and report the area to the user. You can use the following area formulae:

Area of a square = side^2

Area of a rectangle = width × height

Area of a triangle = $\dfrac{1}{2}$ × base × height

Area of a circle = π × radius^2

16. Write a program that will convert a temperature for the user. First, prompt the user for a temperature. Then ask if the temperature entered is in degrees Fahrenheit or degrees Celsius. Convert the temperature to the other scale. The conversion formulae are the following:

$$\text{Degrees Celsius} = \left(\text{Degrees Fahrenheit} - 32\right) \times \frac{5}{9}$$

$$\text{Degrees Fahrenheit} = \text{Degrees Celsius} \times \frac{9}{5} + 32$$

17. Write a program that allows two players to play tic-tac-toe. You do not need to draw the board, but you should report the locations of the pieces after each move, for example, the board might look like this after three moves:

```
1 2 3
4 o 6
X 8 x
```

Allow the user to choose the quadrant in which to move. You can keep track of whether it is x's turn or o's turn. If the user enters a quadrant that is outside of the range 1–9 or that already has a piece in it, they forfeit their move.

18. You and your friends have constructed small, balloon-powered cars using a maximum budget of $3 per car. After racing them, you want to compute the average cost of the cars that crossed the finish line and the average cost of the cars that did not, to see if the cost of materials was a factor in the success or failure of the cars. Write a program that will allow the user to enter, first, the distance of the course, and then the cost and distance traveled of each of eight cars. (That is a total of seventeen inputs.) Compute the average cost of all cars that traveled the distance of the course or more, and the average cost of all cars that traveled less than the distance of the course. (Hint: You will need to keep track of running totals and at least one count.)

Chapter 4

Loops and files

4.1 Finding repetition in a problem

We will return to the turtle module to begin our conversation about problems with repetition, because it is easy to visualize repetition in a drawing. Suppose we wish to draw a picture with the turtle that is a series of boxes stacked on top of each other.

Figure 4-1 is a plan of the drawing that we want to create. This represents a clear definition of the problem. If we were to describe it verbally, we might say that we want to draw a series of five 50 by 50 boxes aligned in a tower without vertical space between them, starting with a bottom left corner of (0, 0), and ending with a bottom left corner of (0, 200). However, the drawing communicates that information and more, because the drawing shows the bottom left coordinate of each box. (We could further add all the coordinates of each box, which might also be helpful.)

Moving to the second problem-solving step, identifying and clearly expressing solutions, we could tackle this problem in several ways. For example, we could draw one large outer rectangle (with bottom left (0, 0) and top right (50, 250)), and then draw the lines inside that define the individual 50 by 50 boxes. Another solution is to draw five 50 by 50 boxes. There are also several variations in the order in which we complete the drawing.

The standards that we know and can use to evaluate solutions are efficiency and readability. There are ways to make either solution efficient, so we will set efficiency considerations aside. We will select the general solution of drawing five 50 by 50 boxes, because it is a closer conceptual match for the problem description, which will make it easy to read and modify.

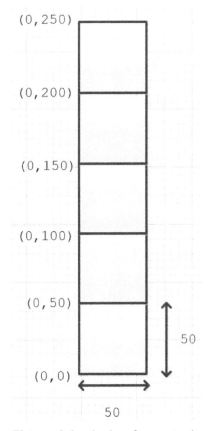

Figure 4-1 A plan for a stack of boxes.

We now have a solution to implement! If we were to implement the solution with the tools we currently have, then our program would be a very long series of turtle commands. Listing 4.1 is the code to draw just two boxes:

```
1   import turtle

2   SIDE = 50
3   # Assumption: turtle starts at 0,0 with a heading of 0.

4   # Draw first box.
5   turtle.forward(SIDE)
6   turtle.left(90)
7   turtle.forward(SIDE)
8   turtle.left(90)
9   turtle.forward(SIDE)
10  turtle.left(90)
11  turtle.forward(SIDE)

12  # Move turtle to start of next box.
13  turtle.penup()
14  turtle.setpos(0,50)
15  turtle.setheading(0)
16  turtle.pendown()

17  # Draw second box.
18  turtle.forward(SIDE)
19  turtle.left(90)
20  turtle.forward(SIDE)
21  turtle.left(90)
22  turtle.forward(SIDE)
23  turtle.left(90)
24  turtle.forward(SIDE)

25  # Move turtle to start of next box.
26  turtle.penup()
27  turtle.setpos(0,100)
28  turtle.setheading(0)
29  turtle.pendown()
```
Listing 4.1

There are a few disadvantages to this code. First, it is very lengthy, and that makes it difficult to read and edit. Second, when we write a lot of repetitive code, there is a possibility of introducing an error (often a copy/paste error, but sometimes simply a typing error). Third, because it is lengthy and repetitive, it is difficult to modify and debug. If we decided that we want to have the boxes start somewhere else in the window, then we will have to calculate the new coordinates, and then scroll through the code, find all of the setpos commands, and update the coordinates. Finally, we should never be performing calculations by hand to type into code. If we are writing a program, the program should be performing the calculations for us!

Python (and other programming languages) have looping structures that you can wrap around code that you want to repeat. When we design using these structures, we can avoid the problems of lengthy, repetitive programs. What we must do is identify what is repeating. We must also identify what is changing in each repetition.

Take a moment to look at the drawing plan for the boxes and Listing 4.1 and see if you can identify what is repeating and what is changing in each repetition.

You hopefully identified that the box-drawing code does not change. That will be repeated for every box, and so it will make the code much shorter and easier to read if we write that code once and wrap a loop structure around it so that it repeats. However, if we repeat drawing the box without moving the turtle to the correct coordinates, then we will not get the drawing that we want.

The code that moves the turtle to the next coordinate also repeats, but there is a change in each repetition. If we can express that change using the programming tools we have, then we can write this whole program in a loop! We will look at the two pieces of code we have that move the turtle to new coordinates:

```
# Move turtle to start of next box.
turtle.penup()
turtle.setpos(0,50)
turtle.setheading(0)
turtle.pendown()
# Move turtle to start of next box.
turtle.penup()
turtle.setpos(0,100)
turtle.setheading(0)
turtle.pendown()
```

There is also our initial assumption, which is related to the movement code:

```
# Assumption: turtle starts at 0,0 with a heading of 0.
```

Most of this code is the same. We lift the pen, set the position, set the heading, and put the pen back down. The only thing that changes is the y coordinate in the heading. Does it change in a predictable way? If it does, then we can write some arithmetic so that Python will calculate that change for us.

We will begin to write the loop, and then examine what we must do to move the turtle to the start of the next box each time through the loop. Listing 4.2 is a first attempt at the program that illustrates the syntax of a `while` loop, which is the first looping structure we will look at.

```
1    import turtle

2    # Assumption: turtle starts at 0,0 with a heading of 0.
3    SIDE = 50
4    num_boxes = 0

5    # Draw five boxes.
6    while num_boxes < 5:
7        turtle.forward(SIDE)
8        turtle.left(90)
```

```
9        turtle.forward(SIDE)
10       turtle.left(90)
11       turtle.forward(SIDE)
12       turtle.left(90)
13       turtle.forward(SIDE)
14       # Move turtle to next box start.
15       turtle.penup()
16       turtle.setpos(0,0)
17       turtle.setheading(0)
18       turtle.pendown()
19       num_boxes = num_boxes + 1
```
Listing 4.2

The syntax of a `while` loop is the keyword `while`, followed by a condition, followed by a colon, and then indented code that is executed conditionally. You might notice this is very similar to an `if` statement. Besides the superficial similarities of keyword, condition, colon, indented code, there is a very important similarity. When control reaches the `while` statement, the condition is evaluated. If it evaluates to `True`, the conditional code is executed. If it evaluates to `False`, the conditional code is ignored.

The crucial difference is what happens after the conditional code executes. In a `while` loop, after the conditional code executes, the condition is evaluated again. If it evaluates to `False`, the conditional code is ignored. If it evaluates to `True`, the conditional code executes, and then the condition is evaluated again. And again, and again … as long as the conditional code is entered, control always returns to the condition, which is evaluated again. That is why it is called a loop—because the flow of control loops back to the top.

If we run this program, we see that it draws the same box five times, so we need to change the y location each time through the loop. Our code that moves the turtle in the original program was:

```
turtle.setpos(0,50)
turtle.setpos(0,100)
```

And if we continued with the full program, it would have continued with:

```
turtle.setpos(0,150)
turtle.setpos(0,200)
```

Do you see a predictable pattern with the *y* coordinate? Each time through the loop, we must add 50 to the *y* coordinate. To do this, we need a variable that will hold a value that changes predictably each time through the loop. In this program, the variable will start at 0, and we will add 50 to it each time through the loop. A meaningful name for this variable is `y`, or `y_coordinate`. Listing 4.3 is the new program:

```
1    import turtle

2    # Assumption: turtle starts at 0,0 with a heading of 0.
3    SIDE = 50
4    num_boxes = 0
5    y_coordinate = 0
```

```
6    # Draw five boxes.
7    while num_boxes < 5:
8        turtle.forward(SIDE)
9        turtle.left(90)
10       turtle.forward(SIDE)
11       turtle.left(90)
12       turtle.forward(SIDE)
13       turtle.left(90)
14       turtle.forward(SIDE)
15       # Move turtle to next box start.
16       turtle.penup()
17       y_coordinate = y_coordinate + 50
18       turtle.setpos(0,y_coordinate)
19       turtle.setheading(0)
20       turtle.pendown()
21       num_boxes = num_boxes + 1
```
Listing 4.3

To evaluate our solution, we should run the program. Figure 4-2 shows the program output.

Although we cannot see the coordinates, the stack of boxes appears to draw in the middle of the screen. To be completely certain, we could run the program in the debugger or insert print statements to print the turtle's coordinates at the start of drawing each box.

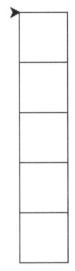

Figure 4-2   Output of the box stack program.

Try this

❖ Modify Listing 4.3 to draw boxes that are 100 on a side, but still stacked on top of each other.

❖ Draw a sketch of a program that draws five boxes in a horizontal row. Include coordinates in your sketch. Identify the repetition in the problem as well as what must change in a predictable way between each repeated block.

❖ Identify the repetition in the problem of printing out a count from 1 to 10. What is repeated, and what must change in a predictable way between each repeated block?

4.2   Desk-checking loops

Before we write more loops, it is important that we can read them. The loop flow of control is very different from sequential and conditional flow. We will desk check a variation of the box-drawing program that simply outputs *x* and *y* coordinates to the console, rather than drawing with the turtle. The simplified program will have less code to step through and it will be easier to show the console output than the turtle drawing. We will also change the number of **iterations** (times the loop executes) from five to three. Listing 4.4 is the simplified code we will desk check.

```
1  num_boxes = 0
2  y_coordinate = 0

3  # Print coordinates of five boxes.
4  while num_boxes < 3:
5      print("X: {}, Y: {}".format(0, y_coordinate))
6      y_coordinate = y_coordinate + 50
7      num_boxes = num_boxes + 1
```
Listing 4.4

Remember that when we create a desk-checking table, we include columns for the line number of the line that is executing, all of the variables, input and output (if any), and tests (if any). Here we will get started with the sequential code on lines 1 and 2. The default flow of control is sequential, so if there is no test which might cause branching or looping (or a function call, which we will get to in Chapter 5), then the flow of control is sequential.

```
1  num_boxes = 0
2  y_coordinate = 0
```

Line #	num_boxes	y_coordinate	num_boxes < 3	Output
1	0			
2	0	0		

We now reach line 4, which is the test. (New lines in the desk-checking table will be highlighted in yellow.)

```
4  while  num_boxes < 3:
```

Line #	num_boxes	y_coordinate	num_boxes < 3	Output
1	0			
2	0	0		
4	0	0	0 < 3 True	

The test evaluates to True, so we execute the conditional (indented) code, which is also called the loop body.

```
5      print("X: {}, Y: {}".format(0, y_coordinate))
6      y_coordinate = y_coordinate + 50
7      num_boxes = num_boxes + 1
```

Line #	num_boxes	y_coordinate	num_boxes < 3	Output
1	0			
2	0	0		
4	0	0	0 < 3 True	

Line #	num_boxes	y_coordinate	num_boxes < 3	Output
5	0	0		X: 0, Y: 0
6	0	50		
7	1	50		

After we have executed the last line of the loop body, control always returns to the start of the loop, which is line 4. The test is executed again.

```
4   while num_boxes < 3:
```

Line #	num_boxes	y_coordinate	num_boxes < 3	Output
1	0			
2	0	0		
4	0	0	0 < 3 True	
5	0	0		X: 0, Y: 0
6	0	50		
7	1	50		
4	1	50	1 < 3 True	

Note that this time the test is 1<3, because the value of num_boxes was updated during the loop body execution. 1<3 evaluates to True, so we execute the loop body again.

```
5       print("X: {}, Y: {}".format(0, y_coordinate))
6       y_coordinate = y_coordinate + 50
7       num_boxes = num_boxes + 1
```

Line #	num_boxes	y_coordinate	num_boxes < 3	Output
1	0			
2	0	0		
4	0	0	0 < 3 True	
5	0	0		X: 0, Y: 0
6	0	50		
7	1	50		
4	1	50	1 < 3 True	
5	1	50		X: 0, Y: 50
6	1	100		
7	2	100		

We have just finished executing line 7—what line executes next? If you said we execute the loop test again on line 4, you are correct! Execution always returns to the loop test after the loop body has finished executing. Now the test is 2<3, because the value in num_boxes was updated to 2 in the loop body, and the test is again True, so we enter the loop body another time.

```
4  while num_boxes < 3:
5      print("X: {}, Y: {}".format(0, y_coordinate))
6      y_coordinate = y_coordinate + 50
7      num_boxes = num_boxes + 1
```

Line #	num_boxes	y_coordinate	num_boxes < 3	Output
1	0			
2	0	0		
4	0	0	0 < 3 True	
5	0	0		X: 0, Y: 0
6	0	50		
7	1	50		
4	1	50	1 < 3 True	
5	1	50		X: 0, Y: 50
6	1	100		
7	2	100		
4	2	100	2 < 3 True	
5	2	100		X: 0, Y: 100
6	2	150		
7	3	150		

One last line will execute: execution will return to line 4 and the loop entry condition will be tested again. This time it will evaluate to False, and the loop body will be skipped. Because there are no lines of code after the loop body, program execution is complete.

```
4  while num_boxes < 3:
```

Line #	num_boxes	y_coordinate	num_boxes < 3	Output
1	0			
2	0	0		
4	0	0	0 < 3 True	
5	0	0		X: 0, Y: 0
6	0	50		

Line #	num_boxes	y_coordinate	num_boxes < 3	Output
7	1	50		
4	1	50	1 < 3 True	
5	1	50		X: 0, Y: 50
6	1	100		
7	2	100		
4	2	100	2 < 3 True	
5	2	100		X: 0, Y: 100
6	2	150		
7	3	150		
4	3	150	3 < 3 False	

With the desk-checking table complete, look at how the variables in the program (num_boxes and y_coordinate) change over time. They both change in a predictable way. Identify the lines of code on which they change value. Identify how many times each variable changes value, and what each variable contributes to the overall program.

Both variables are examples of **steppers**. Steppers are loop variables that take on a predictable sequence of values over the course of loop execution. This distinction is a problem-solving distinction. Steppers are no different to Python than other variables. To a programmer, a stepper is a variable that can be used to solve certain kinds of problems. When we have a problem with a quantity that predictably changes, or if we can solve a problem by using a quantity that predictably changes, then we might use a loop and a variable in a stepper role. A variable in a stepper role can also be used to control a loop.

4.3   The loop control variable

We will focus here on the variable num_boxes in Listings 4.3 and 4.4. This is the stepper variable that we are using to control the execution of our loop, which is a new way to use variables in programs. Here are just the lines of code in Listing 4.4 that include num_boxes:

```
1  num_boxes = 0
4  while num_boxes < 3:
7      num_boxes = num_boxes + 1
```

What is happening here? The variable num_boxes starts with a value that ensures we enter the loop (in other words, the loop entry condition num_boxes < 3 will evaluate to True because num_boxes is given a starting value of 0). Within the loop, it is given a new value that ensures we will eventually exit the loop. Entry into and exit from the loop are determined by the condition num_boxes < 3, so the entry value for num_boxes must be less than three. The exit value for num_boxes must be greater than or equal to 3. Adding to the variable will ensure that it increases from 0 to 3 as the loop executes.

There are three components to loop control: initialization of the loop control variable, testing the loop control variable, and updating the loop control variable. Together they determine how many times the loop will execute. The initializer, test, and updater are labeled in Figure 4-3.

These three lines of code together form a sort of engine that drives the loop. Any other code that we put inside the loop body is brought along for the ride and will execute as

```
1    num_boxes = 0          ◄──────────────  Initializer
4    while num_boxes < 3:   ◄──────────────  Test
7        num_boxes = num_boxes + 1  ◄────   Updater
```

Figure 4-3   Initializer, test, and updater identified.

many times as are determined by the loop control variable. In Listings 4.3 and 4.4, the only function that num_boxes has is to cause the loop to execute five and three times, respectively. The box-drawing code can then be placed inside the loop in Listing 4.3 so that it will execute five times. Any other code we place inside the loop will also execute five times.

Try this

❖ Modify Listing 4.4 so the loop executes five times.
❖ How many times does the loop in Listing 4.4 execute if we change line 1 to num_boxes = 1?
❖ How many times does the loop in Listing 4.4 execute if we change line 7 to num_boxes = num_boxes + 2?

4.4   Loop design errors

We will look at some variations on a very simple loop that repeatedly prints the message "Hello, world!"

Hello world 1	Hello world 2
```i = 0 while i < 10: print("Hello, world!") i = i + 1```	```i = 0 while i > 10: print("Hello, world!") i = i + 1```

Hello world 3	Hello world 4
```i = 0 while i < 10: print("Hello, world!") i = i - 1```	```i = 0 while i <= 10: print("Hello, world!") i = i + 1```

Can you identify the loop control variable in these loops? Since there is only one variable, i, you probably can! But i is the loop control variable because it is initialized before the loop test, it is tested, and then it is updated within the loop body. By looking at the predictable sequence of values that i will take on as this program executes, we can learn how many times each loop will execute.

In the first example, Hello world 1, we see a very typical pattern for a loop control variable. The variable is initialized to 0, the test is a less-than test, and the variable is incremented by 1. If you see this pattern in a loop control variable, then the loop executes n times, where n is the value we are testing against. In this case, the loop executes 10 times. If you desk check, or step through, the code, you will see that i takes on the values 0 through 9, which is 10 values.

How many times does the loop in example Hello world 2 execute? Look carefully at the initializer, the test, and the updater.

If you said the loop executes zero times, you are correct! This loop is never entered. The loop control variable is initialized to zero, and then it is tested to see if it is greater than 10. It is not, so the loop is bypassed.

How many times does the loop in example Hello world 3 execute? Once again, look carefully at the initializer, the test, and the updater. Step through the program, either on paper or mentally.

This is a special kind of (bad) loop called an **infinite loop**! This loop is entered and it is never exited. The loop control variable is decremented each time through the loop, so it is always less than 10, and the test evaluates to True each time it is reached.

Finally, how many times does the loop in example Hello world 4 execute? Step through the program. What values does the loop control variable i take on as this loop executes?

This loop executes 11 times. It is very similar to example Hello world 1. The difference is the test. In Hello world 4, the test is i <= 10, which means that the loop is last entered when i equals 10. In Hello world 1, the test is i < 10, which means that the loop is last entered when i equals 9. If the programmer intended for the loop to execute 10 times, then they have programmed an off-by-one error, when a loop is entered one too many or one too few times. This is a very common kind of error. When you write a program with a loop, you should design your testing to check for off-by-one errors.

Try this

❖ For each loop below, determine how many times the loop executes and exactly what values the loop control variable takes on. Identify the initializer, the test, and the updater for each loop.

a.
```
i = 0
while i < 10:
    print("Hello, world!")
    i = i + 2
```
b.
```
i = 0
while i < 100:
    print("Hello, world!")
    i = i + 10
```
c.
```
i = 0
while i < 100:
    print("Hello, world!")
    i = i * 10
```

(Continued)

(Continued)

```
d. i = 1
   while i < 10:
       print("Hello, world!")
       i = i + 1
```

4.5 Augmented assignment operators

You might have noticed that the increment operation i = i + 1 (or a similar operation with a different variable) is quite common in loops. It is very common, when programming, to add or subtract a number from a variable and assign the result back to the same variable.

Because this is such a common operation, there are assignment operators called **augmented assignment operators** that are shorthand for adding to a variable, subtracting from a variable, dividing a variable by a value, multiplying a variable by a value, modding a variable by a value, and raising a variable to a power, with the result assigned to the original variable.

Here is a table of these operators, with examples of the value in the variable before and after the operation:

Operator	i before	Example	i after	Equivalent to
+=	10	i += 1	11	i = i + 1
-=	10	i -= 1	9	i = i - 1
*=	10	i *= 5	50	i = i * 5
/=	10	i /= 2	5	i = i / 2
%=	10	i %= 3	1	i = i % 3
**=	10	i **= 3	1000	i = i ** 3

Listing 4.4 with augmented assignment operators looks like this:

```
1  num_boxes = 0
2  y_coordinate = 0

3  # Print coordinates of five boxes.
4  while num_boxes < 3:
5      print("X: {}, Y: {}".format(0, y_coordinate))
6      y_coordinate += 50
7      num_boxes += 1
```
Listing 4.5

This is functionally identical to Listing 4.4, but lines 6 and 7 now use augmented assignment statements to increment the variables y_coordinate and num_boxes.

Try this

❖ Predict the outcome of these blocks of code, and then check your predictions using the IDLE console:

a.
```
i = 3
i += 5
```
b.
```
i = 10
i -= 10
```
c.
```
i = 100
i /= 5
```
d.
```
i = 2
i **= 5
```

❖ Rewrite Listing 4.3 using augmented assignment operators.

❖ Write a loop that displays "Hello world" 20 times. Use an augmented assignment operator.

4.6   Loop patterns

The art of designing a loop to solve a problem is in recognizing a repetition, and then defining what stays the same during each iteration and what must change. The change will build (or reduce) in some way toward a solution to the problem, and the loop will end.

4.6.1   Stepper variables

For example, consider a very simple loop to print the numbers from 1 to 10, as in Listing 4.6:

```
1  """A program to print the values from 1 to 10."""

2  i = 1
3  while i < 11:
4      print(i)
5      i += 1
```
Listing 4.6

In this basic loop, we recognize that there is a repetition in counting. But we are not printing the same number repeatedly—the number that is displayed must change each time. Specifically, it must increase by one each time. Once we have printed the number 10, our problem is solved, and the loop can end.

We have already seen this variable pattern, the stepper. A stepper variable can be used to control a loop, but it also might be a part of the problem solution. For example, recall the program we wrote in Chapter 2 that printed a table of final grades computed from different final exam grades, where the final exam is worth 25% of the final grade. The table was produced by performing computations with the user's input.

```
Please enter your average: 92

Final Exam      Final Grade
100             (100*.25) + (92*.75)
90              (90*.25) + (92*.75)
80              (80*.25) + (92*.75)
70              (70*.25) + (92*.75)
```

Do you see repetition in this problem? Identify what stays the same and what needs to change in a predictable way. Hopefully, you see that most of the calculation stays the same for each row of the table, but the value of the final exam, which is both displayed in the final exam column and is used in the calculation, changes in a predictable way. The final exam grade can be a stepper in a program with a loop. We can also see that it has an initial value of 100, it should be 70 the last time it is used in the computation, and it decrements by 10 between computations. Listing 4.7 is a new version of Listing 2.4, which solves the same problem, but uses a loop:

```
1    """Produce a table of final grades, given current average."""

2    # Obtain the current average.
3    average = float(input("Please enter your average: "))

4    # Print the table header.
5    print("{:<15}{:<15}".format("Final Exam", "Final Grade"))

6    # Calculate the final grades for different exam grades
7    # in a loop, using exam grades from 90 down to 70 by 10.
8    average_75_percent = average * .75
9    final_exam = 100
10   while final_exam > 60:
11       # Calculate the grade and display it.
12       final_grade = average_75_percent + final_exam * .25
13       print("{:<15d}{:<15.1f}".format(final_exam, final_grade))
14       # Update the final exam grade for the next iteration.
15       final_exam -= 10
```
Listing 4.7

This program is organized a little differently from Listing 2.4. Each row of the table is calculated and then immediately displayed within the loop, because only one variable is used to hold the result, so we cannot wait until the end of processing to display the output. Each time through the loop, the final_grade value will be replaced with the new calculation.

One advantage to the loop and stepper variable solution is that we can easily change the start and stop values and we can change the increments (maybe showing every grade in smaller increments, like 1 or 5). We can even obtain these values from the user and allow the user to customize the output.

4.6.2   Most-recent holder variables

A loop is a convenient structure for processing a stream of data. Each time through the loop, a new data value is obtained. It might be obtained from the keyboard, a file, another component of the software system, or some other piece of hardware such as a sensor. We will focus on keyboard input.

We will write a variation of our program that computes current based on user input of battery voltage (Listing 3.3). In this program, we will allow the user to type the voltage in directly, and we will also allow them to enter a resistance. To keep this simple we will compute the current for five sets of inputs, but we could easily be more flexible and allow the user to continue entering values until they are finished. Listing 4.8 is a solution to this problem:

```
1  """Compute the current for five circuits from
2     resistance and voltage obtained from the user."""

3  # Initialize the loop control variable.
4  i = 0
5  # Ask for five sets of values, compute
6  # and display the result.
7  while i < 5:
8      voltage = float(input("What is the voltage? "))
9      resistance = float(input("What is the resistance? "))
10     current = voltage / resistance
11     print("The amperage of the circuit is {:.3f}.".format(current))
12     i += 1
```
Listing 4.8

In this example, the input stream is being stored, one set of inputs at a time, in the two variables `voltage` and `resistance`. The calculation is performed, and then we enter the loop again. The next set of inputs is read from the input stream into `voltage` and `resistance`, replacing the old values.

A variable that takes on a new value from a source of input each time a loop executes is called a **most-recent holder**. This is a very common role for a variable in a loop, as we are often writing a loop to process a collection of data, one element at a time.

4.6.3 Accumulator variables

Another common programming pattern is the accumulation of a sum or product of values. The values could be generated from a stepper, or they could come from an input stream. We will write a program that accumulates the sum of the even numbers between 2 and 100. We will use a new kind of variable, an **accumulator**, to hold the sum. The sum will build each time we execute the loop body. We will start by adding two to the sum, and we will be finished when we have added 100 to the sum.

An accumulator variable must be initialized before the loop is entered, because each time the loop executes it will have more value added to it. (It accumulates value as the loop executes.) When an accumulator is a sum, you will generally want to initialize it to zero. Listing 4.9 is a program that sums the even numbers from 2 to 100:

```
1  """Compute the sum of the first 100 even numbers."""

2  # Initialize the sum and first even number.
3  even_sum = 0
4  next_even = 2
5  # Add the next even number to the sum
```

```
 6  # and increment to the next even number.
 7  while next_even < 101:
 8      even_sum += next_even
 9      next_even += 2

10  print("The sum of the even numbers from 2 to 100 " +\
             "is {:d}.".format(even_sum))
```
Listing 4.9

Can you identify the stepper variable and the accumulator variable in Listing 4.9? The stepper takes on a predictable sequence of values, and the accumulator accumulates value into itself each time through the loop.

The stepper is the variable next_even, which takes on the values 2, 4, 6, 8, ..., 100, 102. (The variable is assigned the value 102 the last time through the loop, and then the test next_even < 101 evaluates to False and the loop body does not execute again.)

The accumulator variable is the variable even_sum, which is initialized to 0 on line 3, and then accumulates each even number from 2 through 100 (stored in next_even) into itself as the loop executes.

4.6.4   Most-wanted holder variables

The final pattern we will discuss is the most-wanted pattern. This is a pattern in which your code finds a value in a stream of data that is the best fit for some criteria. For example, you might want to find the largest value entered by the user, or the smallest. If you need to find a best-fit value, you will need one or more variables in a **most-wanted holder** role.

We will first write a relatively straightforward program to find the largest of five values entered by the user. It might be easier to imagine this program if we produce a table of potential inputs. If we assume that they will be entered by the user in the order presented, then we can include a column in our table for the most-wanted holder—the largest value entered by the user *so far*. This table might help to visualize how the solution to a most-wanted problem works.

Largest value so far	New value	Is the new value larger?	New largest value so far
–	10	–	10
10	100	Yes	100
100	–5	No	100 (no change)
100	102	Yes	102
102	14	No	102 (no change)

This problem has one most-recent holder—the new value. Each time through the loop, our program will obtain the new value from the user. It will then compare the new value to the largest value so far (stored in the most-wanted variable). If the new value is larger, then the largest value so far will be replaced by the new value. If the new value is not larger, then the largest value so far will not be changed.

The first value is a special case, because we do not yet have a largest value so far to compare it to. We will use the first value to initialize our most-wanted holder (largest value so far) variable.

In our example, the user first enters 10, which becomes the largest value so far. The second value entered by the user is 100. When the comparison is performed, 100 is larger than 10, and so the value in the largest value so far variable, the most-wanted holder, is replaced with 100. The value 100 is now the largest value so far. When the user enters −5 and the comparison is performed, because −5 is less than 100, the value in the most-wanted holder is not replaced. The problem continues in this way for two more values.

Listing 4.10 solves this problem:

```
1  """Find the largest value entered by the user."""

2  # Obtain the first value to initialize the most wanted holder.
3  largest = float(input("Please enter a value: "))

4  # Obtain four more values from the user in a loop
5  # and find the largest.
6  i = 0
7  while i < 4:
8      number = float(input("Please enter a value: "))
9      if number > largest:
10         largest = number
11     i += 1

12 # Display the largest number entered to the user.
13 print("The largest number entered was {:.1f}.".format(largest))
```
Listing 4.10

Do you see the most-recent holder and most-wanted holder in this program? The most-recent holder is the variable that obtains a new value from an input stream each time through the loop, so that is the variable number, which is receiving a new value from user input on line 8. The most-wanted holder is the variable that is holding the largest value entered by the user so far. You can see that the variable largest is being compared to the most-recent holder, number, on line 9, and the value assigned to largest is being replaced by the value assigned to number if number is larger on line 10. Therefore, largest is the variable which holds the largest value encountered so far in the input stream.

We wrote a program to find the largest value in a stream of input, but most-wanted holders can have a more interesting "best-fit" criteria. You can search for a value in a stream of input that matches any criteria that you can compute.

To illustrate something a little more fun, we will write a program to find the location closest to the Community College of Rhode Island (CCRI) campus in Warwick, Rhode Island, USA, using Global Positioning System (GPS) coordinates (in decimal degrees). We will allow the user to enter five locations, one at a time. We will compute the distance of each location from the CCRI campus, and, if the current location is the closest we have found so far, we will store the details of the location in one or more most-wanted holder variables.

As before, it might be easier to imagine this program if we produce a table of potential inputs. Again we will assume that they will be entered by the user in the order presented, so we can include columns in our table for the most-wanted holders—the information for the location that is closest to CCRI so far.

CCRI's coordinates are 41.712935 (latitude), −71.481696 (longitude)

Location name	Location Latitude	Location Longitude	Distance from CCRI	Closest location so far (name)	Closest location so far (distance)
Boston, MA	42.360082	−71.058880	80.1 km	Boston, MA	80.1 km
New York City, NY	40.712775	−74.005973	237.2 km	Boston, MA	80.1 km
Providence, RI	41.823989	−71.412834	13.6 km	Providence, RI	13.6 km
Newport, RI	41.490102	−71.312829	28.5 km	Providence, RI	13.6 km
Mystic, CT	41.354266	−71.966462	56.7 km	Providence, RI	13.6 km

You might recognize three most-recent holders in this problem: the location name, the location latitude, and the location longitude. Each time through the loop, our program will obtain these values from the user.

Using the latitude and longitude, the distance from CCRI Warwick is computed.

The most-wanted holder variables are the name of the closest location so far and the distance of the closest location so far. We need to store the distance so we can compare it to the distance computed for other locations. We need to store the name so we can report the name of the closest location to the user when they are finished entering locations. We should put the first values entered by the user (or computed based on user data) in these most-wanted holders to initialize them. When the user enters the data for Boston, MA, its name and distance are saved as the closest location to CCRI Warwick *so far*.

Each subsequent time through the loop, after computing the new distance, we will compare it to the value in the distance most-wanted holder. If it is smaller, then the location is closer, and that becomes the new most-wanted value. If it is not smaller, then it is further away (or equidistant), and we will ignore it.

We will therefore have some conditional code within the loop, comparing the new value to the most-wanted value, and executing a replacement assignment statement (or in this case, two assignment statements) if the comparison finds that the new value is the best fit.

Listing 4.11 is a program that solves this problem. In this example, to keep the focus on the variable roles, we use a simple distance formula calculation to compute the distance. This is not accurate for computing distance on a curved surface (and will not give the values in the table above), so the far more accurate code for the haversine method of computing the distance is included below this listing. You might enjoy modifying the program yourself with the haversine code once you are comfortable with the most-wanted holder pattern. (You might also enjoy changing the location we are comparing to your campus, a favorite city, or a favorite landmark.)

```
1    """Compute the distance between two locations."""

2    import math

3    # Define some constants for the calculations.
4    LAT_CCRI = 41.712935
5    LON_CCRI= -71.481696

6    # Get the first set of coordinates from the user and
7    # compute the distance. We will store this in our
8    # most wanted holder variables.
9    closest_location = input("Please enter the location name: ")
10   latitude = float(input("Please enter the latitude: "))
11   longitude = float(input("Please enter the longitude: "))
12   closest_distance = math.sqrt((LAT_CCRI - latitude)**2 + \
                      (LON_CCRI - longitude)**2) * 100

13   # Now loop, getting four new locations, and find the closest.
14   i = 0
15   while i < 4:
16       # Get the inputs and calculate the distance.
17       location = input("Please enter the location name: ")
18       latitude = float(input("Please enter the latitude: "))
19       longitude = float(input("Please enter the longitude: "))
20       distance = math.sqrt((LAT_CCRI - latitude)**2 + \
                      (LON_CCRI - longitude)**2) * 100

21       # Compare to the closest distance and replace if closer.
22       if distance < closest_distance:
23           closest_distance = distance
24           closest_location = location

25       # Update the loop control variable.
26       i += 1

27   # Display the closest location to the user
28   output = "{} is the closest location,".format(closest_location)
29   output +="with a distance of {:.1f} km.".format(closest_distance)
30   print(output)
```
Listing 4.11

Although the distance program in Listing 4.11 obtains three inputs from the user each time through the loop, instead of just one, and performs a mathematical computation, you will notice that it has the same structure as Listing 4.10. In both cases, there are most-recent holders and most-wanted holders. There is a comparison of the most-recent holder to the most-wanted holder, and there is a replacement if the most-recent holder is a better fit than the current most-wanted holder. Look carefully at the structural parts of the problem that are the same, as this is the pattern that you will use to find a value that is the best fit so far as you examine a stream of values one at a time.

4.6.5 The haversine code

To write a more accurate distance calculation program using GPS coordinates, combine the calculations in this code (which uses hard-coded (literal) values for CCRI and Boston rather than getting inputs from the user as an example) with the most-wanted holder code in Listing 4.11.

```
"""Compute the distance between two locations."""
import math
# The hard-coded values for computations.
RADIUS_EARTH = 6371
LAT_CCRI = 41.712935
LON_CCRI= -71.481696
LAT_CCRI_RADIANS = math.radians(LAT_CCRI)
LAT_BOS = 42.360082
LON_BOS = -71.058880
# Perform the calculation of distance.
a = math.sin(math.radians(LAT_BOS - LAT_CCRI)/2)**2 + \
            math.cos(LAT_CCRI_RADIANS)**2 * \
            math.sin(math.radians(LON_BOS - LON_CCRI)/2)**2
distance = RADIUS_EARTH * 2 * \
            math.atan2(math.sqrt(a), math.sqrt(1-a))
```

Try this

❖ Rewrite Listing 4.7 to display final grades based on final exam grades from 100 down to 50 in increments of 5. (Hint: Change the updater and the test of the loop.)
❖ Write a program to obtain five names from the user in a loop. Greet each person by name.
❖ Write a program that will ask the user how many hours they exercised each day for 7 days in a loop. Total the hours and display the total.
❖ Add to your exercise hours program by finding the day on which the user exercised the most hours and display the largest hours value that was entered. To make this more challenging, ask for the day and the hours, and display the name of the day that had the most hours of exercise. (Hint: Use the GPS code as an example.)

4.7 Input validation loops

Loops can be used to validate input and can be more effective than an `if` statement. Listing 4.12 asks the user for an age and validates that the number is positive before proceeding.

```
1  """Validate that the user's input is positive."""
2  # Obtain an age from the user.
```

```
3  age = int(input("Please enter an age: "))

4  # Loop if the age is less than zero
5  # until the user enters a positive value.
6   while age <= 0:
7       print("Age must be a positive number.")
8       age = int(input("Please enter an age: "))
9   assert age > 0

10  # The age is positive, display a message.
11  print("{:d} is a positive value.".format(age))
```
Listing 4.12

In Listing 4.12, the user is in control of the loop through the input that they enter. If the loop is written correctly, the user will be trapped in the loop until they enter valid input.

If the user enters a value on line 3 that is zero or negative, then the loop entry condition on line 6 will evaluate to True and the loop will be entered. The loop consists of a message on line 7 explaining that the user's input was invalid, and another prompt for input on line 8. Because control will always return to line 6 at the end of the loop, the loop will execute until the user enters a value that is greater than zero.

When writing an input validation loop, you want to enter the loop when the input is bad. Therefore, the loop entry condition should describe invalid input. The loop will be bypassed if the user enters valid data before the loop. If execution reaches the first line after the loop, you can assume that the input is valid.

One way to confirm your loop entry condition is correctly written is to place an assert statement after the loop. An assert statement can help you test your assumptions, and you must assume, after an input validation loop, that the input is valid. In Listing 4.12, we wrote, on line 9:

```
assert age > 0
```

The assert statement is a description of valid input. Once execution has moved past a loop, the complement of the loop entry condition is True. If you find it easier to describe valid data with a Boolean expression, then write the assert statement first, and then complement it for the loop entry condition.

Try this

- ❖ Modify Listing 4.12 to validate that the age is between 0 (exclusive) and 120 (inclusive).
- ❖ Write an input validation loop to accept values for year that are between 1900 and the current year.
- ❖ Modify Listing 3.7 to validate that the user has entered "chocolate" or "fruit" at the prompt.
- ❖ Write an input validation loop to accept values "Y", "y", "N", or "n", but no other values. (Note that you are not going to do something if the user entered one of these values, you are just checking to make sure they entered one of these four values before proceeding.)

4.7   Sentinel-controlled loops

The loops that we have written so far have been controlled by stepper variables. This works well for some problems, but there are times when it is more convenient, or necessary, to read input until a certain value is reached, called a **sentinel value**. The sentinel value signals that the end of the data stream has been reached. When the end of a data stream has been reached, if we are processing it in a loop, then the loop should end.

The sentinel value will be the last value in a stream of data. Because it is in the stream of data but it is not, itself, data, it must be distinguishable from the data. It cannot be a value that might naturally occur within the data. If you are reading room temperatures in degrees Fahrenheit, 65 would be a very poor sentinel value because that could easily be a room temperature. Even −1 could be a room temperature if the room were a walk-in freezer. In selecting a sentinel value, it is important that you understand your data very well—especially the full range of values that the data could take on.

We will write a sentinel-controlled loop that reads keyboard input. It will read the ages of runners in a 5K and print out their division. We will have only four divisions to keep the code simple. The divisions will be "Under 12," "12 to under 20," "20 to under 40," and "40+". How will the user let us know when they are done entering ages? The value −1 is a good sentinel value in this example, as it is impossible for a person to be −1 years old.

Listing 4.13 prompts the user for a runner's age and determines and displays the division. The loop continues until the user enters −1 when prompted for a runner's age.

```
1   """Sentinel loop to place runners in the
2       correct division."""

3   # Obtain the runner's age.
4   age = int(input("Please enter the runner's age, -1 to quit: "))

5   # Loop until the user enters -1, printing the division
6   # and obtaining the next age.
7   while age != -1:
8       if age < 12:
9           print("Under 12 division")
10      elif age < 20:
11          print("12 - under 20 division")
12      elif age < 40:
13          print("20 - under 40 division")
14      else:
15          print("40+ division")
16      age = int(input("Please enter the runner's age, -1 to quit: "))
```
Listing 4.13

The most-recent holder variable `age` is the variable that we test for the sentinel value, −1. One potential source of errors in a sentinel-controlled loop is accidentally processing the sentinel value as if it were data. In Listing 4.13, we obtain the value for `age` on line 4 and test it on line 5 before we enter the loop and process it. We know that it will not be −1 after the test on line 7. We then read the value again at the end of the loop, on line 16, and test it when we return to line 7. If it is the sentinel value, we will not enter the loop and process it.

If you must read the data within the loop before processing, then you will need an `if` statement to test for the sentinel value within the loop, so you can bypass the processing if the user has entered the sentinel value. Listing 4.14 is a sentinel loop that averages the runners' ages. It reads the data within the loop, so it must check that the value entered is not the sentinel before adding the value to the total and incrementing the count of runners entered.

```
1  """Sentinel loop to average the runner ages."""

2  # Initialize the sum, count, and age.
3  total_ages = 0
4  count = 0
5  age = 0

6  # Obtain age, add to sum, increment count until the sentinel.
7  while age != -1:
8      age = int(input("Please enter the runner's age, -1 to quit: "))
9      if age != -1:
10         total_ages += age
11         count += 1
12 # If any ages were entered, average them.
13 if count != 0:
14     average = total_ages / count
15     print("The average age is {:.1f}.".format(average))
16 else:
17     print("No ages were entered.")
```
Listing 4.14

It is always possible, with a sentinel loop, that no data will be entered. When you write a sentinel loop, you might need to write code to handle that situation. In Listing 4.14, on line 13, we check that at least one value was entered before computing the average of the runners' ages. If we did not, we would risk a division-by-zero error.

Try this

❖ What are good sentinel values for the following input streams?
Distance between two cities
Population of a city
Weight of a dog
Number of hawks sighted
❖ Rewrite Listing 4.13 to find the oldest and youngest runners. Display the oldest and youngest ages when the loop has finished executing.

4.8   File processing

When a program finishes executing, the data that was stored in its variables is lost. Most of the programs that we interact with daily allow us to save our work to a file and load our work from a file into the program's internal data structures.

We can write programs in Python that can read from files on a disk into variables and write values into files, allowing us to create **persistent data**—data that persist even when our program is not executing. There are basically two kinds of files: binary files and text files. Binary files store information in a format that is not readable to a person. Text files store information as plain text. We will focus on reading and writing text files.

4.8.1   Writing to files

We will first create a very simple program that writes a few values to a file.

```
1    """Write a string, an integer, and a float to a file."""

2    # Open the file in write mode.
3    simple_file = open("three_values.txt", "w")

4    # Write three values to the file.
5    simple_file.write("Hello, world!")
6    simple_file.write(str(5))
7    simple_file.write(str(2.71828))

8    # Close the file.
9    simple_file.close()
```
Listing 4.15

Listing 4.15 first opens a file on line 3. The open function will return a reference to a file object, which allows us to read from the file or write to the file, depending on the mode. The first argument is the name of the file. In Listing 4.15, this is "three_values.txt". The second argument is the mode. The default mode is "r", for read. In Listing 4.15, because we are going to write to the file, we open it by passing in the value "w" for the mode argument, which stands for write. When we open a file in write mode, if there is already a file with that name, it will destroy the existing file. The file that we are creating will be called three_values.txt and it will be in the same directory as Listing 4.15. It is possible to specify a different path with the file name, but to keep all examples simple, we will always read from and write to files in the same directory as the program that is reading or writing them.

One line 3, we store a reference to the file object in the variable simple_file. We will use this variable to work with our file. On lines 5, 6, and 7, we use the write function to write string, integer, and floating-point data to the file. We can write only string data to a text file, so we must cast the integer and floating-point values to strings using the str function before we can write them to the file. Notice that the syntax here is the file object variable (simple_file), followed by a dot, and followed by the word write. We then pass what we want written to the files as an argument enclosed in parentheses.

Finally, we must close the file. If you do not close the file, then none of your data will be written to it. Once again, notice that the syntax is the name of the file object variable, followed by a dot, followed by the word close and empty parentheses.

After we run the program, we can open the file in Python, if we choose *Text files* or *All files* from the drop-down next to the *File name:* box. We will see the file `three_values.txt` in the list of files in the same directory with Listing 4.15. When we open it, this is what we see:

```
Hello, world!52.71828
```

Our file was created and all of our data was written to the file, but with no spaces between the values.

If we want each value to be on a separate line, we must write the newline character after each value. We can change lines 5 and 6 to write a value and a newline by appending `"\n"` to the end of the data.

```
5    simple_file.write("Hello, world!\n")
6    simple_file.write(str(5) + "\n")
```

Now that you are familiar with the syntax and process of writing to a file, we will modify Listing 4.13 to read a runner's name and age from the keyboard, determine the division, and write the name, age, and division to a file on one line.

We already have a loop in Listing 4.13 that reads runner ages and determines their division. We will need to add another most-recent holder variable to hold the runner's name each time through the loop, and we will need to add code to open a file, write each record to the file, and close the file after the user enters the sentinel value.

```
1    """Sentinel loop to obtain, process, and store information
2    about runners."""

3    # Obtain the runner's age.
4    age = int(input("Please enter the runner's age, -1 to quit: "))

5    # Open the file.
6    runners = open("runners.txt", "w")

7    # Loop until the user enters -1 for age,
8    # obtaining name and determining division.
9    while age != -1:
10       name = input("Please enter the runner's name: ")
11       if age < 12:
12           division = "Under 12 division"
13       elif age < 20:
14           division = "12 - under 20 division"
15       elif age < 40:
16           division = "20 - under 40 division"
17       else:
18           division = "40+ division"
19       # Write runner information to the file.
20       runners.write(name + "\t" + str(age) + "\t" + division + "\n")
21       age = int(input("Please enter the runner's age, -1 to quit: "))
22   # Close the runner information file.
23   runners.close()
```

Listing 4.16

You can see, in Listing 4.16, that the basic sentinel loop structure remains the same. A value is obtained from the input stream (the runner's age), and while that value is not the sentinel value, we continue to loop, processing the value and reading the next value from the input stream.

Here we have added obtaining a name from the user as well. Notice that we do not obtain a name until we know that the user has entered a valid age. This is because age is our most-recent holder that we must test for a sentinel value. We must have three pieces of information: age, name, and division, before we write a line to the file.

When we write the data to the file, we are writing all three pieces of information to one line. Between the name and the age, and between the age and the division, we are appending tabs, which is the \t escape character. To place each record of data on its own line, we are placing a newline character \n after the division, which is the end of the record.

If we run the program and enter complete information for four runners, our file runners.txt might look like this:

```
Haneen Aboud       20    20 - under 40 division
Adisa Olawale      30    20 - under 40 division
Jack Jones    15   12 - under 20 division
Wilkins Lopez      45    40 + division
```

You can see that delimiting our records with tabs does not produce output in columns, which is why the format command is the preferable way to produce tables of output. But there is an advantage to a tab-delimited line of data that we will learn in Chapter 6.

4.8.2 Reading from files

Python can also read data from text files. We will begin with a simple file-reading program in which we know that the file that we are reading from contains a string, an integer, and a floating-point value, each on a separate line, in that order. A file that our program can read might look like this:

```
Hello, world!
5
2.71828
```

Listing 4.17 reads each line of the file into a variable and then prints the data to the console.

```
1    """Reading a string, an integer, and a float from a file."""

2    # Open the file in read mode.
3    simple_file = open("three_values.txt")

4    # Read three values from the file.
5    greeting = simple_file.readline()
6    int_number = simple_file.readline()
7    float_number = simple_file.readline()
8    # Print them all.
9    print(greeting, int_number, float_number)
```

```
10   # Close the file.
11   simple_file.close()
```
Listing 4.17

This program assumes that the file `three_values.txt` exists, is in the same directory as the program, and contains three lines of data. These are all assumptions that a program cannot make, so we will cover how to check for the existence of a file and a line of data in this section.

On line 3, we open the file `three_values.txt` without a mode argument. (Previously we used the `"w"` mode argument when we opened a file in write mode.) The default mode is `"r"`, for read. Because it is the default, we do not need to include it when we are opening a file to read from it.

Lines 5, 6, and 7 each read a line of data from the file. When we read a line of data, if we want to save it or process it in some way, we must assign it to a variable. We assign these lines to the variables `greeting`, `int_number`, and `float_number`. We then print the three values in line 9 and close the file in line 11. When we run the program (assuming a file `three_values.txt` that is in the same directory as the program, and containing the values `Hello,  world!`, `5`, and `2.71828` each on a separate line), we get the following output:

```
Hello, world!
5
2.71828
```

You might notice that it does not look quite right. Why are there spaces before the two numbers, and why is each line from the file displayed in a separate line in the output, when we have a single print statement that prints all three values?

If we ask the IDLE console to evaluate the variables, this is what we will see:

```
>>> greeting
'Hello, world!\n'
>>> int_number
'5\n'
>>> float_number
'2.71828\n'
```

You may remember that when we were writing to the file, we needed to insert the newline escape sequence to place each piece of data on a separate line. Whether we create the file programmatically with Python, or if we were to create it in a text editor and press the enter key after each line, a newline would be inserted. The text file contains nonprinting characters that are typed, such as newline, tab, and space. When we read a line, the newline character is also read in with our data.

You also might notice that the two numeric values are not stored as numbers at all, but rather strings. Again, referring back to our work with Listings 4.15 and 4.16, we had to cast our numeric data to the string type using the function `str` before we could write it to the text file.

There is a simple solution to both problems. Listing 4.18 is an updated solution to our simple program that reads three values from a file.

```
1    """Reading a string, an integer, and a float from a file."""

2    # Open the file in read mode.
```

```
3    simple_file = open("three_values.txt")

4    # Read three values from the file.
5    greeting = simple_file.readline()
6    greeting = greeting.strip()
7    int_number = simple_file.readline()
8    int_number = int(int_number)
9    float_number = simple_file.readline()
10   float_number = float(float_number)

11   # Print them all.
12   print(greeting, int_number, float_number)

13   # Close the file.
14   simple_file.close()
```
Listing 4.18

On line 6 in Listing 4.18, we invoke the function strip on the first line that we read from the file, stored in the variable greeting. This function creates a new string that is a copy of the string stored in greeting, but with all **white space characters** (spaces, tabs, newlines) removed from both ends of the string. This will remove the newline character at the end of the string, and also any leading white space. (If you want to strip white space only from the end of a string, use rstrip(), and if you want to strip white space only from the beginning of a string, use lstrip().) Because this function makes a copy of the string and does not alter the original string referenced by greeting, we need to assign the new version of the string to greeting.

To convert the numeric data to the appropriate type, we simply use the casting functions int and float. Casting these strings to numeric types will automatically remove all leading and trailing white space characters and will return the integer or floating-point version of the string. Remember that if you try to cast a value that is not a string representation of numeric data, Python will throw an error.

Now that we have written a simple program to read data from a file, we will look at a program that represents a more typical situation: reading many lines of data from a file and processing them as we read them. We will solve the problem of reading runner ages from a file and calculating an average, very similar to Listing 4.14. In this program, we will obtain runner ages from the file, rather than from the keyboard.

```
1    """Sentinel loop to average runner ages from a file."""

2    # Initialize the sum, count, and age.
3    total_ages = 0
4    count = 0

5    # Open the file and read the first line.
6    ages_file = open("ages.txt")
7    age = ages_file.readline()
8    # Add age to sum, increment count, obtain age until the end of file.
9    while age != "":
```

```
10          age = int(age)
11          total_ages += age
12          count += 1
13          age = ages_file.readline()

14   # If any ages were entered, average them.
15   if count != 0:
16          average = total_ages / count
17          print("The average age is {:.1f}.".format(average))
18   else:
19          print("No ages were entered.")
```
Listing 4.19

There are structural elements of note in Listing 4.19. The file is opened and the first line is read into the most-recent holder variable `age` before we test for the sentinel value. The sentinel value, when reading from a file, is the end of file marker. In Python, we test against the empty string to test for the end of file. You can see this test on line 9.

After we have confirmed, on line 9, that there is data (and not the end of file marker) in the variable `age`, we can convert it to an integer and add it to the accumulator variable `total_ages`. We then increment the variable `count` and read the next line from the file. This can be either another age or the end of file marker, so we return to the top of the loop and check to see if we have read the end of file or another age.

As in Listing 4.14, once we exit the loop, we check the value of `count`, and if at least one age was read from the file, we compute the average of the ages and display it for the user.

4.8.3   Testing if a file exists

If you try to open a file that does not exist, your program will crash with a run-time error. You can check if the file exists before opening it by using Python's `os` library. Listing 4.20 checks for a file and reports whether it exists or not.

```
1    """Program to check whether a file exists."""

2    import os.path

3    # Obtain a file name from the user.
4    file_name = input("Enter the file name: ")

5    # Check if the file is in the same directory as
6    # the program, and report.
7    if os.path.isfile(file_name):
8          print("The file exists.")
9    else:
10          print("That file was not found.")
```
Listing 4.20

You will first need to import the os library, or os.path, as we did here. Before you attempt to open the file, use a test such as the one on line 7 to confirm the file exists. Place all of your processing code within the if block. If the file does not exist, then you can display an error or perform some alternate processing in an else block, depending on the problem that is being solved.

Try this

❖ Create a text file of numbers, one to a line. Write a program to read the numbers in, convert them to float or int (depending on what you put in the file), and print them. Confirm that your program works if you change the number of lines in the file.

❖ Enhance your number-reading program to total the numbers and find the largest and display these values.

❖ Combine the code from Listing 4.19 that tests for a file's existence with code Listing 4.18, which averages runner ages read from a file so that the program will not crash if the file does not exist. Test your program with files that exist and the name of a nonexistent file.

4.9   Counting loops and ranges

In some of the looping examples in this chapter, we have known before we wrote our loop how many times the loop needed to repeat. For example, in Listing 4.3, we wrote code to draw five boxes. In Listing 4.7, we wrote code to create a table with four rows, and in Listing 4.8, we computed the current of five circuits. In each of these examples, we used a stepper variable to control the loop execution. A **stepper variable** is a variable that takes on a predictable sequence of values over the course of a loop's execution. In Listings 4.2 and 4.3, the variable takes on the sequence of 0 through 5 in increments of 1. In Listing 4.7, the variable takes on the values 100 through 60 in increments of −10.

4.9.1   Counting (for) loops

When we know in advance how many times our loop will execute, we can use a counting loop structure to write the loop. A counting loop is often called a **for loop**, because in many languages (including Python) it will start with the keyword for.

We will rewrite Listing 4.8, the program to compute current given voltage and resistance, using a for loop.

```
1    """Compute the current for five circuits from
2        resistance and voltage obtained from the user."""

3    # Ask for five sets of values, compute
4    # and display the result.
5    for i in range(5):
```

```
6          voltage = float(input("What is the voltage? "))
7          resistance = float(input("What is the resistance? "))
8          current = voltage / resistance
9          print("The amperage of the circuit is {:.3f}.".format(current))
```
Listing 4.21

One thing you might immediately notice about Listing 4.21 is that it is quite short. You can see that there is no initializer and no updater for the loop control variable, i. One of the primary advantages of a for loop is that all of the control information is contained in one place, at the top of the loop. This makes for loops very easy to read and write. When you are reading the code, as soon as you encounter line 5, you have all of the information you need to know how many times the loop will execute, and what values the loop control variable will take on each time through the loop. That is not the case with conditional (while) loops, because the initializer is somewhere before the test, and the updater is somewhere within the loop. It is also possible that there are multiple updaters within the loop (and multiple initializers before the loop), which can make a conditional loop harder to read.

4.9.2   Ranges

A counting loop in Python makes use of a structure called a **range**. A range is a sequence of values that is generated by passing one to three arguments to the range function. When a range is used in a counting loop, the loop control variable takes on each value in the range, in order—one for each execution of the loop. Some examples will make this clearer.

In Listing 4.21, on line 5, we generate a range using the range function and the argument 5. When you pass one argument to the range function, it will generate a range of values from zero up to, but not including, the argument, in increments of one. Therefore, the code range(5) generates the values 0, 1, 2, 3, 4.

In the loop in Listing 4.21, the loop control variable takes on the first value in the range, 0, the first time through the loop. It takes on the value 1, the second value in the range, the second time through the loop. The third time it takes on 2, the fourth time it takes on 3, and the last time through the loop, i takes on the value 4, which is the last value in the range. In this loop, i is not being used for any purpose other than to drive the loop. Its purpose is to make the code in the loop body execute five times.

There will be times when you will want a stepper to take on specific values, because it is both driving the loop and being used within the loop. Listing 4.9 is an example of a loop in which the loop control variable is a stepper that is used within the loop. In Listing 4.9, the variable next_even takes on the values of the even numbers from 2 through 102, so that the even numbers from two through 100 can be summed.

The default initial value for the range function is 0, and the default step value is 1. (There is no default stop value, you must provide that argument to the function.) If we need our loop control variable to start at a value other than zero and step in increments other than one, we can pass values in for the start and step arguments to control the start, stop, and step of a range. Listing 4.22 is a rewrite of Listing 4.9 using a range function that includes a start value of 2, a stop value of 101, and a step value of 2.

```
1    """Compute the sum of the first 100 even numbers."""

2    # Initialize the sum.
3    even_sum = 0

4    # Add the next even number to the sum.
5    for next_even in range(2, 101, 2):
6        even_sum += next_even

7    # Display the sum.
8    print("The sum of the even numbers from 2 to 100 " +\
          "is {:d}.".format(even_sum))
```
Listing 4.22

In Listing 4.22, the loop control variable next_even will take on the first value in the range, 2, the first time through the loop. The next value in the range will be 4, because the range function generates values from 2 to 101 (not including 101) in increments of 2. Therefore, the second time through the loop, next_even takes on the value 4, and then 6 the next time through the loop, and then 8 the next time through the loop, up in increments of two until it is 100 the last time through the loop.

You cannot see what the range function generates, but if you convert the result to a list, you can see the values in list form. You can use this trick to predict what values different ranges will generate and confirm them in the console. Here are a few examples:

```
>>> list(range(5))
[0, 1, 2, 3, 4]
>>> list(range(5,10))
[5, 6, 7, 8, 9]
>>> list(range(0, 10, 2))
[0, 2, 4, 6, 8]
>>> list(range(1,1))
[]
>>> list(range(5, 0, -1))
[5, 4, 3, 2, 1]
```

It is a good idea to predict the results of different ranges and confirm your answers until you are completely comfortable with how the function works and can predict its outcome reliably. It is important to remember how the range function will interpret one, two, or three arguments. If you provide one argument, it is the stop value. If you provide two arguments, they will be interpreted as the start and stop. If you want your range to have a step value other than one, you must include all three arguments.

4.9.3   When to choose counting loops

Counting loops are a good choice when we know in advance how many times the loop will execute. But what does that mean? As a general rule of thumb, if you can use a stepper for a loop control variable, then you can write a counting loop.

For some loops, the choice of a stepper as a loop control variable is more obvious than for others. If we know we are going to produce a table with 10 rows, for example, or obtain six input values from the user, then we can use the literal values 10 and 6 in our ranges.

If we must repeat an action some number of times (say n), then we can write a loop that uses a loop control variable such as i and range(n), and the loop will execute n times and will be very easy to read. The value can be a literal, or it can be a value that is stored in a variable. A value stored in a variable might be computed before the loop, or it might be a value obtained from the user. Listing 4.23 asks the user how many values to read in a loop, and then reads in (and sums) those values.

```
1    """Compute the sum of the first 100 even numbers."""

2    # Initialize the sum.
3    value_sum = 0

4    # Obtain the number of values to read.
5    num_values = int(input("How many values? "))

6    # Read in and sum the values.
7    for i in range(num_values):
8        value = int(input("Enter a value: "))
9        value_sum += value

10   # Display the sum.
11   print("The sum is {:d}.".format(value_sum))
```
Listing 4.23

In Listing 4.23, you can see that the value entered by the user in line 5 is stored in the variable num_values and is then used as the stop argument to the range function. The loop will execute num_values times. We do not know what value the user might enter, but we know when we are writing the program that the value entered by the user is the number of times we want the loop to execute. Contrast this with a sentinel loop, in which we do not know the loop should end until we read the sentinel value in the input stream, some time during loop execution.

"Knowing in advance" refers to the flow of control. Is the number of executions known in the program before the first loop test is reached, so that we can use it as a stop value for the range, or a test value in a while statement?

If we learn when the loop should stop after we enter the loop, then we cannot choose a counting loop. (Or we should not. It is possible, with some ugly coding, to force it to work.) For example, when we are reading each line in a file, we do not know until we have read the end of file marker (usually inside the loop) that the loop must end. Another example of a conditional loop is one that executes until the user chooses quit, or in a game, until a game-ending condition is met, such as a player winning, or a goal being achieved.

4.9.4 Solving a counting loop problem

If we recognize a predictable pattern in our data that controls when we will stop processing, then we can use that predictable pattern to construct a counting loop. Suppose we are to write a program that will predict all the years in this century in which a cicada with a 13-year periodic cycle will emerge, assuming that the cicada last emerged in 2018.

There is only one output to this problem, so it is easy to define and test. The program should compute the values 2018 + 13, or 2031 for the next year in which the cicada will emerge, 2018 + 13 + 13, or 2044 for the next year, 2018 + 13 + 13 + 13 or 2057 for the third year, and on as long as we are still in the 21st century. If you compute this by hand or on a calculator, you will probably just add 13 to the last year you calculated to get the next year, starting with 2018.

The next step in the problem-solving process is to define one or more solutions. You might recognize that the adding-on pattern is the pattern of a stepper variable, because it is a predictable sequence of values. Each new value is 13 more than the last. You know that you can write a conditional (while) loop or a counting (for) loop to reproduce this predictable pattern, but a for loop is the better choice when you are using a stepper to control your loop. The next step is to figure out the pattern so that you can implement the solution.

Looking back on your calculations, you realize that you started calculating at 2018, and you incremented by 13 each time. You know that you will stop at the last value that is less than 2100, because we are only interested in cicada appearances in this century. Listing 4.24 solves this problem. To test the program, because there is only one possible output, you can compute the output by hand and then compare it to the output produced by the program. Remember that a common error in looping programs is an off-by-one error, in which the loop executes one too many or one too few times.

```
1   """Compute and print cicada emergence every 13 years
2       since 2018 in the 21st century."""

3   # Define constants for the start and end years
4   # and the emergence period.
5   START_YEAR = 2018
6   END_YEAR = 2100
7   PERIOD = 13

8   # Display the years the cicada will emerge.
9   print("Cicadas will emerge in the following years:")
10  for emergence_year in range(START_YEAR, END_YEAR, PERIOD):
11      print("{:d}".format(emergence_year))
```
Listing 4.24

4.9.5 Desk-checking counting loops

Reading and desk-checking a counting loop is very similar to reading and desk-checking a while loop. After the loop body has executed, control returns to the top of the loop, which is the line with the loop keyword (while or for).

We will desk check the first three iterations of the loop in Listing 4.24.

The program begins with four lines that execute sequentially up to line 10, where the loop begins.

```
5    START_YEAR = 2018
6    END_YEAR = 2100
7    PERIOD = 13
9    print("Cicadas will emerge in the following years:")
```

Line #	START_YEAR	END_YEAR	PERIOD	emergence_year	Output
5	2018				
6	2018	2100			
7	2018	2100	13		
9	2018	2100	13		Cicadas will emerge in the following years:

On line 10, we begin the for loop. In this loop, the loop control variable will take on each value in the generated range, once for each iteration of the loop. The range contains the values 2018, 2031, 2044, 2057, 2070, 2083, and 2096. The loop control variable emergence_year references the value 2018 the first time through the loop. (New lines in the desk-checking table will be highlighted in yellow.)

```
10   for emergence_year in range(START_YEAR, END_YEAR, PERIOD):
```

Line #	START_YEAR	END_YEAR	PERIOD	emergence_year	Output
5	2018				
6	2018	2100			
7	2018	2100	13		
9	2018	2100	13		Cicadas will emerge …
10	2018	2100	13	2018	

The loop body is entered, and line 11 executes.

```
11   print("{:d}".format(emergence_year))
```

Line #	START_YEAR	END_YEAR	PERIOD	emergence_year	Output
5	2018				
6	2018	2100			
7	2018	2100	13		
9	2018	2100	13		Cicadas will emerge …

Line #	START_YEAR	END_YEAR	PERIOD	emergence_year	Output
10	2018	2100	13	2018	
11	2018	2100	13	2018	2018

At the end of the loop body execution, control returns to line 10, where the loop control variable takes on the next value in the range.

```
10    for emergence_year in range(START_YEAR, END_YEAR, PERIOD):
```

Line #	START_YEAR	END_YEAR	PERIOD	emergence_year	Output
5	2018				
6	2018	2100			
7	2018	2100	13		
9	2018	2100	13		Cicadas will emerge …
10	2018	2100	13	2018	
11	2018	2100	13	2018	2018
10	2018	2100	13	2031	

Because there is a new value in the range for the loop control variable, the loop body executes again.

```
11    print("{:d}".format(emergence_year))
```

Line #	START_YEAR	END_YEAR	PERIOD	emergence_year	Output
5	2018				
6	2018	2100			
7	2018	2100	13		
9	2018	2100	13		Cicadas will emerge …
10	2018	2100	13	2018	
11	2018	2100	13	2018	2018
10	2018	2100	13	2031	
11	2018	2100	13	2031	2031

Again, control returns to the loop header in line 10, where there is a new value for the loop control variable, so the loop body executes again.

```
10    for emergence_year in range(START_YEAR, END_YEAR, PERIOD):
11        print("{:d}".format(emergence_year))
```

Line #	START_YEAR	END_YEAR	PERIOD	emergence_year	Output
5	2018				
6	2018	2100			
7	2018	2100	13		
9	2018	2100	13		Cicadas will emerge …
10	2018	2100	13	2018	
11	2018	2100	13	2018	2018
10	2018	2100	13	2031	
11	2018	2100	13	2031	2031
10	2018	2100	13	2044	
11	2018	2100	13	2044	2044

This pattern continues through the last value in the range. When the last value in the range is reached, the loop body executes a final time, then the loop header executes a final time (as with a while loop, when the loop test executes and evaluates to `False`) and then control continues with the first line after the loop body.

Try this

❖ Write `range` expressions to generate the following sequences of numbers. Confirm your ranges in the IDLE console by casting your range to a list:
0, 3, 6, 9, 12
1, 2, 3, 4, 5
10, 20, 30, 40, 50, 60, 70
5, 10, 15, 20
❖ What happens if you use a negative step value in a range function? Write a loop that counts down from 10 to 1.
❖ Convert Listing 4.3 from a conditional (while) loop to a counting (for) loop.
❖ Convert Listing 4.6 from a conditional (while) loop to a counting (for) loop and desk check your loop.
❖ Convert Listing 4.7 from a conditional (while) loop to a counting (for) loop.

4.10   Nested loops

Loops (while and for) and conditional statements (if) are **compound statements**, which means they contain other statements. The statements inside a compound statement can be simple statements (such as an assignment statement or print statement) or they can be other compound statements, such as loops and conditional statements.

In Listing 4.10, for example, line 7 is the beginning of a compound looping statement. Within the loop body, there are two assignment statements (on lines 8 and 11), but there is also another compound statement, a conditional statement, on lines 9 and 10.

```
7     while i < 4:
8         number = float(input("Please enter a value: "))
9         if number > largest:
10            largest = number
11        i += 1
```

When you are designing a solution to a computational problem, you will include simple and compound statements where they are needed to solve the problem, including within other compound statements.

There is a category of problems for which your solution will require loops immediately nested within each other, and this is generally what is meant when we refer to "nested loops."

We will consider one loop nested within another, but there can be as many levels of nesting as are needed. You will use a nested loop when you have a set of steps that are themselves repeated. For example, in a structure such as a calendar, we can iterate over the 7 days of the week and repeat the iteration for each of the 52 weeks of the year. Another example is a clock. We can iterate over the 60 minutes in an hour and repeat the iteration for each of the 24 hours in a day. In a deck of cards, we can iterate over the cards ace through king, and repeat the iteration for each of the four suits.

We will develop a program to display the room numbers for a three-floor apartment building. Each floor of the building has eight rooms, as shown in Figure 4-4.

We will first develop a loop to display the eight room numbers of a single floor of the apartment building. We will then enhance the program to display the room numbers for every floor in the building.

We can display each room number for eight rooms using a while loop controlled by a stepper. Even though a for loop is a better choice when we are using a stepper variable, we will use a while loop so that every part of the process (initialization, test, update) is explicit. This will clarify the way a nested loop works.

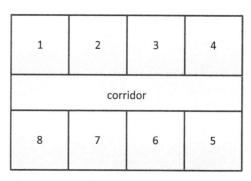

Figure 4-4 An apartment floor.

We can display the room numbers with the following loop:

```
room = 1
while room < 9:
    print("Room number {:d}".format(room))
    room += 1
```

We now want to repeat printing the eight room numbers once for each floor, which is three times. Figure 4-5 shows the three floors of the building. When we want to repeat something, we wrap it in a loop.

```
floor = 0
while floor < 3:
    print("Floor number {:d}".format(floor))
```

```
# Loop through the rooms and print.
room = 1
while room < 9:
    print("Room number {:d}".format(room))
    room += 1


floor += 1
```

Each loop by itself is straightforward enough. We have an inner loop with room as the loop control variable which iterates from 1 to 8, printing the value of room. We have an outer loop with floor as the loop control variable which iterates from 1 to 3, printing the value of floor. In addition to that, the inner loop executes completely (printing rooms from 1 to 8) each time we enter the outer loop.

The program prints the floor value 0, then iterates through the inner loop printing room numbers from 1 to 8. When the inner loop is complete, the value in floor is updated, the outer loop test is executed, and the

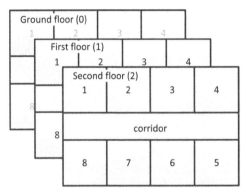

Figure 4-5 An apartment building.

program enters the outer loop again. It prints the floor value 1, then iterates through the inner loop printing room numbers from 1 to 8. The entire process repeats another time for the floor value 2.

A final version of the program is Listing 4.25. In the final version of the program, we use the floor number to compute a room number that is one through eight, 101–108, or 201–208 by multiplying the floor number by 100 and then adding the room number.

```
1   """Display the numbers for an apartment building
2      with three floors and eight rooms per floor."""

3   # Initialize the value of floor.
4   floor = 0

5   # Loop over three floors, printing the room number.
6   while floor < 3:

7       # Loop through the rooms and print.
8       room = 1
9       while room < 9:
10          room_number = floor * 100 + room
11          print("Room number {:d}".format(room_number))
12          room += 1

13      # Update to the next floor.
14      floor += 1
```
Listing 4.25

Try this

❖ Modify Listing 4.24 so that the apartment building has five floors with 15 rooms per floor.

❖ Write a nested loop to display the hours and minutes as if on a digital clock. For example, 00:00 through 23:59. (Hint: Start by writing a loop to display the minutes and do not worry about displaying 0 as 00.)

❖ Write a loop to display the cards in a deck. (Hint: Start by displaying 1 for Ace and 13 for King, and then use an `if` statement to display `"Ace"`, `"Jack"`, `"Queen"`, and `"King"` instead of 1, 11, 12, and 13.)

4.11   Finding repetition in a problem (again)

We will write a program that reads vocabulary words from a file in two languages, and then prints the word in both languages. (The program can be enhanced to quiz the user on one of the languages, but here we will focus only on reading both words from the file and printing them to the screen in a table.) The file will be structured with a header which lists the two languages each on a separate line, followed by a series of two-line records of the word in the first language followed by the word in the second language.

For example, if the two languages are English and German, then we might have a file that contains the following data, which is one header and two vocabulary records:

```
English
Deutsch
school
die Schule
book
das Buch
```

The output of the program would then look like this:

```
English        Deutsch
school         die Schule
book           das Buch
```

To fully understand the problem, we should imagine different file configurations that are possible from the description that is given. For example, we might ask if it is possible that the file will be empty, or that the file will have a header but no vocabulary records. (If it has a header and vocabulary records, can we assume that they will be complete? That is, if there is a word in the first language, will it always be followed by the translated word in the second language? If not, then we will have a garbage in—garbage out situation, because our program cannot be expected to determine the language of a word or verify that the data in the file is correct.) Will the user enter the file name, or will it be a literal in our program? How long might the vocabulary words be? (This is important for setting the field width of the columns in our output.)

Having asked these questions and received answers, we will make the following assumptions:

- ❖ The records in the file will be complete.
- ❖ The file will contain a header record, but it can contain from zero to a very large number of complete vocabulary records.
- ❖ Vocabulary words might be as long as 30 characters.
- ❖ The user will supply the name of the file.

The next problem-solving step is to propose and evaluate solutions. We should review all of the tools in our programming toolbox and match the tools to the problem. We should recognize that we will need to display formatted output, but before that, we will need to read from a file. How much are we reading from a file? We know that there will be two lines which are the header lines, and we can read those in from the file and produce the first line of the table, the header, using those two values.

But then we can have from zero to many additional records, which are two lines from the file that will be displayed together as the next line in the table.

So we will read two lines from the file:

```
English
Deutsch
```

And we will produce a header for a table of output:

```
English              Deutsch
```

But then the program must read zero to many more sets of lines from the file and produce a line of the table. We hopefully recognize that we will need a sentinel-controlled loop to do this, reading each line of the file until we reach the end of file marker.

We have written programs that read from a file until the end, but we have not written programs that must read two lines at a time. What is tricky about this is getting the order correct. If we look at our sample file and take the processing one step at a time, as a program must, it is easier to work out. We must read a line, check that it is not the end of file, and if it is not, we can read the next line in the record and print out the record as one line of our table. We then read another line, check that it is not the end of file, read the next line, print them out, until we finally do reach the end of file.

The first read is the initializer for our loop control variable. We then test. The processing consists of reading the next line and printing out, and then we update the loop control variable by reading again from the file.

Listing 4.26 is a solution to this problem.

```
1    """Read vocabulary information from a file
2       and produce a table."""
3
4    # Obtain the file name from the user, check
5    # that it exists, and open it if so.
6    import os.path
7    file_name = input("Please enter the file name: ")
8    if os.path.isfile(file_name):
9        vocabulary_file = open(file_name)
```

```
9       # Read the header record from the file
10      # and print the table header.
11      language1 = vocabulary_file.readline().strip()
12      language2 = vocabulary_file.readline().strip()

13      print("{:35s}{:35s}".format(language1, language2))

14      # Read the vocabulary from the file until the end
15      # and print the vocabulary table lines.
16      vocabulary1 = vocabulary_file.readline().strip()
17      while vocabulary1 != "":
18          vocabulary2 = vocabulary_file.readline().strip()
19          print("{:35s}{:35s}".format(vocabulary1, vocabulary2))
20          vocabulary1 = vocabulary_file.readline().strip()

21  # Display an error if the file was not found.
22  else:
23      print("That file was not found.")
```
Listing 4.26

You might notice that reading a line of text from the file and stripping the white space was accomplished in one step on lines 11, 12, 16, 18, and 20 by first invoking the `readline` function, which returns a string, and then invoking the `strip` function directly on the result of the `readline` function. This was done here to save space, but you could accomplish this in two steps, as we have done previously in this chapter. You might also have noticed that we used a column width of 35 in our output table. This is to accommodate words of length 30 with enough space to separate the columns visually.

The part of the program that processes the vocabulary records is found in lines 16–20. To illustrate how this works, imagine we have the sample file:

```
English
Deutsch
school
die Schule
book
das Buch
```

The first two lines of the file have been read into the variables `language_1` and `language_2` on lines 11 and 12, and our file variable, `vocabulary_file`, is now pointing to the next line, which contains the word `school`.

```
11      language1 = vocabulary_file.readline().strip()
12      language2 = vocabulary_file.readline().strip()
```

Line 16 is the initializer for the loop control variable, in which we read a vocabulary word in the first language from the file. This reads the word `school` from the file into the variable `vocabulary1`. The file variable is now ready to read the next line in the file, `die Schule`.

```
16          vocabulary1 = vocabulary_file.readline().strip()
```

We then test to see if we have reached the end of file. Because we have not, we then enter the loop, and on line 18 the program reads die Schule into the variable vocabulary2. The file variable now points to the next line in the file, book.

```
18          vocabulary2 = vocabulary_file.readline().strip()
```

We now have two matching words in the variables vocabulary1 and vocabulary2, and so we print them as a line in the table on line 19. On line 20, we update the loop control variable by reading the next word in the first language. The line book is read into the variable vocabulary1.

```
19          print("{:35s}{:35s}".format(vocabulary1, vocabulary2))
20          vocabulary1 = vocabulary_file.readline().strip()
```

Control now returns to line 17 to test the loop entry condition. This process repeats until we read the end of file marker on line 20, the test fails on line 17, and we exit the loop.

The final problem-solving step is to evaluate the result. We must thoroughly test Listing 4.26, comparing it to the expected behavior. If we test the program against a bad file name, a file with a header only, a file with a header and one record only, files with a variable number of records (including very many records), and files with variable-length words (including words up to 30 characters long), we find that the program performs according to specifications.

4.12   Challenge accepted!

1. Write a guess-the-number program that randomly generates an integer between 1 and 100 and allows the user to guess until they correctly guess the number. Let them know if each guess is too low, too high, or correct.

2. Write a program that will calculate areas for the user. The program should begin by presenting the user with a menu of different shapes and a quit option. (e.g., it could present Square, Circle, Rectangle, Triangle, and Quit.) It should prompt the user to make a selection from the menu. Depending on the choice, it will then prompt the user for the dimensions needed to compute the area, it will compute the area, and report the area to the user. (Construct your loop so that if the user chooses Quit, the program will stop running.) You can use the following area formulae:

$$\text{area of a square} = \text{side}^2 \qquad\qquad \text{area of a rectangle} = \text{width} \times \text{height}$$

$$\text{area of a triangle} = \frac{1}{2} \times \text{base} \times \text{height} \qquad\qquad \text{area of a circle} = \pi \times \text{radius}^2$$

3. Write a program that uses a loop to allow two players to play tic-tac-toe until the board is filled. You do not need to draw the board, but you should report the locations of the pieces after each move, for example, the board might look like this after three moves:

```
1  2  3
4  o  6
X  8  x
```

Allow the user to choose the quadrant in which to move. You should keep track of whether it is x's turn or o's turn. Use an input validation loop so if the user enters a quadrant that is outside of the range 1–9 or that already has a piece in it, the program prompts them to enter another value. (For an extra challenge, you can check for a win and end the game if one of the players wins.)

4. Write a program using turtle graphics that draws a flower by repeatedly drawing overlapping circles or diamond shapes in a circle until the circle is filled. Obtain the length of a petal and the number of petals from the user. Two examples are shown below.

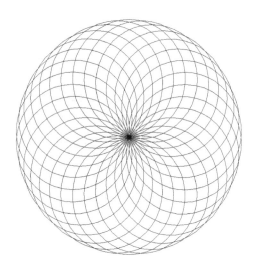 

5. Rewrite Listing 4.26 to quiz the user on the vocabulary words by showing the user the word in the first language and asking for the word in the second language, then comparing the result and telling the user if their answer is right or wrong.

6. Rewrite the following program from the Chapter 2 challenges using a loop: Write a program to obtain the following information for five videos: name, the number of views, the number of likes, and the number of dislikes. Compute the percentage of likes and dislikes (out of the total likes + dislikes) for each video and display a table of the results with columns for name, percentage of likes, and percentage of dislikes. Use a consistent column width for each column and display one decimal place for the percentages. The first row should contain meaningful headers.

7. Rewrite this fractal program from the Chapter 2 challenges using a loop. Prompt the user for the number of times the program should reduce the circle size in half. (e.g., in the drawing, the circle size is split three times.) Create a turtle graphics program to draw a fractal composed of some number of circles. Begin with one large circle in the center of the screen. Then draw a circle 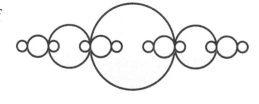 half the diameter of the large circle on each side of the circle. Then repeat that for the next set of circles, and for one more set. The final drawing, for three splits, should look like the image.

8. Rewrite Listing 4.26 to repeatedly obtain a file name from the user until a valid file name is entered.

9. Write a turtle graphics program to draw a chess board. (A board that is eight squares by eight squares.) Using the `begin_fill` and `end_fill` commands described in the Chapter 1 challenges, fill every other square with a color (like a chess board).

10. Write a program to obtain usage statistics for a website from the user. It should prompt the user for the number of page views each day for 10 days. It should then report the average number of page views, the highest number of page views, and the lowest number of page views.

11. Create (by hand) a text file of fortunes, with one fortune to a line. The first line of the file should be the number of fortunes in the file. Write a program to randomly generate a fortune for the user by opening the file, reading the number of fortunes in the file, and then randomly generating a number between 1 and the number of fortunes in the file. The program should then read that fortune from the file and display it for the user. (e.g., if there are 10 fortunes in the file, then the first line of the file would be 10, and the next 10 lines would each contain a fortune. If the program randomly generated the number 4, then the program would read the first four fortunes from the file and display the fourth fortune for the user.)

12. Write a program that obtains race times for a 10K road race from the keyboard and counts the number of runners who completed the race in less than 35 minutes, the number of runners who ran the race in 35 minutes up to 45, the number of runners who ran the race in 45 minutes up to 55, and the number of runners who ran the race in 55 minutes or more. Print a table of results with the time range in the left column and the number of runners in that category in the right column. (Hint: Use multiple accumulators to count the runners in the different categories.) As a variation, put the race times in a file and read the data from a file rather than the keyboard.

13. Write a program to obtain rainfall values from the user for each day in a week, for each week in a month of 5 weeks. Calculate and display the total rainfall for each week and for the month. (Hint: Use a nested loop.)

14. Write a program to compute and print the hailstone sequence for a given number. The hailstone sequence is generated based on the following rule:

    ✦ If the number is divisible by 2, then divide the number by 2 and proceed with the result.
    ✦ If the number is not divisible by 2, then multiply the number by 3 and add 1, and proceed with the result.

    For example, for the number 16, the sequence is: 16, 8, 4, 2, 1

    For the number 9, the sequence is: 9, 28, 14, 7, 22, 11, 34, 17, 52, 26, 13, 40, 20, 10, 5, 16, 8, 4, 2, 1

    The Collatz conjecture is that the sequence will eventually reach the value one. Ask the user for a positive integer, and then loop, computing the hailstone sequence, until you reach one. Display the full sequence and the number of steps required to reach one.

15. Write the following variation of the hailstone program: find and print the highest value reached during the computation process for a given number. For example, for the number 16, 16 is the highest value reached. For 9, 52 is the highest value reached.

16. Write the following variation of the hailstone program: compute and display the hailstone sequence for each number from 10 to 20, inclusive. Display the number that takes the most steps to reach one, and the number that takes the fewest steps.

17. You probably remember the now-classic game of Planks and Bones from the Chapter 3 challenges. Each player is given three dice. In the first round, they roll all three dice. In the second round, they may reroll one die, two dice, or all three dice, and they may do the same in the third. The goal is to achieve three of a kind (e.g., three 5's) or three in a row (e.g., 2, 3, 4). At the end of the three rounds, the game is scored as follows: add the values on the dice. Multiply by two if the user rolled three of a kind or three in a row. The player with the higher score wins. (The rounds can be repeated for as long as the players like, with the scores accumulating between rounds.) Write a program that will allow two players to play the game for as many sets of three rounds as they choose. You may simplify the game by allowing only three of a kind (no three in a row). The program should start by simulating the roll of the three dice for each user using the

random library and reporting both sets of rolls. It should then ask each user which dice (if any) they would like to reroll, and it should reroll those dice only. It should do that again for the third round, and then total the dice, multiply by two if either player scored three of a kind, and tell the users their score. Scores should accumulate between sets of rounds. For example, one set of the game might look like this:

```
Player 1 rolled: 2, 5, 6
Player 2 rolled: 1, 5, 2
Player 1, would you like to re-roll the 2? (Y or N) Y
Player 1, would you like to re-roll the 5? (Y or N) Y
Player 1, would you like to re-roll the 6? (Y or N) N
Player 2, would you like to re-roll the 1? (Y or N) Y
Player 2, would you like to re-roll the 5? (Y or N) N
Player 2, would you like to re-roll the 2? (Y or N) Y

Player 1 rolled: 3, 6, 6
Player 2 rolled: 4, 5, 1
Player 1, Would you like to re-roll the 3? (Y or N) Y
Player 1, Would you like to re-roll the 6? (Y or N) N
Player 1, Would you like to re-roll the 6? (Y or N) N
Player 2, would you like to re-roll the 4? (Y or N) Y
Player 2, would you like to re-roll the 5? (Y or N) N
Player 2, would you like to re-roll the 1? (Y or N) Y

Player 1 rolled: 1, 6, 6
Player 2 rolled: 5, 5, 5
Player 1's score is 13. Player 2's score is 30.
Would you like to continue? (Y or N) N
```

18. You work for a radio station that gives out prizes to the first caller from the surrounding town with the lowest temperature that morning and the first caller from the surrounding town with the highest temperature that morning. Write a program to read temperature data from a file that is formatted as town name on one line followed by morning temperature on the next line, for an unknown number of towns. Find the town with the highest and lowest temperature and print out the name and temperature of the town with the highest temperature and the name and temperature of the town with the lowest temperature.

Chapter 5

Functions

5.1 Defining functions

Suppose you are assigned the task of drawing a personal flag with the turtle graphics module. You are given artistic freedom to draw whatever you like, so long as it is in the shape of a rectangle. You decide to create a flag made of stripes of different colors that represent your interests and your family and friends.

You might begin by writing the comments for the program, resulting in something like this:

```
"""Draw a personal flag."""
# Draw the bottom stripe in green for school color.
# Draw the second stripe in gold for honors.
# Draw the third stripe in brown for running (track).
# Draw the fourth stripe in red for Chinese heritage and family.
# Draw the fifth stripe as a horizontal rainbow for friends.
```

Your program would be very easy to read if the code could also be that simple!

The comments that describe the steps of the algorithm are a way of decomposing (breaking) the program into steps. The steps provide a high-level overview of how the program will solve the problem.

Most programming languages include the ability to define functions. A function is a block of code that has a name. When you need the block of code to execute, you use the name of the function in your program. We can define a function for each of the steps in the algorithm above.

Listing 5.1 is an example of a program that will draw the bottom stripe of the flag.

```
1    import turtle

2    def draw_green_stripe():
3        """Draw the green stripe of the flag."""
4        # Move the turtle to the correct position.
5        turtle.penup()
6        turtle.setpos(-100,0)
7        turtle.setheading(0)
```

```
8         turtle.pendown()
9         # Draw the rectangle.
10        turtle.color("green")
11        turtle.begin_fill()
12        for i in range(2):
13            turtle.forward(200)
14            turtle.left(90)
15            turtle.forward(25)
16            turtle.left(90)
17        turtle.end_fill()

18   # Draw the green stripe.
19   draw_green_stripe()
```
Listing 5.1

On line 2, you can see a new keyword, `def`, followed by the name `draw_green_stripe`, followed by parentheses `()` and a colon `:`. Below that is indented code from lines 3–17. Lines 2–17 are a function definition. The function definition in this program associates the name `draw_green_stripe` with the indented code that follows it.

Defining a function is not the same as executing the code for a function. The lines of code from 2–17 define a function, but that code does not execute when it is first encountered as the Python interpreter processes the file. The name `draw_green_stripe` is registered for later use, for when it is called. The code executes only when the function name is used with parentheses, as on line 19.

On line 19, the function is **invoked**, or **called**. This means that the code associated with the name `draw_green_stripe` will execute. The flow of control will jump from line 19 to lines 2–17, and when they are finished executing, control will return to line 19, after the function call.

The parentheses in the definition and in the call are necessary. You may remember that when we call functions that are part of the Python language or the Python libraries, such as `random.randint`, `turtle.penup`, `round`, and `math.sqrt`, we always put parentheses after the call. Sometimes we put arguments within the parentheses, as with `random.randint(1,6)`, `round(4.5)`, and `math.sqrt(25)`, and sometimes we do not, as with `penup()` (and also `draw_green_stripe()`). The parentheses signal to Python that the name is the name of a function and we want the code to execute.

Try this

❖ Define a function called `greet_user` to display a `"Hello, world!"` message. Invoke (call) the function.

❖ Invoke your `greet_user` function three times. What is the output of your program?

❖ Define two functions called `say_hello` and `say_goodbye`. Invoke first `say_hello` and then `say_goodbye`. What is the output of your program? Reverse the order of the function definitions. Is there any change? Reverse the order of the calls. Is there any change? Remove the calls. Is there any change? Put the calls back in and remove the definitions. Is there any change?

5.2   Functional decomposition

If we continue working on the flag-drawing program, we can imagine defining a function for each stripe of the flag. If we do, then the main program will be a series of function calls, like this:

```
"""Draw a personal flag."""
# Draw the bottom stripe in green for school color.
draw_green_stripe()
# Draw the second stripe in gold for honors.
draw_gold_stripe()
# Draw the third stripe in brown for running (track).
draw_brown_stripe()
# Draw the fourth stripe in red for Chinese heritage and family.
draw_heritage_stripe()
# Draw the fifth stripe as a horizontal rainbow for friends.
draw_rainbow_stripe()
```

Even without the comments, this code is very easy to read. One quality that makes it easy to read is the names of the functions. The rules for choosing a name (also called an **identifier**) for a function are the same as the rules for choosing a name (identifier) for a variable: only letters, numbers, and underscores are allowed, it may not begin with a number, and it may not be a Python keyword. The conventions are similar as well: you should begin a function name with a lowercase letter, and you should use underscores to separate complete words in a function. Most importantly, a function name should be meaningful. When you are naming functions, you should choose a name that describes what the function does. If you are choosing between naming a function `green_stripe` and `draw_green_stripe`, the name `draw_green_stripe` is better because it describes a process. The name `green_stripe` would be more appropriate for a variable, because it describes a thing.

Our flag-drawing program is also easy to modify. If there is a problem with the brown stripe, we can quickly find, debug, and edit the function that draws the brown stripe without the distraction of all the other code. If we want to add a stripe, we can define and call a new function.

Breaking a problem into smaller steps is called **functional decomposition**. One advantage of functional decomposition is that you can focus on the steps required to solve the problem in a general way without thinking about the details. Once you have the general steps listed, you can then focus on the details of one piece of the problem at a time. In our flag example, we focus first on the entire flag drawing and the order of the stripes, and then in each function, we focus on the details of drawing only one stripe.

Another advantage to functional decomposition is that you can avoid repeating code by placing it in a function and calling it multiple times. Review the code for the function `draw_green_stripe`, and compare it to the code for `draw_gold_stripe`:

draw_green_stripe()	draw_gold_stripe()
``	```
def draw_green_stripe():	def draw_gold_stripe():
"""Draw the green stripe."""	"""Draw the gold stripe."""
# Move the turtle.	# Move the turtle.
turtle.penup()	turtle.penup()

(Continued)

draw_green_stripe()	draw_gold_stripe()
turtle.setpos(-100,0)	turtle.setpos(-100,25)
turtle.setheading(0)	turtle.setheading(0)
turtle.pendown()	turtle.pendown()
# Draw the rectangle.	# Draw the rectangle.
turtle.color("green")	turtle.color("gold")
turtle.begin_fill()	turtle.begin_fill()
for i in range(2):	for i in range(2):
turtle.forward(200)	turtle.forward(200)
turtle.left(90)	turtle.left(90)
turtle.forward(25)	turtle.forward(25)
turtle.left(90)	turtle.left(90)
turtle.end_fill()	turtle.end_fill()

Do you see code that is repeated? The code that draws the rectangle is the same in both functions. When code is duplicated in a program, there is the risk of making an error by typing or copy/pasting incorrectly. If you find that you are copying and pasting code, there is probably a better way. The most likely improvements are a loop or a function.

Another risk with duplicated code is that it is more difficult to change. If we decide to change the size of the flag, making the rectangles longer, for example, we would have to modify the code to draw the rectangle in all of our stripe-drawing functions. Every time we edit code, there is a chance we will make an error. Editing the same functionality multiple times multiplies the risk of error.

A good solution to the problem of duplicated code is to remove the rectangle-drawing code into its own function and call that from our stripe-drawing functions. Listing 5.2 is the flag-drawing program with code for the first two stripes. It includes a separate function to draw the rectangle which is called from each of the stripe-drawing functions.

```
1    import turtle

2    def draw_rectangle():
3        """Draw a rectangle of length 200 and height 25."""
4        for i in range(2):
5            turtle.forward(200)
6            turtle.left(90)
7            turtle.forward(25)
8            turtle.left(90)

9    def draw_green_stripe():
10       """Draw the green stripe of the flag."""
11       # Move the turtle to the correct position.
12       turtle.penup()
13       turtle.setpos(-100,0)
14       turtle.setheading(0)
15       turtle.pendown()
```

```
16        # Draw the rectangle.
17        turtle.color("green")
18        turtle.begin_fill()
19        draw_rectangle()
20        turtle.end_fill()

21   def draw_gold_stripe():
22        """Draw the gold stripe of the flag."""
23        # Move the turtle to the correct position.
24        turtle.penup()
25        turtle.setpos(-100,25)
26        turtle.setheading(0)
27        turtle.pendown()
28        # Draw the rectangle.
29        turtle.color("gold")
30        turtle.begin_fill()
31        draw_rectangle()
32        turtle.end_fill()

33   def main():
34        """Draw a personal flag."""
35        draw_green_stripe()
36        draw_gold_stripe()

37   main()
```
Listing 5.2

On lines 19 and 31, you can see the calls to `draw_rectangle` from within `draw_green_stripe` and `draw_gold_stripe` functions. You might also notice that there is a `main` function which calls each of the stripe-drawing functions. Program execution begins with the call to `main`, at the bottom of the file. It is a common programming practice to begin execution with a function called `main`.

When you compared the two functions side-by-side, did you find other parts of the functions that are similar, but not exactly the same? We will learn shortly how we can abstract similar (but not identical) functionality into one function using parameters.

Try this

❖ Add a function to draw the brown stripe. Have it call the `draw_rectangle` function. Call the `draw_brown_stripe` function from the `main` function.

❖ Write a program to display the lyrics of *All Around the Mulberry Bush*. Define a function called `print_pop` that displays the "Pop! Goes the weasel" line. Define functions to display the different verses of the song and have them invoke the `print_pop` function. (Hint:

(Continued)

(Continued)

The structure is the same as the flag-drawing code's structure.) You can substitute a favorite song if it has a repeated lyric that you can put in a separate function.

Here are the lyrics to the first three verses:

(1) All around the mulberry bush / The monkey chased the weasel / The monkey thought 'twas all in good fun / Pop! Goes the weasel; (2) A penny for a spool of thread / A penny for a needle / That's the way the money goes / Pop! Goes the weasel; (3) Up and down the city road / In and out the Eagle / That's the way the money goes / Pop! Goes the weasel.

5.3 Flow of control

Before we learn more about functions, we should take some time to clarify the flow of control. We will desk check Listing 5.3, which is a program with a similar structure to the flag-drawing program, but with less code.

```python
1   import random

2   def print_item():
3       """Randomly generate an item."""
4       item_number = random.randint(1,3)
5       if item_number == 1:
6           print("There is a laptop here.")
7       elif item_number == 2:
8           print("There is a cold cup of coffee here.")
9       else:
10          print("There is nothing else here.")

11  def print_classroom():
12      """Describe a classroom."""
13      print("You are in a classroom with a whiteboard " +\
                "and computers. Let's start programming!")
14      print_item()

15  def print_great_hall():
16      """Describe the great hall."""
17      print("You are in giant space full of tables " +\
                "and friendly-looking students. Let's study!")
18      print_item()

19  def main():
20      """Describe the building."""
21      print_great_hall()
```

```
22        print("You decide to visit another area.")
23        print_classroom()

24        main()
```
Listing 5.3

Before we begin desk checking, read the code over and see how much of it makes sense. The program is a very simplistic adventure game that simply describes rooms but offers the user no opportunity to move around. The print_item function randomly generates an item to put in a location.

There is only one variable, and that is found in function print_item. Our focus in desk checking this program is primarily on flow of control—understanding when lines of code execute in a program with functions.

As you know, the default flow of control is sequential. Execution will begin at the top of the program, where, on line 1, the random library is imported. Control then reaches line 2, the start of the function definition for print_item. The function does not execute at this time, but the name is registered for later use. Control jumps to lines 11, 15, and 19, where the names for functions print_classroom, print_great_hall, and main are registered for later use. The first executable line of code is line 24, which is the invocation, or call, to function main.

Once again, new lines of code will be highlighted in yellow, but to keep the table brief, we will abbreviate the lines that have already executed.

```
1    import random
2    def print_item():
11   def print_classroom():
19   def main():
24   main()
```

Line #	item_number: print_item	Output
1		
2		
11		
15		
19		
24		

When the function main is called on line 24, control jumps to function main, on line 19. Flow of control proceeds sequentially within main. On line 21, there is another function call, to the function print_great_hall.

```
19   def main():
21       print_great_hall()
```

Line #	item_number: print_item	Output
1, 2, 11, 15, 19, 24		
19		
21		

Control jumps to line 16, the first line of print_great_hall. Within function print_great_hall, once again, control proceeds sequentially. Line 17 is a print statement split over two lines. Line 18 is a call to another function—print_item.

```
15    def print_great_hall():
17        print("You are in giant space full of tables " +\
                "and friendly-looking students. Let's study!")
18        print_item()
```

Line #	item_number: print_item	output
1, 2, 11, 15, 19, 24, 19, 21		
15		
17		You are in giant space full of tables and friendly looking students. Let's study!
18		

Control now jumps to function print_item on line 2. On line 4, a number between 1 and 3 is randomly generated and stored in the variable item_number. We will assume the value 2 is generated. The test on line 5 executes, item_number == 1, and because this evaluates to False, control jumps to line 7, the first elif. Here the test is item_number == 2, which evaluates to True, and so line 8 will execute, and the rest of the if-elif-else block will be bypassed.

```
2    def print_item():
4        item_number = random.randint(1,3)
5        if item_number == 1:
7        elif item_number == 2:
8            print("There is a cold cup of coffee here.")
```

Line #	item_number: print_item	output
1, 2, 11, 15, 19, 24, 19, 21, 15		
17		You are in giant space full of tables and friendly looking students. Let's study!
18		

Line #	item_number: print_item	output
2		
4	2	
5	2 (number==1 False)	
7	2 (number==2 True)	
8		There is a cold cup of coffee here.

Now that we have finished executing a function, control returns to where the function was called. The function print_item was called from line 18. This is also the end of a function (print_great_hall), so control will return to where this was called, on line 21. That line is finished executing, so line 22 will execute.

```
21        print_great_hall()
22        print("You decide to visit another area.")
```

Line #	item_number: print_item	output
1, 2, 11, 15, 19, 24, 19, 21, 15		
17		You are in giant space full of tables and friendly looking students. Let's study!
18		
2		
4	2	
5	2 (number==1 False)	
7	2 (number==2 True)	
8		There is a cold cup of coffee here.
18		
21		
22		You decide to visit another area.

On line 23, there is another function call, to print_classroom. We will leave completing the desk check as an exercise.

Try this

❖ Finish desk checking Listing 5.3.

❖ Step through Listing 5.3 in the debugger and confirm your desk check.

❖ Add another location to Listing 5.3 by adding a function and a function call. Add more options to function `print_item`. Desk check the enhanced program.

5.4   Parameters

We will again compare the `draw_green_stripe` and `draw_gold_stripe` functions from Listing 5.2. We had previously abstracted out the rectangle-drawing functionality to remove repeated code. There is other code in the two functions that is similar, but not identical. Look at the functions and find the similar code. Identify what is the same and what is different in each function.

`draw_green_stripe()`	`draw_gold_stripe()`

```def draw_green_stripe():```
```   """Draw the green stripe."""```
```   # Move the turtle.```
```   turtle.penup()```
```   turtle.setpos(-100,0)```
```   turtle.setheading(0)```
```   turtle.pendown()```
```   # Draw the rectangle.```
```   turtle.color("green")```
```   turtle.begin_fill()```
```   draw_rectangle()```
```   turtle.end_fill()```
	```def draw_gold_stripe():```
	``` """Draw the gold stripe."""```
	``` # Move the turtle.```
	``` turtle.penup()```
	``` turtle.setpos(-100,25)```
	``` turtle.setheading(0)```
	``` turtle.pendown()```
	``` # Draw the rectangle.```
	``` turtle.color("gold")```
	``` turtle.begin_fill()```
	``` draw_rectangle()```
	``` turtle.end_fill()```

You might notice that both functions are the same except for the starting y coordinate of the stripe and the color of the stripe. (And the names and comments, of course!)

`draw_green_stripe()`	`draw_gold_stripe()`

```def draw_green_stripe():```
```   """Draw the green stripe."""```
```   Move the turtle.```
```   turtle.penup()```
```   turtle.setpos(-100,0)```
```   turtle.setheading(0)```
```   turtle.pendown()```
```   # Draw the rectangle.```
```   turtle.color("green")```
	```def draw_gold_stripe():```
	``` """Draw the gold stripe."""```
	``` # Move the turtle.```
	``` turtle.penup()```
	``` turtle.setpos(-100,25)```
	``` turtle.setheading(0)```
	``` turtle.pendown()```
	``` # Draw the rectangle.```
	``` turtle.color("gold")```

draw_green_stripe()	draw_gold_stripe()
turtle.begin_fill() draw_rectangle() turtle.end_fill()	turtle.begin_fill() draw_rectangle() turtle.end_fill()

You have seen functions in Python that take parameters to specialize the way the function behaves. For example, random.randint takes two parameters that determine the range of the randomly generated number. We can also write our own functions that take parameters to specialize their behavior.

What information will specialize our function, so that it draws a stripe, but not exactly the same stripe every time? The information we need to pass in is the values that are different for each function. We can write a draw_stripe function that takes the location and color of the stripe as parameters and draws a stripe at the specified location in the specified color. If we do that, then we will need only one draw_stripe function to draw all the solid-color stripes in the flag (instead of draw_green_stripe, draw_gold_stripe, etc.).

Listing 5.4 is our new flag-drawing program.

```
1    import turtle


2    def draw_rectangle():
3        """Draw a rectangle of length 200 and height 25."""
4        for i in range(2):
5            turtle.forward(200)
6            turtle.left(90)
7            turtle.forward(25)
8            turtle.left(90)


9    def draw_stripe(color, y):
10       """Draw a flag stripe in color at (-100, y)."""
11       # Move the turtle to the correct position.
12       turtle.penup()
13       turtle.setpos(-100,y)
14       turtle.setheading(0)
15       turtle.pendown()
16       # Draw the rectangle.
17       turtle.color(color)
18       turtle.begin_fill()
19       draw_rectangle()
20       turtle.end_fill()
21   def main():
22       """Draw a personal flag."""
```

```
23          draw_stripe("green", 0)
24          draw_stripe("gold", 25)

25      main()
```
Listing 5.4

On line 9, we define the `draw_stripe` function, which takes two **formal parameters**, `color` and `y`, enclosed in parentheses. The formal parameters are variables within the function `draw_stripe` that are named in the parameter list. Within the function, you should assume that these parameter variables already have values when the function begins executing. You can see the parameter `y` being used on line 13, where it is used to set the turtle's position. The parameter `color` is used on line 17, where it sets the turtle's pen and fill color.

On lines 23 and 24, we see two calls to the `draw_stripe` function with **actual parameters**, also called **arguments**, being passed in. On line 23, we call `draw_stripe` with the actual parameters `"green"` and 0. The value of the first parameter in the actual parameter list, `"green"`, is associated with the first parameter in the formal parameter list, `color`. The second parameter in the actual parameter list, 0, is associated with the second parameter in the formal parameter list, `y`. This means that the first time `draw_stripe` is called, when control jumps to line 9, `color` has the value `"green"` and `y` has the value 0. After the function executes, control returns to line 24, where the `draw_stripe` function is called again, this time with the values `"gold"` and 25. Control jumps again to line 9, but this time color has the value `"gold"` and `y` has the value 25. The different parameters specialize the behavior of the function. The function always draws a filled rectangle, but in the first call, the function draws a green stripe at (−100, 0), and in the second call, it draws a gold stripe at (−100, 25).

The number and order of formal parameters and actual parameters must match. You cannot call a function with the wrong number of parameters, or Python will throw a run-time error. Python determines what values to copy into the formal parameters based on order. (The first actual parameter is copied to the first formal parameter, the second actual parameter is copied to the second formal parameter, etc.) You cannot call `draw_stripe` and pass the *y* coordinate first and the color second, because then they will be matched to the wrong formal parameters, and Python will throw a run-time error when you try to set the turtle's position to (−100, `"green"`).

We will switch back to console programming and look at a different program that uses parameters. In Listing 4.26, we wrote a program to read vocabulary words from a file and display them in a table. Listing 5.5 is a vocabulary quiz that uses a function called `quiz_word` that takes three parameters: the word in the user's first language (`word1`), the word in the language the user is being quizzed on (`word2`), and the name of the language the user is being quizzed on (`language`).

```
1    def quiz_word(word1, word2, language):
2        """Quiz the user on word in language 2."""
3        answer = input("What is {} in {}? ".\
                        format(word1, language))
4        if answer == word2:
5            print("Correct!")
6        else:
```

```
7              print("No, {} in {} is {}.".\
                    format(word1, language, word2))

8    def main():
9        """Quiz the user on vocabulary."""
10       quiz_word("book", "kitab", "Arabic")
11       quiz_word("school", "madrasa", "Arabic")

12   main()
```
Listing 5.5

In this program, the function `quiz_word` is invoked twice in the `main` function: on lines 10 and 11. Here is the program running with the user answering both questions correctly:

```
What is book in Arabic? kitab
Correct!
What is school in Arabic? madrasa
Correct!
```

The first time the function is invoked, the value "book" is associated with the parameter `word1`. The value "kitab" is associated with the parameter `word2`, and the value "Arabic" is associated with the parameter `language`. On line 13, when the program prompts the user with "What is {} in {}? ".format(word1, language), "book" is the value associated with the parameter variable `word1`, and "Arabic" is the value associated with the parameter variable `language`, so the program displays "What is book in Arabic?"

We can combine this program with the program in Listing 4.26. Listing 5.6 reads vocabulary from a file and quizzes the user.

```
1    """Read vocabulary information from a file
2       and quiz the user."""

3    import os.path

4    def quiz_word(word1, word2, language):
5        """Quiz the user on word in language 2."""
6        answer = input("What is {} in {}? ".\
7                    format(word1, language))
8        if answer == word2:
9            print("Correct!")
10       else:
11           print("No, {} in {} is {}.".\
12                   format(word1, language, word2))

13   def main():
14       # Obtain the file name from the user, check
15       # that it exists, and open it if so.
```

```
16          file_name = input("Please enter the file name: ")
17          if os.path.isfile(file_name):
18              vocabulary_file = open(file_name)

19              # Read the header record from the file.
20              language1 = vocabulary_file.readline().strip()
21              language2 = vocabulary_file.readline().strip()

22              # Read the vocabulary from the file until the end
23              # and quiz the user.
24              vocabulary1 = vocabulary_file.readline().strip()
25              while vocabulary1 != "":
26                  vocabulary2 = vocabulary_file.readline().strip()
27                  quiz_word(vocabulary1, vocabulary2, language2)
28                  vocabulary1 = vocabulary_file.readline().strip()

29          # Display an error if the file was not found.
30          else:
31              print("That file was not found.")

32  main()
```
Listing 5.6

The code here is all code you have seen before, but it is put together in a new way. The `quiz_word` function is taken from Listing 5.5 and "plugged in" to Listing 5.6 where it can be used in a slightly different way. Instead of hard-coding the actual parameters (using literal values), the parameter values are read from the file into variables and the variables are used as the actual parameters in the function call on line 27.

Actual parameters that are integers, floats, strings, or Booleans can be literals (as in Listing 5.5 on lines 10 and 11) or variables (as in Listing 5.6 on line 27). The value is copied from the actual parameter to the formal parameters in the function, so either the literal value is copied to the formal parameter, or the value from the actual parameter is copied to the formal parameter.

On line 24 in Listing 5.6, the value of the first vocabulary word in the user's language is read into the variable `vocabulary1`. On Line 26, the value of the vocabulary word in the practice language is read into the variable `vocabulary2`. On line 27, these values, along with the value `language2`, which was read from the file on line 21, are passed as actual parameters to the function `quiz_word`.

Control jumps to line 4, where the value in `vocabulary1` is copied to the variable `word1`, the value in `vocabulary2` is copied to the variable `word2`, and the value in `language2` is copied to the variable `language`. (Remember that it is the order that Python uses to determine which value gets copied to which formal parameter.) The parameter variables can then be used to quiz the user.

One thing you might notice is that when actual parameters are variables, they do not have to be named the same as the formal parameters. Python pays no attention to the names—it is concerned only with the number and order of the parameters. You cannot communicate with Python through the names of your variables, except to assign in to them or ask Python to evaluate them. Variable names are for writing code that is readable to you and other programmers. The names of your actual parameters (if they are variables) should make sense in the context of the calling function (in this example, the calling function is `main`). The names of your formal parameters should make sense in the context of the called function (in this example, the called function is `quiz_word`). For example, within `quiz_word`, you would not use the parameter names `word_English`, `word_German`, `language_German`, because `quiz_word` works for words in any language. But if you were specifically writing an English-to-German quiz, you might use those variable names in your main program.

Try this

❖ Add a function call to `draw_stripe` in Listing 5.4 to draw the brown stripe.

❖ Add more vocabulary questions to the quiz in Listing 5.5 by adding more calls to the function `quiz_word`. Change the vocabulary and language in the quiz.

❖ If you add an extra parameter to a call to `draw_stripe` in Listing 5.4, you get the following error:

```
TypeError: draw_stripe() takes 2 positional arguments but 3
were given
```

What do you think that means?

❖ What happens if you change the order of parameters in the calls to `draw_stripe` in Listing 5.4? What happens if you remove the parameters from the call? Try to make sense of the errors that Python throws so you can recognize them if you accidentally make these mistakes.

❖ In Listing 5.5, change the order of the parameters in the calls to function `quiz_word` on lines 10 and 11. Does the program still work? What does it do?

5.5   Returning values

One of the most important qualities of functions is the ability to return values. If you think back to the functions `random.randint`, `round`, and `math.sqrt`, you will remember that they each evaluated to a value—the result of generating a random number in the correct range, rounding the number that you passed as a parameter, or taking the square root of the number that you passed as a parameter, respectively. Listing 5.7 shows these functions being demonstrated in a program.

```
1    """Program to demonstrate function returns."""

2    import math, random

3    # Generate a random number between 1 and 100.
4    rand_num = random.randint(1, 100)
5    print("Your lucky number is {}!".format(rand_num))

6    # Take the square root, round it, and print.
7    root = math.sqrt(rand_num)
```

```
8    rounded_root = round(root)
9    print("Or maybe it's {}.".format(rounded_root))
```
Listing 5.7

On line 4, the `random.randint` function is invoked with the parameters 1 and 100. The function will generate a random number within that range and, from the perspective of our program, it will evaluate to a random value in the range of 1–100. We must then do something with that value. In our program, we assign it to the variable `rand_num`, print it on line 5, and use it as an argument to the `math.sqrt` function on line 7.

But what is happening inside the `random.randint` function? We know that it has two formal parameters representing the bounds within which it should generate a random value. It uses those values to generate a random number, and then it returns the number. The two parameters are the inputs to the function, and the result, the random number, is the output.

When we are designing a program with functions, we should think of functions in terms of their inputs, processing, and outputs. A function is a part of a program to which you can pass some data, so the function can compute the result for you. Functions like `random.randint`, `round`, and `math.sqrt` are so commonly used they exist in libraries for many programming languages and can be (and are) "plugged in" to many different kinds of programs. When we are writing functions, we probably will not be writing libraries, and our functions will be more specific to the problem we are solving.

Suppose you are given the problem of reducing a fraction, such as $\dfrac{16}{24}$, to its equivalent fraction in lowest terms. The first thing you must do is to find the greatest common divisor of the numerator, 16, and the denominator, 24. After you have done that, you simply divide the numerator and denominator by that number, and you have your fraction in lowest terms. The greatest common divisor of 16 and 24 is 8. Therefore, $\dfrac{16}{24} = \dfrac{16 \div 8}{24 \div 8} = \dfrac{2}{3}$.

But how do you find that greatest common divisor? Fortunately, there is a brilliant algorithm for solving this problem, developed by the mathematician Euclid. It would be nice if you could write a function that takes the numerator and denominator as parameters and give you back the greatest common divisor. It is also nice if you can set that part of the problem aside while you write the rest of the program, and then research the Euclidean algorithm and write your greatest common divisor function when you understand how it works. (There actually is such a function in Python already, in both the `math` and `fractions` libraries, called `math.gcd` and `fractions.gcd`. But it will be fun to write our own, it will lend a little insight into how functions are written, and we can imagine a situation where you might need to translate your code to a language that does not have a built-in gcd function.)

If we write the fraction-reducing program first, we might write something like this:

```
"""Reduce a fraction to lowest terms."""


def main():
    """Obtain a fraction from the user and reduce."""
    # Obtain the fraction.
    numerator = int(input("Please enter the numerator: "))
```

```
    denominator = int(input("Please enter the denominator: "))

    # Find the greatest common divisor.
    fraction_gcd = gcd(abs(numerator), abs(denominator))

    # Divide the numerator and denominator by the gcd.
    new_numerator = numerator // fraction_gcd
    new_denominator = denominator // fraction_gcd

    # Display the reduced fraction
    print("The fraction is {}/{}.".\
        format(new_numerator, new_denominator))

main()
```

You can see that here we are expecting the gcd function, which we have not yet written, to find the greatest common divisor of our numerator and denominator and evaluate to that value. We store the result in the variable fraction_gcd, which we can then use to reduce our numerator and denominator values. In our previous example, if the numerator and denominator are 16 and 24, we expect the gcd function to evaluate to 8.

The completed program with the gcd function written is in Listing 5.8.

```
 1   """Reduce a fraction to lowest terms."""

 2   def gcd(a, b):
 3       """Compute and return the gcd of a and b
 4          using Euclid's algorithm."""
 5       remainder = b % a
 6       while remainder != 0:
 7           b = a
 8           a = remainder
 9           remainder = b % a
10       return a

11   def main():
12       """Obtain a fraction from the user and reduce."""
13       # Obtain the fraction.
14       numerator = int(input("Please enter the numerator: "))
15       denominator = int(input("Please enter the denominator: "))

16       # Find the greatest common divisor.
17       fraction_gcd = gcd(abs(numerator), abs(denominator))

18       # Divide the numerator and denominator by the gcd.
19       new_numerator = numerator // fraction_gcd
20       new_denominator = denominator // fraction_gcd
```

```
21          # Display the reduced fraction
22          print("The fraction is {}/{}.".\
                format(new_numerator, new_denominator))

23   main()
```
Listing 5.8

The function gcd is defined on lines 3–11. Recall that when we invoke it, on line 17, we are passing in the numerator and denominator of our fraction. The values in the numerator and denominator variables are copied into the formal parameters a and b. Why did we choose not to call the formal parameters numerator and denominator? The gcd function will find the greatest common divisor of any two numbers. They do not have to be the numerator and denominator of a fraction. So, in the context of the program that is reducing a fraction, numerator and denominator are meaningful names for these variables. But in the context of the gcd function, they are too specific. They refer only to one sort of problem in which we might want to find the greatest common divisor. So, we will call the variables a and b.

Lines 5–9 of the function calculate the greatest common divisor of a and b using Euclid's algorithm. But on line 10, there is something new! The keyword return, followed by an expression. This expression could be a literal value, a variable, or a more complex expression. On line 10 we are returning our result, which is the value in the variable a.

The expression following the return keyword is the expression that the function evaluates to. Reviewing line 17, where we invoke the function, we expect the call gcd(abs(numerator), abs(denominator)) to evaluate to a value that we can store in the variable fraction_gcd. That value is whatever is returned in the return statement within the function. In the example in which we pass 16 in for a and 24 in for b, when the algorithm is finished executing, a will have the value 8, and so 8 is the value returned by the function. That is assigned into the variable fraction_gcd on line 17.

The return statement ends execution within the function. If there were lines of code after line 10 in the function, they would never execute, because the return statement returns control to the function call (line 17 in Listing 5.8). It is possible to have more than one return statement from a function, but it makes it difficult to read and debug a function, so it is best if you design your functions with only one return statement, as the last statement of the function. You can do this by using a variable to hold the result of the function and returning the variable at the end of the function's code.

You might also notice that we have been including a docstring comment after the **function header** (the first line of the function, beginning with the keyword def). This is a Python convention. The docstring comment after the function header should describe what the function does and should include what the function returns. One advantage to documentation conventions is that they can be used by programming tools to assist programmers. Figure 5-1 shows the tool tip in IDLE for the gcd function when the programmer types the function name and the opening parenthesis. You might notice that this is the docstring comment from our program. IDLE can show us the parameters to the function, but it cannot show what

```
>>> gcd(
       (a, b)
       Compute and return the gcd of a and b
       using Euclid's algorithm.
```

Figure 5-1   Tool tip generated from docstring.

the function returns. This is why we include information about the value returned by the function in the docstring.

Try this

❖ Write a function that takes the length and width of a rectangle as parameters and returns its area (length × width). Write a program to invoke the function and display the result.
❖ Write a function that takes a positive integer as a parameter, sums the values from 1 to the parameter, and returns the result. (You can use a loop to do this or you can use the formula $\frac{n(n+1)}{2}$.) Write a program to invoke the function and display the result.

5.6   Input-processing-output (IPO) charts and structure charts

Programmers use diagrams to highlight certain aspects of programs and hide distracting details. This allows programmers to communicate and reason about the details of the system that are important in specific contexts. One way you can categorize the different kinds of diagrams used to model software systems is static and dynamic. A **static diagram** shows a way that the program is organized, and a **dynamic diagram** shows the way that the program functions while it is running. A dynamic diagram will communicate something about flow of control, and a static diagram will communicate something about the structure of the code.

5.6.1   Input-processing-output charts

We will look at two kinds of static diagrams that communicate information about functions, using Listing 5.8 as an example. The first is an Input–Processing–Output chart, or IPO chart. An IPO chart describes a function, with a focus on the data that is coming in (through parameters) and the data that is going out (through the return value).

Here is an IPO chart for the gcd function in Listing 5.8.

gcd		
Input	**Processing**	**Output**
int a,b	Use Euclid's algorithm to find the greatest common divisor of a, b.	int gcd The greatest common divisor of a, b.

The first row of the chart shows the name of the function, and the second row is the headings Input, Processing, Output. The third row describes the function. The first column, Input, lists the parameters of the function and the types of the parameters. Function gcd in Listing 5.8 takes two integer parameters, a and b. The last column, Output, lists the type of the return value and describes what it is. Function gcd returns the greatest common divisor of a and b, which is an integer. The middle column, Processing, describes how the function transforms the input(s) into the output.

The IPO chart can be used to communicate how to design and program a function, if it is given as part of the specification, or how to use a function, if it is given as documentation of a function that has already been written. This diagram provides information on how the function can be used as a component in a larger program. The parameters and the return value are the ways the component connects to the larger program. The programmer using the function will need to connect it to their program by passing in the requested inputs, and they will use the output it will return, or evaluate to. They can use the return value by assigning the output into a variable, as we do in Listing 5.8, or by embedding it in a larger expression. The information that is in the IPO chart is very similar to the information in the tool tip that IDLE provides for a well-documented function. Knowing the inputs to and output from a function is critical to using it correctly.

5.6.2 Structure charts

Structure charts show how functions are connected to other functions through calls and parameters. They are sometimes called module charts or hierarchy charts. Figure 5.2 is a structure chart representing the lowest terms program in Listing 5.8.

Each function in a structure chart is represented by a box labeled with the function's name. An arrow in a structure chart shows a call, or invocation. The arrow in Figure 5-2 is from the box representing the `main` function to the box representing the `gcd` function because, in the program, `main` calls `gcd`. Along the arrow are data flows representing the data that is passed between the two functions. The data flows are small circles with an arrow indicating which direction the data flows (to or from the calling function). The parameters flow from the calling function, `main`, to the called function, `gcd`, because they are inputs to the function. The return value flows from the called function, `gcd`, back to the calling function, `main`, because it is an output from the function.

The chart in Figure 5.2 is quite simple, because there are only two functions represented. If you have a function that calls several other functions, then you would have many more boxes and arrows. The order of the boxes and arrows in a structure chart is not important. The order of calls and the number of calls is not communicated in a structure chart. That is dynamic information that is not part of a structure chart. The structure chart shows only which functions call which other functions, what data is passed between them, and the direction of the flow of data.

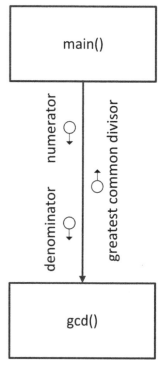

Figure 5-2 Structure chart.

Try this

❖ Write IPO charts for some of Python's built-in functions that we have already used: `random.randint`, `round` (remember that round can take two input values), and `math.sqrt`.
❖ Draw a structure chart for Listing 5.4.

Chapter 5: Functions 153

5.7   Code blocks, namespaces, and scope

5.7.1   Code blocks and namespaces

A script is a block of code (it is also called a **module**). A function is also a block of code. Blocks of code have their own namespaces, which is the directory of programmer-defined names that can be used in that block. You define a name when you define a function or assign a value to a variable. Listing 5.9 has four blocks of code and therefore four namespaces. The four blocks are the module and the functions `function_a`, `function_b`, and `main`.

```
1    """Illustrate namespaces."""

2    def function_a(param_a):
3        local_var_a = 0

4    def function_b(param_b):
5        local_var_b = 0

6    def main():
7        local_var_m1 = 5
8        local_var_m2 = 10
9        function_a(local_var_m1)
10        function_b(local_var_m2)

11   main()
```
Listing 5.9

Figure 5-3 illustrates the code blocks in Listing 5.9.

When we define functions we are associating names with blocks of code. When we assign values into variables for the first time, we are associating names with values. Python puts those names into the appropriate namespace, where they are visible to the block of code associated with the namespace. For a name to be visible means the code can use that name. If a function name is visible, the function can be invoked. If a variable name is visible, it means the variable can be evaluated.

The names defined within a block are visible only within the block's namespace. Therefore, the names defined within a function's namespace are visible only within the function. These names include the parameter variables as well as any variables defined within the function, which are called **local variables**.

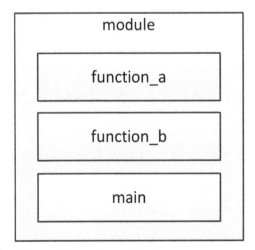

Figure 5-3   Code blocks.

Python has a function called `dir()` that will show the names that are defined in a namespace. We can modify `function_a` to print its namespace using the `dir()` command.

```
def function_a(param_a):
    local_var_a = 0
    print(dir())
```

The output of this modification is:

```
['local_var_a', 'param_a']
```

Within `function_a`, the variables `local_var_a` and `param_a` are defined and can be used. Any code we write within `function_a` may use these variables (or create new ones). We cannot see `local_var_b`, `param_b`, `local_var_m1`, and `local_var_m2`.

We can add the command to print the namespace for the module before or after the call to the `main` function.

```
main()
print(dir())
```

This results in some very interesting output.

```
['local_var', 'param']
['__annotations__', '__builtins__', '__doc__', '__file__', '__
loader__', '__name__', '__package__', '__spec__', 'function_a',
'function_b', 'main']
```

The first line is the result of our `print` statement from `function_a`. The rest of this is the output from the `print` statement in the module, after the call to `main`.

If we ignore the names that begin and end with a double underscore (such as `__doc__`), we see that there are three names defined in the module: `function_a`, `function_b`, and `main`. This means that we can invoke these functions from any code we write in the module.

If we add the same print statement at the end of the main module, we see this:

```
['local_var_m1', 'local_var_m2']
```

Do you wonder why we can use the names `function_a` and `function_b` within the function code block `main`? You might notice that they are not part of the local namespace in `main`.

When Python encounters a name within a block of code, it looks first within that block's namespace for the name. If it does not find it, then it will look in the surrounding namespace. It will continue to do this until it finds the name. If it cannot find the name, it will throw an error. Within the `main` function, Python looks for the name `function_a`. It does not see it—it sees `local_var_m1` and `local_var_m2`. So, it looks at the surrounding block's namespace, which is the module's namespace. We saw above that `function_a`, `function_b`, and `main` are all defined in the module's namespace, and so this is the namespace that is used to resolve the call to `function_a` to a function definition.

5.7.2   Shadowing

If we define a name within a block that is also defined in the surrounding block, the new name **shadows** the old name. For example, if we had a variable in the module (the program) called `local_var_a`, it would be visible within the module, within the main function, and within `function_b`, but it would not be visible within `function_a`, because `function_a` has defined its own variable called `local_var_a`, and this name will shadow (hide) the name in the namespace of the surrounding block. (Remember that Python looks first within the local block's namespace to resolve a name, and then in the surrounding block.) Listing 5.10 illustrates shadowing. Read the code and predict the output.

```
1    """Illustrate shadowing."""

2    def shadowy():
3        var = 0
4        print(var)

5    def main():
6        shadowy()
7        print(var)

8    var = 10
9    print(var)
10   main()
```
Listing 5.10

Program execution begins on line 8, where the variable `var` is associated with the value `10`. Within the module's namespace, then, we have the variable `var` and the two functions `shadowy` and `main` defined. The value associated with `var` is printed. The module then invokes the function `main`, which immediately invokes the function `shadowy`. The function `shadowy` has its own local variable `var`, which shadows the variable in the module. Python resolves the name `var` to the local variable and never looks beyond the local namespace. The local variable is assigned the value `0` and is then printed. Control returns to `main`, where the value associated with `var` is printed. Python will look within the namespace of `main` to find this name, but will not find it, so it will look to the outer namespace, which is the module namespace. It will therefore print the value `10`, the value associated with the variable `var` in the module's namespace. Control then returns to the module after the call to `main`, which is the end of the program.

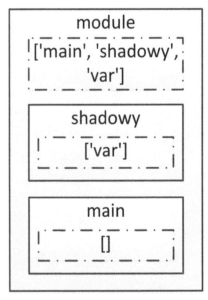

Figure 5-4 Shadowing.

Do you suspect that the `import` command has something to do with namespaces? When we use the `import` command to import an external module, we are adding the name of that module to the current namespace. Once we do that, it is visible and defined and we can use that module's name to access its local namespace.

5.7.3   Best practices

You might have noticed that in our programs with functions, all functions manage their own data. There is no pool of data that all functions work with and modify defined in the module namespace.

(Except when illustrating shadowing!) Designing a program in this way makes it easier to ensure that the data is not accidentally corrupted. It also allows for more freedom in naming variables, as you do not have to think of a unique and meaningful name for every piece of data in a very large program (where the same name might be the best name for two different variables). Another advantage is that a function's access to data is documented through its parameter list.

When you design programs with functions, you should define your variables locally (within functions). If you need data to be shared between functions, you should do so through parameter passing and return values. The only names that should be defined in the module namespace are imported modules, functions, and constants.

5.7.4 Module namespace

We will return to Listing 5.9 and the output of the `print(dir())` command in the module, because it shows a lot of Python's defined names that we have seen only in the debugger.

```
['local_var', 'param']
['__annotations__', '__builtins__', '__doc__', '__file__',
'__loader__', '__name__', '__package__', '__spec__', 'function_a',
'function_b', 'main']
```

If you are curious about these defined names, you can print them or examine them in the debugger. Figure 5-5 shows the debugger just before line 11 executes in Listing 5.9.

You can see that the names `function_a`, `function_b`, and `main` are associated with values that include the word "function," the name of the function, and then "at" followed by a hexadecimal value. That value represents the location in memory where the code for the function can be found. This allows control to jump to that code when the function is invoked.

Do you recognize the value associated with the name `__doc__`? That is the docstring that we wrote for the module (line 1 of Listing 5.9) (Figure 5-5).

Another interesting value here is `__name__`. The value associated with `__name__` is the string "`__main__`". This value means that the module is being executed as a program (as opposed to being imported into another program, with the `import` statement). You will sometimes see programs that are written with code something like the following:

```
if __name__ == "__main__":
    main()
```

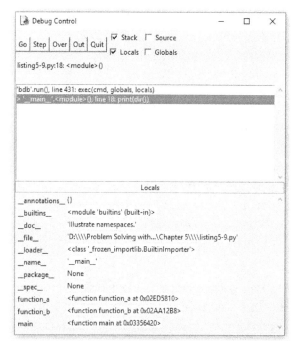

Figure 5-5 The debugger showing the module namespace. *Copyright © 2001–2018 Python Software Foundation; All Rights Reserved.*

This code is checking to see if the module is being run as a program or being imported. If it is being run as a program, then the indented code will execute. In this case, that is starting program execution with the function `main`. We will not use that code in this book, but if you see it being used by other programmers, you now know what it means.

Try this

❖ Add a `print(dir())` command to `function_b` in Listing 5.9. Predict the output, and then run the program to confirm your prediction.

❖ Move the `print(dir())` command in `function_a` in Listing 5.9 to the beginning of the function (before `param_a` is defined). Predict the output, and then run the program to confirm your prediction. Are you surprised? You cannot evaluate a variable until it has a value, but Python creates the directory of names before the code executes.

❖ Add `print(dir())` commands to both functions in Listing 5.8. Predict the output, and then run the program to confirm your prediction.

5.8   The math module, revisited

In most programming languages that you will learn, there will be libraries of commonly used functions that you can use in your programs. We have seen a few of the libraries that are available with Python already: the `random` library, the `turtle` library, the `os` library, and the `math` library. (Another word for these libraries is modules.)

We used the math library in Listing 2.2, where we saw the `math.log`, `math.pow`, and `math.sqrt` functions. We also used the `abs` and the `round` functions, two of Python's built-in functions that perform math operations. (If you type `dir(__builtins__)` in the console you can see a full list of Python's built-in names. These are the names that are highlighted in purple in IDLE by default.)

We will talk about a few additional functions in the `math` module. You can read the full Python documentation for the `math` module here:

https://docs.python.org/3/library/math.html

Python's built-in `round` function will round a floating-point number to the nearest integer (and you may recall that when the floating-point value is exactly between two integers, it will round to the nearest even integer). There are two functions in the math library that are related to round: `ceil` and `floor`.

The `math.ceil` function will raise a floating-point value to the nearest integer that is greater than or equal to the floating-point argument. The `math.floor` function will lower a floating-point value to the nearest integer that is less than or equal to the floating-point argument. This console session illustrates round, math.ceil, and math.floor:

```
>>> import math
>>> round(3.7)
4
>>> math.ceil(3.7)
4
>>> math.floor(3.7)
3
```

The math library also has trigonometric functions such as sin, cos, and tan. The trigonometric functions take their arguments in radians, so it might be useful to know the math.radians function, which converts its argument from degrees to radians, and the math.degrees function, which converts its argument from radians to degrees. Some of these functions were used in the haversine code in Chapter 4.

The sine and cosine of an angle can be used to calculate the (x, y) coordinates of a point on a circle's perimeter. Listing 5.11 is a program that stamps the turtle around the perimeter of a circle every 20 degrees, illustrating the use of some of the trigonometric math functions.

```
1   """The turtle travels around the globe."""
2   import turtle, math

3   def main():
4       # Set the turtle's shape and color.
5       turtle.shape("turtle")
6       turtle.color("green")
7       # Set the circle size.
8       radius = 100
9       # Loop through 360 degrees.
10      for num_degrees in range(0, 360, 20):
11          # Calculate the coordinates.
12          num_radians = math.radians(num_degrees)
13          x = radius * math.cos(num_radians)
14          y = radius * math.sin(num_radians)
15          # Stamp the turtle.
16          turtle.penup()
17          turtle.setheading(num_degrees + 90)
18          turtle.setpos(x,y)
19          turtle.pendown()
20          turtle.stamp()

21  main()
```
Listing 5.11

On line 13 of Listing 5.11, the function math.cos is invoked with the parameter num_radians. The function will evaluate to the cosine of the argument num_radians. Because the function evaluates to a floating-point value, it can be used in code as a float. Floating-point values can be used in assignment statements, in tests, and in mathematical expressions, as you see in Listing 5.11. On line 13, the result is multiplied by the value of `radius` before the final result is stored in the variable `x`.

Programmer-defined functions can also be used anywhere a value of the return type can be used. In Listing 5.8, we had the code:

```
17          fraction_gcd = gcd(abs(numerator), abs(denominator))
19          new_numerator = numerator // fraction_gcd
```

We could have also written:

```
new_numerator = numerator // gcd(abs(numerator), abs(denominator))
```

In Listing 5.8, it was better practice to store the result of `gcd` in a variable, because it was immediately used in two expressions (calculating the numerator and denominator), and it would have been inefficient to call the function twice. But if it is being called only once, the single-line, embedded version is the way many programmers would write the code. You might find the two-line version easier to understand (and it is also easier to debug, because the result of the function call is stored in a variable), but with practice you will find the single-line version equally easy to read.

In addition to functions, the math library also has some built-in constants that might be useful, including `math.pi`, `math.tau`, and `math.e`. You can use these in expressions that call for pi, tau (2 * pi), or e.

Try this

* ❖ Research another command in the `math` library, such as `hypot`, `exp`, or `trunc`. Use it in a program.
* ❖ Research what other libraries are available with Python. Can you find one for creating graphical user interfaces (windows, menus, etc.)? Can you find one that will perform time zone conversions? What else looks interesting?
* ❖ Use functions in the `math` library to write expressions that are equivalent to the following mathematical formulae:

$$\text{population}^{2.5} \qquad \text{digit} * 10^2 \qquad \frac{16^2}{8}$$

$$\frac{4\pi r^3}{3} \qquad \frac{1}{2}g(t1-t2)^2 \qquad \sqrt{b^2 - 4ac}$$

5.9   Input validation functions

There are times when it is easier to write a function to validate input than to validate it within the input validation loop. One reason we might prefer to write a function to validate input is if the conditions that describe valid input are complex.

We will work with our longitude conversion example from Chapter 3. This example illustrates that an input validation function can make the input code easier to read. Input validation functions are also reusable (which is good for security) and are easier to modify (because we know that all of the input validation code is in the validation function).

You might remember from Chapter 3 that it is somewhat complicated to validate the coordinates entered for longitude if they are entered in DMS format. The user must enter either the letter "E" or "W," and they must enter degrees that are up to 180 with minutes and seconds that are less than 60, or degrees that are exactly 180 with minutes and seconds that are exactly 0.

Listing 5.12 is a program that uses an input validation function to verify the input before calculating the longitude in DD format and displaying the result to the user. (Note that the variable name `direction` has been shortened to `dir` to make the code more readable in textbook format. Variable names should be complete words and not abbreviations.)

```python
1  """Convert a longitude from DMS to DD format."""

2  def valid_longitude(degrees, minutes, seconds, direction):
3      """Validate that the user has entered a valid longitude."""
4      valid = False
5      # Check that the direction is E or W.
6      if direction == "E" or direction == "W":
7          # Check that minutes and seconds are less than 60.
8          if minutes < 60 and seconds < 60:
9              # Check that degrees is < 180 or exactly 180
10             # (okay only if minutes and seconds are 0).
11             if degrees < 180:
12                 valid = True
13             elif degrees == 180 and minutes == 0 and seconds == 0:
14                 valid = True
15     return valid

16 def main():
17     # Obtain longitude values from the user.
18     degrees = int(input("Please enter the degrees: "))
19     minutes = int(input("Please enter the minutes: "))
20     seconds = float(input("Please enter the seconds: "))
21     dir = input("Enter E or W: ")

22     # Validate the input values.
23     while not valid_longitude(degrees, minutes, seconds, dir):
24         print("That is not a valid longitude.")
25         degrees = int(input("Please enter the degrees: "))
26         minutes = int(input("Please enter the minutes: "))
27         seconds = float(input("Please enter the seconds: "))
28         dir = input("Enter E or W: ")

29     # Convert to DD format (absolute distance).
30     longitude_dd = degrees + minutes/60 + seconds/3600
```

```
31          # If west of the prime meridian, multiply by -1.
32          if dir == "W":
33              longitude_dd = longitude_dd * -1

34          # Display the DD longitude to the user.
35          print("The longitude in decimal degrees format is {:.6f}." \
                .format(longitude_dd))
```

```
36   main()
```
Listing 5.12

The input validation function, `valid_longitude`, is on lines 2–15, but we will look first at where the function is invoked, on line 23. Remember that in an input validation loop, we want to obtain input from the user until they enter valid input. We therefore need a loop entry condition that describes invalid input.

A loop entry condition must be a Boolean condition. Input validation functions therefore generally return a Boolean result. Our function is called `valid_longitude` and returns a `True` result if the longitude values are valid. Our loop entry condition is therefore `not valid_longitude`, indicating an invalid longitude value.

Within the function, we use a flag variable because the conditions for validation are not simple. On line 4, we set our flag variable, called `valid`, to `False`. We then check the conditions under which the input is valid, and if all the conditions are met, we set the flag variable to `True`. At the end of the function, we return the flag variable.

You may have noticed that the function does not have an action name, such as `validate_longitude`. This was a conscious decision designed to make the loop entry condition more readable. The entry condition `while not valid_longitude` is very close to a natural language statement and describes the conditions under which we will enter the loop and obtain new input values from the user.

Try this

❖ Listing 5.12 does not check for values that are negative. Rewrite `valid_longitude` to return `False` if any of the values entered are negative.

❖ Longitude coordinates can "wrap around" if the user enters a value over 180 or less than zero. Use the `%` operator to adjust the `degrees` value in Listing 5.12 so that it is always between 0 and 180.

❖ Write an input validation function that takes a value for a year and returns `True` if the year is between 1900 and the current year, and `False` otherwise. What is a good name for this function?

❖ Write an input validation loop that uses your input validation function as a loop entry condition to obtain a year from the user that is between 1900 and the current year.

5.10 Problem-solving with functions

We will now apply the problem-solving process to a computational problem, one that is particularly well suited to our new knowledge of functions.

Imagine that you have been asked to write the following program:

> Write a program that will read records from a file that describe a turtle graphics image composed of circles and rectangles. Read each record from the file and draw the correct shape. Rectangle records will be five lines long, with data in the following order: the word "rectangle", the x coordinate, the y coordinate, the length, and the width. Circle records will be four lines long, with data in the following order: the word "circle", the x coordinate, the y coordinate, and the radius of the circle. You should obtain the name of the file from the user. You may not assume the file name references a valid file. You may assume that if the file is valid, it contains zero to many complete records and no incomplete records.

Refer back to the problem-solving steps that we have been using throughout the book, and think about what you would do first, if you were given this problem to solve. Think not only about what the first step is, but also how we have accomplished it in past problems.

If we said that we need to define the problem, well done! If you further remembered that we often start with clarifying our assumptions and asking questions about ambiguities, then you are off to a very good start. We already know that, if there are any records, they will be complete. We might ask if the records can be in any order in the file, and what the records might look like. Will the numerical values be floating-point values? Will the words "rectangle" and "circle" always be all lowercase, and will they always be spelled correctly? What should we do if we encounter a word that is not "circle" or "rectangle"? (What other questions can you think of?)

We might also try to think up several sample files ourselves and try to create files that challenge our assumptions and are not average case files. We should confirm those files with the client. We will provide one sample here, with a single rectangle record and a single circle record and leave developing other sample inputs to you. A two-record file might look like this:

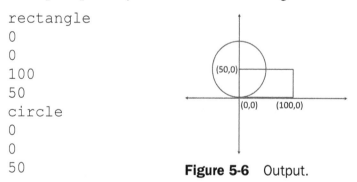

```
rectangle
0
0
100
50
circle
0
0
50
```

Figure 5-6 Output.

For each file that we develop, we should show the corresponding output. This gives us practice solving the problem by hand, which will help us develop an algorithm. It gives us examples we can use as a starting point for test cases, and it gives us examples that we can confirm with our client. The sample file above should produce a drawing like Figure 5-6.

The problem-solving process is not always linear. Even if you have produced a drawing by hand for every sample file that you have developed, it might be helpful to write the Python commands to draw the different shapes based on file data. Do you get the same shapes with your Python code, or have you identified inconsistencies in the way you have interpreted the file data? Is there missing information that you filled in when you were drawing by hand that you will need to consider when you write the program? You may or may not use the code that you write in your final program, but sometimes implementing small parts of the solution can help you define the problem. For example, in writing the code to produce a turtle graphics image like Figure 5-6, you might realize that you were assuming a starting heading of 0 degrees for both the rectangle and circle drawings. Heading is not part of the data in the file. Should the heading be 0 degrees? You now have another ambiguity to discuss with the client.

In solving this problem, we will focus particularly on the process of functional decomposition. The next step in the process is to identify and clearly express solutions, and then choose among those solutions. One approach to functional decomposition is to list the tasks that must be accomplished, and then subtasks, and design some solutions with the responsibility for accomplishing those tasks located in individual functions. For example, some of the tasks in this program include obtaining a file name from the user, validating that the file exists, reading a record from the file, determining if the record is a circle or a rectangle, drawing a circle or a rectangle, and repeating that process until the end of the file is reached. A subtask of drawing is getting the turtle ready to draw (setting its coordinates and heading).

Select tasks from the list above and place them into functions. Determine the inputs to and output from the functions, and how the data will pass to the functions so they can accomplish their work. If they are returning a value, determine what function needs the value to complete its work. Most importantly, do not get overwhelmed! Functions allow us to consider this program one tiny piece at a time.

Figures 5-7 and 5-8 are structure charts that represent two different functional decompositions for this problem. (You may have thought up another, or several others.) We should determine which is the better solution, and then begin implementation.

Do you see any advantages or disadvantages to either of these decompositions? A good rule of thumb is for each function to have a single responsibility. By that criteria, Figure 5-7 looks like a better decomposition of the problem because there is only one function reading a record, and one function to draw each of the shapes. But does `read_record` really have one responsibility, or many? If we were to add a shape type, we would have to change `read_record` to know how to read the new shape type, and we would also have to write a new function to draw the new shape.

The design in Figure 5-8 gives all rectangle responsibility (reading and drawing) to one function, and all circle responsibility to one function. If were to add a shape, we could write one new function

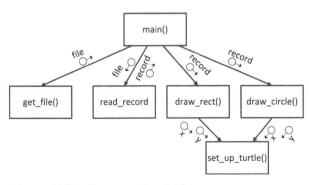

Figure 5-7 Proposed solution.

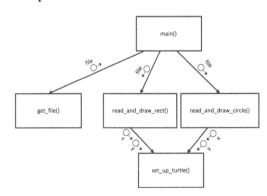

Figure 5-8 Another proposed solution.

to read and draw the new shape. (Be careful not to overdesign for what-if scenarios that will never occur. There are enhancements in the Challenge accepted! section that ask for you to add more shapes, so this is a reasonable enhancement to consider when we are evaluating the initial design.)

There are other ways you can consider these two designs. With our current toolkit, we do not know how to pack a full record of information into one data item that we can return from a function or send to another function. (There are several ways to do this, and you will learn one of them in Chapter 6.)

Based on these criteria, we should begin to develop and test the functions in the chosen design. A function is like a small program with a single responsibility. When phrased this way, you might realize that each function becomes an opportunity to define the problem, identify, express, and evaluate solutions, implement a solution, and evaluate the result. If you are working with a well-designed system, you probably already have a good specification to start with. A function's specification is, in part, its IPO chart and the structure chart, and this should be your starting point for many of these steps.

Testing an individual function before connecting it to the program is called **unit testing**. We should verify that the function takes the specified number and type of parameters, and that it returns the specified result. We should then design test cases for the function, just as we design test cases for a full program. When we have a working function, we can connect it to the rest of the system.

Listing 5.13 is an implementation of the design in Figure 5-8, with one function left as an exercise for you to design, implement, and test.

```
1    """Draw a turtle graphics image from
         instructions in a file."""

2    import turtle, os

3    def set_up_turtle(x, y):
4        """Move the turtle into position at heading 0."""
5        turtle.penup()
6        turtle.setpos(x, y)
7        turtle.setheading(0)
8        turtle.pendown()

9    def read_and_draw_rect(file):
10       """Read square information and draw."""
11       x = float(file.readline())
12       y = float(file.readline())
13       length = float(file.readline())
14       width = float(file.readline())
15       set_up_turtle(x, y)
16       for i in range(2):
17           turtle.forward(length)
18           turtle.left(90)
19           turtle.forward(width)
20           turtle.left(90)
```

```
21   def read_and_draw_circle(file):
22       """Read circle information and draw."""
23       x = float(file.readline())
24       y = float(file.readline())
25       radius = float(file.readline())
26       set_up_turtle(x, y)
27       turtle.circle(radius)

28   def get_file():
29       """Return a valid file obtained from the user."""
30       file = open("drawing.txt")
31       return file

32   def main():
33       """Draw the image described in a file."""
34       file = get_file()
35       # Read from the file as long as it's a valid shape type.
36       drawing_type = file.readline().strip()
37       while drawing_type == "rectangle" or \
                drawing_type == "circle":
38           # Draw the correct shape.
39           if drawing_type == "rectangle":
40               read_and_draw_rect(file)
41           elif drawing_type == "circle":
42               read_and_draw_circle(file)
43       drawing_type = file.readline().strip()

44   main()
```
Listing 5.13

Read through Listing 5.13 and connect it to Figure 5-8. Identify the function calls and the data that is flowing in to each function (through parameters) and out (through return values). This program will work even though the function get_file is little more than a **stub**—a piece of code that stands in for something else. The function get_file is connected to the program. It is invoked, and it returns a value. But it does not obtain a file name from the user and validate it. It is a temporary piece of code that allows us to develop the rest of the program.

The final step in the problem-solving process is to evaluate the result. We should develop test cases from our specifications. We might consider testing the following cases: a bad file name (once we have implemented function get_file), an empty file, a file with a bad shape name (e.g., "retagle"), files with floating-point values for coordinates and sizes, a file with only one shape record, a file of all rectangles, a file of all circles, and a file with many records of both types mixed together. Can you think of other test cases that maintain our assumptions but test the limits of what the program should do? (e.g., we will not try an incomplete record, or records with data of the wrong type, because we were told we could assume complete records.)

Once you have practiced developing programs with functions, you will find they can make your work much easier. Once again, a function is like a small program with a single responsibility, so if you can devise a way to break the larger task into small responsibilities, then you can focus on solving one small problem at a time.

5.11   Challenge accepted!

1. Redesign the `quiz_word` function to be more general. It should take a question and a correct answer as parameters and return a Boolean result of `True` if the user answered the question with the correct answer, and `False` otherwise. Design a program to read quiz questions from a file, quiz the user, and compute and display the percentage of questions that were answered correctly. Write a series of Python questions (maybe about functions!) and test your program.

2. Redesign the `draw_stripe` function to be more general. It should take an *x* coordinate, *y* coordinate, length, width, and color, and should use turtle graphics to draw the rectangle specified by the parameters. Complete the flag-drawing program with the new function.

3. As in the last problem, redesign the `draw_stripe` function to be more general. It should take an *x* coordinate, *y* coordinate, length, width, and color, and should use turtle graphics to draw the rectangle specified by the parameters. Use the function to draw a chessboard. (A chessboard is a board of equal-sized rectangles in eight rows and eight columns, with alternating black and white squares.) Find the repetition in the problem and use a loop or nested loop to draw the squares.

4. Complete Listing 5.13 by designing, implementing, and testing the `get_file` function.

5. Enhance Listing 5.13 to include other shapes, such as lines and shaped stamps. Decide how these will be represented in the file, and then write functions to read the information and draw the shape. You can further enhance the program to include color for all of the shapes. (This will change the length of the records in the file, as you will need another line for color. What if there is an invalid color word?)

6. Write a function that takes a floating-point value as a parameter and returns the associated letter grade. Use the letter grade values that are used by your school or you can return values in a 10-point range down to 60, for example, 90–100 is an A, 80 up to but not including 90 is a B, 70 up to but not including 80 is a C, 60 up to but not including 70 is a D, and all grades below 60 are an F. Use your function in a program that prompts the user for a floating-point value and returns the letter grade. Write and use an input validation function that ensures the value the system processes is between 0 and 100.

7. Write a function that takes a price and a discount percentage as parameters and returns the discounted price. (e.g., if the price is 49.99 and the discount is 20%, the function should return 39.99.) Use the function in a program that prompts the user for the price and the discount percentage and tells them the discounted price. Write and use an input validation function that ensures the value for price is greater than 0. Write and use an input validation function that ensures the value for discount is between 0 and 100.

8. Finding the greatest common divisor of two numbers can be thought of geometrically, as a tiling problem. The greatest common divisor is the side of the largest square tile that you can use to completely fill an *a* × *b* space. Using the `gcd` function from Listing 5.8, write a program to draw an *a* × *b* rectangle and then fill it with square tiles that are the size of the greatest common

divisor of *a* and *b*. Write a function that takes parameters for the (*x, y*) coordinate of each tile and the size of the side to draw each square. The image shows the greatest common divisor of 354 and 66 is 6. There are 11 6 × 6 tiles vertically by 59 6 × 6 tiles horizontally.

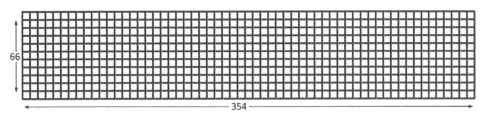

9. For a much more challenging variation on the last problem, modify the gcd function so that it tiles as much of the empty space with squares of side *a* as it can each time it calculates new values for *a* and *b*. For example, in this image of the greatest common divisor of 354 and 66, five 66 × 66 squares fill 66 × 330 of the rectangle, leaving 24 × 66 unfilled. That is then filled with two 24 × 24 squares, leaving 18 × 24 unfilled. That is filled with one 18 × 18 square, leaving 6 × 6 unfilled. That is then filled with three 6 × 6 squares, and the original 354 × 6 rectangle is tiled. Six is the greatest common divisor of 66 and 354.

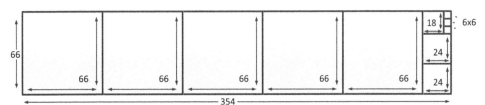

10. Write a program that will calculate areas for the user. The program should begin by presenting the user with a menu of different shapes and a quit option. (e.g., it could present Square, Circle, Rectangle, Triangle, and Quit.) It should prompt the user to select from the menu. Each of the user's choices should be implemented as a function (except for quit). Each function should prompt the user for the dimensions needed to compute the area, compute the area, and report the area to the user. You can use the following area formulae:

$$\text{area of a square} = \text{side}^2 \qquad\qquad \text{area of a rectangle} = \text{width} \times \text{height}$$

$$\text{area of a triangle} = \frac{1}{2} \times \text{base} \times \text{height} \qquad \text{area of a circle} = \pi \times \text{radius}^2$$

11. Write a program that uses a loop and functions to allows two players to play tic-tac-toe until the board is filled. You do not need to draw the board, but you should report the locations of the pieces after each move, for example, the board might look like this after three moves:

```
1  2  3
4  o  6
X  8  x
```

Design a functional decomposition of the problem, including a function to obtain the user's move and a function to validate the user's move.

12. Write a program using turtle graphics that allows the user to select the type of terrain for quadrants of a map. Write separate functions to draw each kind of terrain. For example, if you have

a square with nine quadrants, the user might choose to fill it with two quadrants of forest, four with rock, and three with water. In the drawing here, the user has not yet finished completing the map. You may choose whatever types of terrain you like, and you may choose how to draw them. In this drawing, a separate function draws the dots within the squares, and all of the terrain functions use this dot-drawing function. The dot function takes color and the coordinates of the square as parameters, and draws a randomly sized dot at a random location within the boundaries of the square in the color passed.

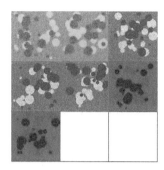

13. Rewrite this program from the Chapters 2 and 4 challenges using functions: Write a program to obtain the following information for five videos: name, the number of views, the number of likes, and the number of dislikes. Compute the percentage of likes and dislikes (out of total likes + dislikes) for each video and display a table of the results with columns for name, percentage of likes, and percentage of dislikes. Use a consistent column width for each column and display one decimal place for the percentages. The first row should contain meaningful headers. Write a function to perform the percentage computation and a function to print a row of the table.

14. Rewrite this program from the Chapter 4 challenges using functions: Write a program that calculates website usage statistics from data in a text file. You should construct a text file by hand that is formatted as follows:

```
Page name
Day 1 views
Day 2 views
...
Day 10 views
Page name
Day 1 views
Day 2 views
...
Day 10 views, etc.
```

The program should read in each record (the name of the page followed by 10 days of usage statistics), average the number of page views, and print a table of page names (left column) and average page views (right column). You should check that the file exists. The file might be empty, but if there are records in the file, you may assume they are complete. Use the problem-solving process to design, implement, and test your program. Create IPO charts for each function and a structure chart for your program.

15. Redesign the Planks and Bones game from the Chapters 3 and 4 challenges using functions. Use the problem-solving process to design, implement, and test your program. Create IPO charts for each function and a structure chart for your program.

16. Design a program using turtle graphics and functions that draws a block of a two-dimensional cityscape by allowing the user to choose the next type of building to be drawn on the block. Give the user a menu of building types and allow them to choose from the menu. The program should then draw their choice. Repeat this process until the block is filled. You can choose the number and type of different buildings available. Write a separate function to draw each different type of building. As an extra challenge, you can give the user the option to customize your

building, for example, by choosing the number of windows or stories, or whether it has an awning or rooftop garden. (You can be creative with your buildings and include anything that might fill the city space, such as a park, art installation, waterfront, city garden, performance area, etc.) Pass these choices as parameters to the drawing function.

17. Write a program that will randomly generate a fortune for the user by calling a series of functions to generate the lines in the fortune. For example, the first function could randomly generate and print a greeting to the user. The second function could randomly generate and print a prediction about the user's success at work. The third function could randomly generate and print a prediction about the user's future career. Write at least four functions that will each randomly generate a part of the fortune.

18. A classic functions programming problem is the projectile motion problem. Write a program that prompts the user for the initial angle (in degrees) and the initial velocity (in m/s) of a projectile (such as a ball) that is being thrown or launched. Write functions to calculate the x and y coordinates of the projectile that take, as parameters, the initial velocity, the initial angle, and the amount of time that has elapsed since the projectile was launched. Write a function that will plot a dot at an (x, y) coordinate in the turtle graphics window. (In the image, the (x, y) coordinates were multiplied by 100 when plotted in order to see the curve. You could scale using hard-coded values or you could calculate the size needed based on the values entered by the user, which is a harder problem. The curve represents a projectile launched at a 60 degree angle at a velocity of 20 m/s drawn in intervals of .2 seconds.) Write a program to compute the (x, y) position of the projectile every .2 seconds and plot it until the projectile reaches the ground (a y coordinate of 0). Use the following formulae:

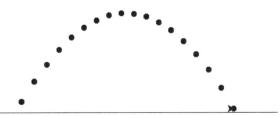

$$x = initial\ velocity \times \cos(launch\ angle) \times time$$

$$y = initial\ velocity \times \sin(launch\ angle) \times time - \frac{1}{2} \times 9.8 \times time^2$$

Chapter 6

Lists

6.1   Collections and indexing

In this chapter we will look at a new data type, called a list. Lists allow you to associate many different values with one name. You can work with the entire list of values, or you can work with individual values within the list. A list can grow and shrink as a program is running, so it is a flexible way to store data if you do not know how many data elements there will be until the program is executing.

In this IDLE console session, we declare a list called `college_credits`, which represents the number of credits that 10 students in an introductory Python course have completed so far in college. We then ask IDLE to evaluate the variable `college_credits`.

```
>>> college_credits = [15, 12, 0, 21, 30, 27, 40, 0, 6, 16]
>>> college_credits
[15, 12, 0, 21, 30, 27, 40, 0, 6, 16]
```

The syntax for declaring a list is a comma-delimited list of expressions, enclosed in square brackets `[]`. In our example, each of the integers between the square brackets is an element of the list `college_credits`. To access an individual element in the list, we use the name of the list followed by the **index** of the element in square brackets. Another word for index is **subscript**, and we will use both in this book. This IDLE console session illustrates evaluating the first value in the list and changing the second.

```
>>> college_credits[0]
15
>>> college_credits[1] = 14
>>> college_credits
[15, 14, 0, 21, 30, 27, 40, 0, 6, 16]
```

You might notice that the index of the first element in the list is 0, and the index of the second element in the list is 1. In most programming languages, structures that contain other elements (such as lists and strings) begin indexing at 0. For clarity, from now on we will write, "the element at index 0" rather than "the first element," as the latter could mean either the element at index 0 or at index 1. As is often the case, natural language is more ambiguous than code.

Another way that we will refer to elements in a list is by saying the name of the list, followed by the word "sub" (short for subscript), followed by the index. For example, `college_credits` sub 0 is 15. `college_credits` sub 2 is 0.

Figure 6-1 is a typical representation of a list that a programmer might draw to help plan or understand an algorithm that works with a list. It is a drawing of the list `college_credits`. Inside the boxes are the values in the list. The indices ("indices" is the plural of "index") are drawn over the boxes.

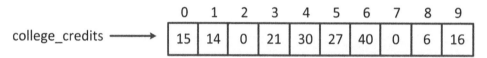

college_credits →

0	1	2	3	4	5	6	7	8	9
15	14	0	21	30	27	40	0	6	16

Figure 6-1 List drawing.

The valid indices for our list of 10 elements are 0, 1, 2, 3, 4, 5, 6, 7, 8, and 9. Because we begin indexing at 0, the index of the last element of a list will always be one less than the length of the list.

Lists can contain any data type that we have seen so far, including lists. (More on that later.) In the following IDLE console session, lists of floats, strings, and Boolean values are created.

```
>>> cities = ["Providence", "Hanoi", "Monrovia"]
>>> weights = [1.34, 2.58, 1.73, 2.01]
>>> has_pets = [True, True, False, True, False, False]
>>> type(cities)
<class 'list'>
>>> type(cities[0])
<class 'str'>
>>> type(weights[0])
<class 'float'>
>>> type(has_pets[0])
<class 'bool'>
```

In this session, first, you can see declarations for three lists of different types. The first list, `cities`, contains string data. The second, `weights`, contains floating-point data, and the third, `has_pets`, contains Boolean data.

When we ask Python the type of the list `cities`, it responds that it is a list. When we ask Python the type of `cities[0]` (read this as "cities sub zero"), it tells us it is a string. This is because `cities[0]` has the value `"Providence"`, which is a string. Similarly, `weights[0]`, which has the value `1.34`, is type `float`, and `has_pets[0]`, which has the value `True`, is type Boolean (`bool`).

We can evaluate the value at a particular index in a list and we can associate a value to a particular index in a list, just as we can with other variables. If we want to perform a calculation on a weight from the list `weights` (such as convert from kilograms to pounds), we can use a single value from the list in a computation, just as we can use any float in a computation.

```
>>> pounds = weights[0] * 2.20462
>>> pounds
2.9541908
```

In this example, `weights[0]` is being evaluated. It evaluates to the value stored at index 0 in the list `weights`, which is `1.34`.

If the list element is on the left side of the assignment operator, then we are assigning into the list, or associating a new value with that index of the list. If we want to associate the value in pounds at weights[0], we use an assignment statement with weights[0] on the left side.

```
>>> weights[0] = pounds
>>> weights
[2.9541908, 2.58, 1.73, 2.01]
```

Although the syntax is new, list elements behave in the same way as the variables you have been working with all along. It is a good idea to practice with the syntax, so you can more easily see the patterns that come with storing values in a list.

Try this

- ❖ Declare a list called `names` that contains the names of five people. Write a statement to print the value at index 0. What is the index of the last value in your list? Write a statement to change the last name in your list. Print your list to confirm your change.
- ❖ Draw a representation like Figure 6-1 for your `names` list.
- ❖ What is the data type of `names[0]`? What is the data type of `names`?
- ❖ How many elements are in the lists `cities`, `weights`, and `has_pets`? What is the index of the last element in each of these lists? Draw a representation like Figure 6-1 for each of these lists.
- ❖ What happens if you try to access `cities[3]`? Why?

6.2   Loops and lists

6.2.1   Stepper-controlled loops

Loops are a natural way to process a list. You can write a loop to visit each element of a list and process it, just as you can write a loop to read each line of a file and process it, or you can write a loop to obtain a value from the user through the console and process it. Many of the algorithms and variable roles that you have already learned for processing files and data from the console are the same for processing lists. You can sum the elements in a list, or find the element with a best fit property, for example.

We will look at how to write a loop to iterate over a list, and then we will revisit some of the algorithms that we use to process streams of data.

We will use a loop that is controlled by a stepper variable to visit each element of a list. A stepper variable takes on a predictable sequence of values. No matter what data is contained in our list, and no matter how long the list is, we can always visit each location in the list by using the following predictable sequence: begin at index 0 and add one until we reach the last element. The index of the last element is one less than the length of the list.

Python has a built-in function called `len` that returns the length of the argument that is passed to it, if the argument is a collection type such as a list. This means that we can write looping code that will work for any size list, by using the `len` function to tell us when to stop.

Listing 6.1 is a program that creates a list of the first eight planets in our solar system, and loops over the list using a stepper variable to print the values in the list.

```
1    """Display eight planets."""

2    def main():
3        # Declare the list of planets.
4        planets = ["Mercury", "Venus", "Earth", "Mars", \
                     "Jupiter", "Saturn", "Uranus", "Neptune"]

5        # Loop over the list and print the planets.
6        i = 0
7        while i < len(planets):
8            print(planets[i])
9            i += 1

10   main()
```
Listing 6.1

Can you identify the stepper variable in this program—the variable that takes on a predictable sequence of values? It is the variable i, which is taking on the values 0 through `len(planets)`, or 0 through 8. (Oops, does that feel like a mistake? Have no fear, we will not enter the loop when i is 8.) When i is assigned the value 8 on line 9 and we return to the loop entry condition i < `len(planets)`, the test fails. We want to be very careful to write the loop entry condition so that we do not try to index into our list using the value that is the length of the list, because that value is always one greater than the last index in the list. So within the loop, i takes on the values 0 through 7, which are the indices of the elements of the `planets` list.

This looping pattern is one that we have used many times before. The pattern is stepper = 0, stepper < some value, stepper += 1, and is a typical looping pattern for iterating over the elements of a collection, such as a list. That is why we learn it and use it even when we are not looping over a collection that begins indexing at 0. It is a good habit to write loops this way when possible.

If you do not follow this pattern when processing a list, you risk off-by-one errors, which can cause a run-time exception (a crash) when you are iterating over a list. Listing 6.2 demonstrates an off-by-one error by using a different pattern for the stepper variables.

```
1    """Demonstrate an off-by-one error."""

2    def main():
3        # Declare a list of cities.
4        cities = ["Providence", "Hanoi", "Monrovia"]

5        # Loop over the list and print the cities,
6        # but one too many times!
```

```
7        i = 0
8        while i <= len(cities):
9            print(cities[i])
10           i += 1

11   main()
```
Listing 6.2

When we run the program in Listing 6.2, here is the output we get:

```
Providence
Hanoi
Monrovia
Traceback (most recent call last):
  File "D:/listing6-2.py", line 14, in <module>
    main()
  File "D:/listing6-2.py", line 11, in main
    print(cities[i])
IndexError: list index out of range
```

Do you recognize what is different about the looping pattern? Instead of checking for the iterator, i, being less than the length of the list, we check for less than or equal to. This results in the loop being entered when i is equal to the length of the list, which is one past the final index in the list. You can see that the loop executed successfully for i equal to 0 through 2, printing the values in the list. But when i reached 3, Python threw a "list index out of range" error. An off-by-one error can be an out of range run-time error like this one, or an error that results in some, but not all, loop elements being processed (e.g., if the output was Providence and Hanoi, but not Monrovia, or if it was Hanoi and Monrovia, but not Providence). When you have a loop error, the debugger is an excellent tool for finding the error.

6.2.2   For loops

A for loop is a natural way to iterate over the elements of a list. Previously we had iterated over a range. For example, here is a for loop that will print the numbers 0 through 9 using a for loop and a range:

```
for i in range(10):
    print(i)
```

In this code, i takes on the value of each element in the range, once for each time the loop body executes. You can also use a for loop to iterate over a collection, such as a list. When you use a for loop that way, the iterator variable takes on the value of each element in the list, once for each time the loop body executes. Listing 6.3 is a program that prints out the first eight planets, using a for loop instead of a while loop.

```
1    """Display eight planets."""

2    def main():
3        # Declare the list of planets.
```

```
4          planets = ["Mercury", "Venus", "Earth", "Mars", \
                       "Jupiter", "Saturn", "Uranus", "Neptune"]

5          # Loop over the list and print the planets.
6          for planet in planets:
7              print(planet)

8      main()
```
Listing 6.3

This program prints each of the planets in the list. In the `for` loop starting on line 6, the variable `planet` will take on first "Mercury", and then the loop body (line 7) will execute and Mercury will be printed. Control then returns to line 6 and the variable `planet` will take on the value "Venus", and Venus will be printed on line 7. This will repeat until the variable `planet` takes on the value of the last element in the list, "Neptune", and prints it.

In this program, you might notice we do not use the variable name `i` for the loop control variable. Here we are not using the index of the elements to control the loop, but rather the elements themselves. The variable that is taking on the value of each element in the list should have a name that describes one element in the list. In a list of planets, one element in the list is a planet. In a list of names, one element is a name. In a list of grades, one element is grade. Naming the variables well makes the code easier to read. On line 7, we are printing a planet name. We are not printing the index of the planet in the list, or the whole list itself.

You might immediately see the advantage to using a for loop to iterate over a list—if you write a simple loop like the one in Listing 6.3, you cannot write code with an off-by-one error. This makes the for loop a good choice if you are going to iterate over a list and process each element. The disadvantages are that you cannot easily replace an element in the list, and you cannot easily iterate in more complicated ways, such as processing two same-sized lists at the same time, or processing some elements, but not all.

You can use a for loop to iterate over the indices of a list, using a range. Listing 6.4 is our planet program using a for loop that iterates over the indices of the list.

```
1      """Display eight planets."""

2      def main():
3          # Declare the list of planets.
4          planets = ["Mercury", "Venus", "Earth", "Mars", \
                       "Jupiter", "Saturn", "Uranus", "Neptune"]

5          # Loop over the list and print the planets.
6          for i in range(len(planets)):
7              print(planets[i])

8      main()
```
Listing 6.4

The for loop on line 6 might require a little unpacking. Expressions that are arguments to functions have the highest precedence, so work from the inside out when you have nested function calls. The first expression to be evaluated will be `len(planets)`, which will evaluate to 8 in our example. The for loop then becomes `for i in range(8)`, where `range(8)` is the values 0, 1, 2, 3, 4, 5, 6, 7. The loop control variable `i` will take on each of these values, once for each time the loop body executes. The loop body uses the loop control variable `i` to index into the list on line 7.

This construct has the advantage that you can both access and modify the element in the list, and the advantage of maintaining the loop control variable for you. (That is, you do not have to write a separate initializer and updater.) It does share some disadvantages with a for loop that iterates over the elements of a list, in that you cannot easily write loops that process only some of the list. We will generally use a while loop and use the index of the list elements to iterate over a list.

6.2.3 Some common loop algorithms

We can use the same variable roles to process lists in loops that we use to process other streams of data. Listing 6.5 is a program that totals and averages a week of daily rainfall measurements.

```
1    """Sum and average the values in a list."""

2    def main():
3        # Declare list of rainfall data.
4        inches = [0, .2, .22, .16, 0, .31, 0]

5        # Loop over the list and sum the values.
6        total = 0
7        average = 0
8        i = 0
9        while i < len(inches):
10           total += inches[i]
11           i += 1

12       # Average the values.
13       if len(inches) != 0:
14           average = total / len(inches)

15           # Display the total and average.
16           print("The total rainfall is {:.2f} and the " + \
                     "average is {:.2f}.".format(total, average))
17       else:
18           print("There is no rainfall data.")

19   main()
```
Listing 6.5

When we are writing a loop to sum values in a stream of data, we need a variable in an accumulator role. Do you recognize the accumulator variable in Listing 6.5? On line 6, we initialize the variable total to 0 prior to the list processing. The loop then visits each element in the list in order, and on line 10 adds the value of the element to the value already in total. When loop execution completes, the sum of the values in the list have been accumulated into total.

After the loop has finished processing the list, we compute the average of the values by dividing the value in the variable total by the size of the list, which is the number of values that were accumulated into the sum. Before computing the average, it is a good idea to test that we will not be dividing by zero. If the list had been empty, its length would be zero. Dividing by zero would cause a zero division run-time exception.

Suppose we want to find the highest rainfall value. When we are searching for a best-fit value, we use a most-wanted holder variable. The most-wanted holder variable will hold the highest value we have found so far as we examine every element in the list. When we are searching for a best-fit value in a list, it is useful to store the index of the highest value, rather than the highest value itself. This is because we sometimes want to process the location where the value is stored.

Continuing with our rainfall example, we can easily see (because there are only seven values) that the highest value is .31, which is stored at index 5. If you imagine processing thousands of items, it is easier to understand why an algorithm that uses a most-wanted holder variable is needed to find the largest item in the list. Listing 6.6 finds the highest rainfall value, storing the index in a most-wanted holder variable.

```
1    """Find the highest rainfall value."""

2    def main():
3        # Declare list of rainfall data.
4        inches = [0, .2, .22, .16, 0, .31, 0]

5        # Loop over the list and find the largest.
6        i_largest = 0
7        i = 1
8        while i < len(inches):
9            if inches[i] > inches[i_largest]:
10               i_largest = i
11           i += 1

12       # Display the largest value.
13       if len(inches) != 0:
14           print("The largest value is {:.2f}."\
                     .format(inches[i_largest]))
15       else:
16           print("There is no rainfall data.")

17   main()
```
Listing 6.6

This loop is a little bit different from the loops we have written previously. Read the loop code carefully, starting on line 6 with initializations, through line 11, which is the updater, and find the code that is different from previous list-processing loops and figure out why it is written the way it is.

Did you identify the most-wanted holder? On line 6, we initialize i_largest to the value 0. We then initialize our loop control variable to 1 and begin indexing into the list at index 1. Did you notice that, and did you figure out why? One way to initialize the most-wanted holder is to set it to the first value in the collection, and then compare it to each subsequent element, one at a time. If the subsequent element is a better fit, we store that value in the most-wanted holder.

In this program, we are storing the index of the largest rainfall value in the most-wanted holder variable, which is i_largest. We initialize it by setting it to the index of the first value in the collection, which is index 0. Within the loop, we compare to the next element, indexed by i, which is index 1 our first time through the loop. If the value at index i is larger, then we will replace i_largest with the value in i. If not, we will keep the value in i_largest as the index to the largest element we have found so far.

If you encounter a list-processing loop that is difficult to understand, then you can desk check it, drawing a representation of the list to help you distinguish the indices from the elements, or you can run the code in the debugger and watch the program execute step by step.

When we are desk checking a list-processing loop that has index variables (like i and i_largest in Listing 6.6), it is sometimes useful to represent these variables as pointers to elements in the list. We can visually desk check some algorithms this way. Figure 6-2 represents the program after line 7 has executed, when i_largest evaluates to 0 and i evaluates to 1. Because these variables are both indices into the list, we show them pointing to elements of the list.

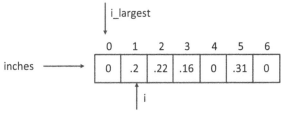

Figure 6-2   After line 7 in listing 6.6.

On line 9, the test inches[i] > inches [i_largest] evaluates to True, because .2, the value at inches[i], is larger than 0, the value at inches[i_largest] (you can see that by looking at where the arrows point in Figure 6-2). Because the test evaluates to True, the code on line 10 executes and i_largest takes the value of i, which is 1. After this line of code has executed, we might draw our representation to look like Figure 6-3.

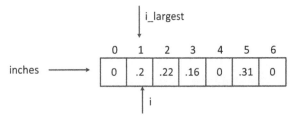

Figure 6-3   After line 10 in listing 6.6.

On line 11, the value in i is incremented, and so we need to move the arrow for i along our list so that it references the element at index 2, as in Figure 6-4. We can proceed this way until the loop entry condition fails and we reach line 13.

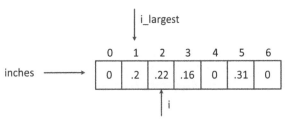

Figure 6-4   After line 10 in listing 6.6.

We will write one more list-processing program. Listing 6.7 is a program to count the days on which no rain fell.

```
1    """Count the days no rain fell in a list of rainfall data."""

2    def main():
3        # Declare list of rainfall data.
4        inches = [0, .2, .22, .16, 0, .31, 0]

5        # Loop over the list and count the days no rain fell.
6        num_dry = 0
7        i = 0
8        while i < len(inches):
9            if inches[i] == 0:
10               num_dry += 1
11           i += 1

12       # Display the number of days no rain fell.
13       print("No rain fell on {} days.".format(num_dry))

14   main()
```
Listing 6.7

You will notice that in this code, we are back to the usual pattern of iterating over the entire list using a loop control variable that indexes into the list. The variable num_dry is being used to count the number of elements in the list that have a value of 0. The loop visits each element and tests to see if the value is 0. If the element evaluates to 0, num_dry is incremented.

Try this

❖ Add a planet name to the lists in Listings 6.1, 6.3, and 6.4 (perhaps "Planet Nine"). Do they still work? Why or why not?
❖ Complete the visual desk check of Listing 6.6.
❖ Modify Listing 6.7 to count the number of days rainfall was over .2 inches.
❖ Write a program to iterate over a list of names and count the number of names that are five characters long or longer. You can use the len function with strings to find their length (e.g., len("Izabele") will evaluate to 7).
❖ What other interesting ways can you process a list of rainfall data or of names?

6.3   Slicing, concatenating, and copying

6.3.1   Variables and memory

You have often seen operations in which we associate a value with a variable using an assignment statement. When we write an assignment statement such as x = y, where x and y are two integers, for example, we know that whatever previous value may have been associated with x is gone, and x now references the same value that y references.

You can think of that copying operation as working by copying the memory address of the value associated with y into x's memory location. Figure 6-5 illustrates the assignment statement x = y.

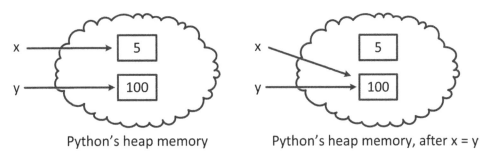

Python's heap memory   Python's heap memory, after x = y

Figure 6-5   Integer assignment of variables.

This may be different from how you have previously thought of assignment. You might have visualized variables as chunks of memory holding data directly, but in Python, they hold the address of the data. This is efficient because memory addresses are quite small and easy to copy, whereas the data they point to can be large.

If there is not already a block in memory allocated with the value being assigned into the variable, then a block of memory is allocated to hold that value. This is illustrated in Figure 6-6.

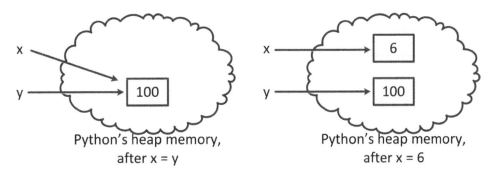

Python's heap memory,   Python's heap memory,
after x = y   after x = 6

Figure 6-6   Integer assignment of a literal.

You can see that assigning a new value to x has no effect on y. A tool that we can use to illustrate this, and that you can use to experiment with this yourself, is Python's id function. You can use the id function by passing it an argument that is a variable name or a literal value. It will evaluate to a value that is unique to that variable or literal, and that you can consider the address of the argument in memory. The following console session shows the id's of x and y after the operations in Figures 6-5 and 6-6.

```
>>> x = 5
>>> y = 100
>>> id(x)
497669232
```

```
>>> id(y)
497670752
>>> x = y
>>> id(x)
497670752
>>> x = 6
>>> id(x)
497669248
>>> y
100
```

Look carefully at the id's of x and y. They are 497669232 and 497670752, respectively, after the initial assignment statements in which the two variables are given different values. This is reflected in the left side of Figure 6-5. After x is assigned the value of y, x has the id 497670752, which is the same as y's id. This is reflected in the right side of Figure 6-5. The variable x is then assigned a new value, giving it a new id of 497669248, and y is evaluated, showing that it is still referencing the value 100. This is illustrated in Figure 6-6.

Copying a reference to a list works in the same way. If you have two lists x and y, and you write the assignment statement x = y, then both variables x and y will reference the same list in memory. If you assign a new list to x, then new memory will be allocated for the list and x will reference that, leaving y untouched.

Lists get tricky because we can change the values of list elements. If we have two lists x and y, and we assign x = y, and then change the value in x[0], the value in y[0] will also change, because they are referencing the same list. Figure 6-7 illustrates this.

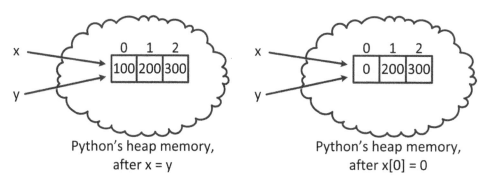

Python's heap memory, after x = y   Python's heap memory, after x[0] = 0

Figure 6-7   Assignment with lists.

A simple assignment statement is therefore not the way to copy a list if you want a copy of the data that is independent of the original list. Here we will look at three ways that you can copy the list and get a completely new list in memory, one that is independent of the original list. To do so, though, we must first learn about two operations on lists.

6.3.2   Concatenation

We looked at string concatenation when we learned about different ways to format text output. String concatenation uses the + operator to create a new string by appending two strings together.

(e.g., `"Hello "` + `"world!"` results in the new string `"Hello world!"`.) We can concatenate lists in the same way, resulting in a new list. The following IDLE console session demonstrates concatenating lists.

```
>>> numbers = [1, 2, 3]
>>> more_numbers = [10, 20, 30]
>>> all_numbers = numbers + more_numbers
>>> all_numbers
[1, 2, 3, 10, 20, 30]
```

How would you confirm that `all_numbers` is an entirely new list? You could use the `id` function to check the ids of the three lists, or you could change values in one list and see if there were side effects in the others. In this case, you would find you had three different lists.

You can use concatenation to copy lists by concatenating the empty list `[]` with the list you want to copy. This will result in a completely new list that has the same elements as the original list. The following IDLE console session demonstrates how you can use list concatenation to duplicate a list.

```
>>> numbers = [1, 2, 3]
>>> copy_numbers = numbers + []
>>> copy_numbers
[1, 2, 3]
>>> id(copy_numbers)
98659824
>>> id(numbers)
98464992
```

6.3.3   Slicing

Another useful operation is list slicing. Slicing also produces a new list from an old list, but with slicing, you can take a subset of the list being sliced. You slice a list by giving the indices of the piece that you want. We will look at the list `numbers` and a visual representation of the list in Figure 6-8, which will help in understanding the slicing operation.

```
numbers = ["555-0000", "555-1111", "555-2222", "555-3333"]
```

Figure 6-8   The numbers list.

To slice a list, you use the list name followed by square brackets, like indexing. Instead of putting an index in the square brackets, you specify the slice that you want. For example, if we want a new list which consists of the two middle values in the list numbers, we would write:

```
two_numbers = numbers[1:3]
```

The slice value before the colon is the starting index of the slice. The slice value after the colon is the index that is one beyond the end of the slice. In our example, we are taking the slice from the value at index 1 up to but not including the value at index 3. This results in `two_numbers` evaluating to the following new list:

```
["555-1111", "555-2222"]
```

You can leave the start, end, or both start and end values empty. If you do this, a default of index 0 (the start of the list) is used for the starting index, and a default of the size of the list (one past the ending value) is used for the ending index. See if you can predict the results of the following slicing operations:

```
mystery1 = numbers[:3]
mystery2 = numbers[2:]
mystery3 = numbers[:]
```

In the first slicing operation, a default of 0 is used for the first index. We are therefore slicing `numbers` from index 0 up to but not including index 3, and so `mystery1` will evaluate to the following new list:

```
['555-0000', '555-1111', '555-2222']
```

In the second slicing operation, a default of 4 (the length of the list) is used for the second index. We are therefore slicing `numbers` from index 2 up to but not including index 4, giving this new list for `mystery2`:

```
['555-2222', '555-3333']
```

Finally, what is in `mystery3`? We are using a default starting index of 0, and a default ending index up to but not including 4. If you figured out that this is the way to make a duplicate of an entire list, well done! The list `mystery3` is a copy of our original list `numbers`.

If you find it difficult to remember that a slice is the first index "up to but not including" the second index, there is another way of visualizing a list for slicing that some people use. It is not good for visualizing indexing, but it works well for understanding slicing operations. With this visualization, you imagine the indices are between the list elements, rather than directly over them, starting with index 0 to the left of the first element. Figure 6-9 is an illustration of this method of visualizing slicing.

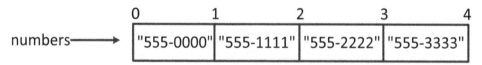

Figure 6-9   Slicing visualization.

6.3.4   The copy method

Lists also have a built-in `copy` **method**. (A method is a function that operates on an object of a particular type. When we use the **dot notation** following a variable or literal value, we are using a method that will work for variables or literals of that type.) The following IDLE console session illustrates the use of the `copy` method.

```
>>> numbers
['555-0000', '555-1111', '555-2222', '555-3333']
>>> copy_numbers = numbers.copy()
>>> copy_numbers
['555-0000', '555-1111', '555-2222', '555-3333']
>>> id(numbers)
```

```
98896952
>>> id(copy_numbers)
98858048
```

In this session, the `copy` method is invoked on the list `numbers` and the result is assigned to a new list variable, `copy_numbers`. The id's of both variables are then displayed to demonstrate that `copy_numbers` is a duplicate of the list `numbers`, and not simply another pointer to the same memory location.

Try this

❖ Create a list of your favorite comedy movies, and a second list of your favorite dramas. (Or select two different genres if you do not enjoy drama or comedy movies.) Use list concatenation to make a third list that is all of your favorite movies.

❖ Using your new list of all movies, make copies using the three copy strategies described in this section: concatenation with the empty list, slicing, and the `copy` method.

❖ Using your new list of all movies, write a slicing operation to return a list that is every element except the element at index 0.

❖ Using your new list of all movies, write a slicing operation that will work for any size list to return a new list that is every element except the last element.

6.4   Operations on lists

6.4.1   Adding to a list

We have not yet talked about how to add values to lists that have already been created. Lists will be much more useful to us if we can create them dynamically, as the program is running. We will be able to add values to a list from user input, from a file, or from computations.

We will look at two ways to add elements to an existing list. The first is the `append` method. The `append` method takes an argument and adds it to the end of a list. The other operation is `insert`, which takes two arguments: an index and an element. The `insert` method will add the element into the list before the index argument. This moves all the elements that were in the list from the element at index to the end of the list to the right, increasing the length of the list by one.

The following console session illustrates the use of `append` and `insert`. You might experiment with these operations, so you understand how they work in different contexts, such as inserting into or appending to an empty list, inserting at the beginning or end of a list, and inserting beyond the end of a list. Can you generate error messages with these operations?

```
>>> values = [10, 20, 30, 40]
>>> values.append(0)
>>> values
[10, 20, 30, 40, 0]
>>> values.insert(1, 100)
>>> values
[10, 100, 20, 30, 40, 0]
```

Note that Python does not try to make any sense out of the values in the list. If you use the `append` method, the value you pass as the argument to `append` will be put at the end of the list. If you use the `insert` method, the value you pass as the second argument will be placed at the index you specify in the first argument. Python will not attempt to order the list if you append or insert (because it does not know the order of the list). You are responsible for maintaining a meaningful ordering to your lists, if there is one.

6.4.2   Finding an element in a list

We could write an algorithm to find a particular element in a list, but lists have an `index` method that will find an element within a list for us. The `index` method will return the index of the element passed as an argument. The search can also be constrained by `start` and `end` parameters that will specify a slice of the list within which to search. The following IDLE console session demonstrates the `index` method.

```
>>> numerals = ["I", "II", "III", "IV", "V", "I"]
>>> numerals.index("II")
1
>>> numerals.index("I", 1, 6)
5
>>> numerals.index("VI")
Traceback (most recent call last):
  File "<pyshell#5>", line 1, in <module>
    numerals.index("VI")
ValueError: 'VI' is not in list
```

Here we define a list of Roman numerals and ask first for the index of the string `"II"`, which is at index 1 in the list. This expression evaluates to 1. We then ask for the index of the string `"I"`, looking only between index 1, up to but not including index 6. The string `"I"` is found in two locations in the list: index 0 and index 5. Because we specify the range 1:6, the second instance is found and the index of that instance is returned.

Python throws an exception if the element you are searching for is not in the list (or in the specified range, if a range is specified). Before you ask a list for the index of an element, you should confirm the element is in the list. You can do this with the `in` operator. For example, before asking for an index, we can write:

```
if "VI" in numerals:
    i = numerals.index("VI")
else:
    i = -1
```

If we write our code this way, then `i` will contain the index of the string `"VI"`, or, if the string is not in `numerals`, the `else` clause will execute and `i` will contain the index −1. It is actually possible to use a negative index into a list (negative indices index backward from the end of the list), so you should determine an error value that makes sense for your application and that you can test for before processing.

6.4.3   Removing from a list

Python offers two ways to remove an item from a list, one that uses the index of the element, and one that uses the element itself. The `remove` method will remove the first instance of the element that you pass as an argument. We can demonstrate using the numerals list again.

```
>>> numerals
['I', 'II', 'III', 'IV', 'V', 'I']
>>> numerals.remove("I")
>>> numerals
['II', 'III', 'IV', 'V', 'I']
>>> numerals.remove("VI")
Traceback (most recent call last):
  File "<pyshell#22>", line 1, in <module>
    numerals.remove("VI")
ValueError: list.remove(x): x not in list
```

There are two instances of the string `"I"` in the list numerals to start. After we ask `numerals` to remove `"I"`, the first instance has been removed. When we ask `numerals` to remove `"VI"`, which is not in the list, Python throws an error.

Before attempting to remove an element from a list, use the `in` operator to avoid errors. For example, we could write:

```
if "VI" in numerals:
    numerals.remove("VI")
```

This will prevent errors and remove the first occurrence of the element from the list only if the element is in the list.

To remove an item or slice using the index, use the `del` statement. This is not a method, so it does not use the dot notation. The syntax is the word `del` followed by the list name and the index or slice in square brackets. The following IDLE console session demonstrates the `del` statement.

```
>>> numerals
['I', 'II', 'III', 'IV', 'V', 'I']
>>> del numerals[5]
>>> numerals
['I', 'II', 'III', 'IV', 'V']
>>> del numerals[0:2]
>>> numerals
['III', 'IV', 'V']
```

Finally, we can remove all elements from a list using the `clear` method. The following IDLE console session demonstrates the `clear` method:

```
>>> numerals
['I', 'II', 'III', 'IV', 'V', 'I']
>>> numerals.clear()
>>> numerals
[]
```

6.4.4   Processing a list

We will look at three of the very useful methods Python offers for processing a list. In Listing 6.7, we wrote a program to count the number of days that there was no rainfall by counting the occurrences of the value 0 in our list called `inches`. Python lists have a built-in method called `count`, which will count the occurrences of a value, passed as an argument, in a list.

Do not worry—your time learning an algorithm to count values in a list was still well spent. While the `count` method will count exact instances of a value, it will not perform more complicated tallying, such as counting values over a threshold (such as days with rainfall greater than .2 inches) or counting values that meet more complicated criteria. The algorithm that you learned can be adapted to many different situations.

When you are simply counting the instances of a value in a list, however, use the `count` method. The following IDLE console session demonstrates its use.

```
>>> numerals
['I', 'II', 'III', 'IV', 'V', 'I']
>>> numerals.count("I")
2
>>> numerals.count("VI")
0
```

We often want to sort our data. The Python list type offers a `sort` method that will sort a list. It will modify the original list, so if you want the list to keep its original order, make a copy before you sort. If you are sorting a list of numeric data, then the ordering will be lowest to highest. If you are sorting string data, the order will be lexicographic. (The Unicode values of the string characters will be used to determine how individual characters compare to each other, starting with the first character of each string.) There are optional parameters that you can use to specialize the way the sort works that we will not discuss here, but you can reference the Python documentation to learn more about sorting and to find additional list methods.

The following console session makes a copy of the rainfall data so that the original order is preserved and sorts the copy. It then uses another list method, `reverse`, to reverse the order of the list. The `reverse` method also modifies the list, so you should again make a copy if you do not want the original order lost (although invoking the reverse method a second time will restore the order of the list before it was reversed).

```
>>> inches = [0, .2, .22, .16, 0, .31, 0]
>>> copy_inches = inches.copy()
>>> copy_inches
[0, 0.2, 0.22, 0.16, 0, 0.31, 0]
>>> copy_inches.sort()
>>> copy_inches
[0, 0, 0, 0.16, 0.2, 0.22, 0.31]
>>> copy_inches.reverse()
>>> copy_inches
[0.31, 0.22, 0.2, 0.16, 0, 0, 0]
```

Try this

- ❖ Create a list of favorite movies. Write code to add a movie to the list, both at the end and within the list (as if you forgot your third favorite movie, for example, and wanted to insert it after the first two movies).
- ❖ Copy your list, and then sort the copy. Copy the sorted list, and then reverse the order.
- ❖ Delete your least favorite movie from the list using the `remove` method.
- ❖ Delete the last three movies from the list.

6.5   Lists and functions

Lists can be passed as parameters to functions and lists can be returned from functions, just like other data. Listing 6.8 contains a function, `random_rolls`, that creates a list of one thousand random values between 1 and 6 and returns the list. A `main` function invokes the `random_rolls` function and then uses the `count` method to count the number of each value between 1 and 6 that was generated.

```
1    """Count randomly generated numbers."""
2    import random

3    def random_rolls():
4        """Generate and return a list of 1000 random rolls."""
5        # Create an empty list to hold the rolls.
6        rolls = []
7        # Generate 1000 random rolls.
8        for i in range(1000):
9            rolls.append(random.randint(1,6))
10       # Return the list of random values.
11       return rolls

12   def main():
13       """Count the frequency of randomly generated numbers."""
14       # Get 1000 random numbers between 1 and 6.
15       numbers = random_rolls()

16       # Count and display the number of each value.
17       for i in range(6):
18           print("The number of {}'s generated was {}."\
                    .format(i+1, numbers.count(i+1)))

19   main()
```
Listing 6.8

We will look first at the `random_rolls` function. This function creates an empty list on line 6. In the loop on lines 8 and 9, it uses the `append` method to add a randomly generated number to the list. Each time line 9 executes, the list grows by one as a new randomly generated value is appended to the end. On line 11, it returns the list, which is now a list of 1,000 random numbers between 1 and 6.

The `main` function invokes the `random_rolls` function on line 15, assigning the result to the variable `numbers`. On lines 17 and 18, the `main` function loops over the values that we are counting (1–6), passing them in to the `numbers.count` method and displaying the result to the user. Because the range generates the values 0 through 5 the way we have written it, we pass `i+1` to the `numbers.count` method so that it will count the occurrences of the values 1 through 6.

As with all functions that return values, you must assign the list that is returned from a function to a variable to use it or you must use it within an expression. If you do not assign it to a variable or use it, the value that is returned is lost.

Returning lists from functions is straightforward, but you must be careful when passing lists as parameters to functions. Unintended side effects can occur if you are not careful. When parameters are passed to functions in Python, they are **passed by value**, which means that the value of the actual parameter (where the function is being called) is copied to the formal parameter variable (in the function). You can think of it as an assignment statement, remembering that the variables in different functions exist in different scopes, and are therefore entirely different variables from each other, even if they have the same name.

As an example, in Listing 6.9, the value referenced by the variable x is passed to the function `no_side_effect` on line 10. Within the function `no_side_effect`, the value that the formal parameter variable x references is changed to `10` on line 4. This has no effect on the actual parameter variable x back in `main`, because the variable x in `no_side_effect` and the variable x in `main` are two different variables that reference first the same, and then different, values. See if you can predict the output of Listing 6.9.

```
1    """Demonstrate pass by value parameters."""

2    def no_side_effect(x):
3        """Change the value of the parameter x."""
4        x = 10
5        print("In no_side_effect, x = {}.".format(x))

6    def main():
7        """Pass an actual parameter to no_side_effect."""
8        x = 5
9        print("Before no_side_effect, x = {}.".format(x))
10       no_side_effect(x)
11       print("After no_side_effect, x = {}.".format(x))

12   main()
```
Listing 6.9

Did you predict the output? Here it is:

```
Before no_side_effect, x = 5.
In no_side_effect, x = 10.
After no_side_effect, x = 5.
```

If that is not what you predicted, and you do not immediately see your error, then there is something about parameter passing that is not entirely making sense, and you should review this. Step through this code in the debugger, pose questions, make modifications, and keep at it until it makes sense. (It will!)

What is most important to note is that no matter what the function might do to its parameter variable, there is no effect on the actual parameter that was passed to the function when it was called. This is not true with lists. Functions can modify lists, and the key to understanding that is to think of parameter passing in the same way that you think of assignment statements. The value that the actual parameter references is copied to the formal parameter variable. When the parameters are lists, the value that is copied is a pointer to the memory location where the original list resides. When you pass a list as a parameter, the reference to the list is copied to the formal parameter, and the formal and actual parameter variables have access to the same list.

You must therefore be very clear about whether your functions are going to modify lists that are passed to them. If it is not clear that a function is supposed to modify a list, and the function does modify a list, then it is an unintended side effect of the function that could cause errors in the program.

Listing 6.10 is like Listing 6.9, except a list, rather than an integer, is passed as a parameter. Predict the output of Listing 6.10.

```
1    """Demonstrate pass by value parameters with lists."""

2    def side_effect(x):
3        """Change the value of the parameter x."""
4        x[0] = 10
5        print("In side_effect, x = {}.".format(x))

6    def main():
7        """Pass an actual parameter to side_effect."""
8        x = [5, 5, 5, 5]
9        print("Before side_effect, x = {}.".format(x))
10       side_effect(x)
11       print("After side_effect, x = {}.".format(x))

12   main()
```
Listing 6.10

Did you predict the output? If we follow the flow of control, we begin with the call to main on line 12. Within main, the list x is given a value on line 8. The list is then printed on line 9. What is printed will be the same value the list was given on line 8. The function side_effect is then called, passing x as an actual parameter. The address of x is copied to the formal parameter x in the function `side_effect`, so that both functions are referencing the same list in memory. On line 4, the element at index 0 is changed to 10. Because that is the same list referenced by the actual parameter in `main`, both variables now reference the list [10, 5, 5, 5]. That list is printed on line 5 in the function `side_effect`, and then again on line 11 in function `main`. The output of the program is shown here:

```
Before side_effect, x = [5, 5, 5, 5].
In side_effect, x = [10, 5, 5, 5].
After side_effect, x = [10, 5, 5, 5].
```

If you are invoking a function that makes a change to a list passed as a parameter, you can pass a copy of the list to the function to preserve the original list. We could have written `main` to prevent the side effect by making a copy of the list x and passing the copy, as shown here:

```
6    def alternate_main():
7        """Pass an actual parameter to side_effect."""
8        x = [5, 5, 5, 5]
9        print("Before side_effect, x = {}.".format(x))
10       y = x.copy()
11       side_effect(y)
12       print("After side_effect, x = {}.".format(x))
```

Here, we make a copy of x and pass the copy to the function `side_effect`. The function changes the list y, but the list x is unchanged. The function `alternate_main` now has both lists—the original and the one that was changed by the function.

Try this

❖ Write a function called `increment` that takes a list of integers as a parameter and adds one to each element in the list.

❖ Write a `main` function that creates a list of integers and passes it to the function `increment`. Print the list in `main` before and after the function call.

❖ Write a `main` function that creates a list of integers, copies it, and passes the copy to the function `increment`. Print both lists in `main` before and after the function call.

❖ Write a function called `safe_increment` that takes a list of integers as a parameter, copies the list, adds one to each element in the copy, and returns the copy.

❖ Write a `main` function that creates a list, prints it, and invokes `safe_increment`. It should store the result of the function call to a different list, then print both lists.

6.6   Lists and files

6.6.1   Splitting strings

A string can be split into a list of substrings, using a delimiter character (or characters) that you specify and that Python will use to determine where to split the string. The string will be split into the substrings that were between the delimiter characters and stored in a list, which is returned from the splitting operation. This is useful for many applications, including reading data from a file that is delimited (separated) by tabs or commas.

This IDLE console session demonstrates splitting a string that is delimited by commas.

```
>>> colors = "red, green, blue, orange, yellow"
>>> list_colors = colors.split(",")
>>> list_colors
['red', ' green', ' blue', ' orange', ' yellow']
```

In this console session, a string called `colors` is created which is composed of different color words separated by commas. The `split` method is then invoked on the string, passing as an argument a string containing a comma. This string is used as the delimiter. The `split` operation breaks the string each time it encounters the comma, storing each substring as a new element in a list. That list is returned from the `split` operation and stored in the variable `list_colors`. One thing you might notice about the strings in `list_colors` is that the space that was after the commas but before the new color words is included as part of the strings. If the desired result was to have color words only in the returned list (and no spaces), then the original string should contain no spaces, or the delimiter `", "` (comma space) should be used, provided that a comma and space is consistently used in the string. (Or each string in the resulting list could be stripped of white space.)

If you wish to split a tab-delimited string, you can use the escape sequence for a tab, as demonstrated in this console session:

```
>>> colors = "red\tgreen\tblue\torange\tyellow"
>>> print(colors)
red	green	blue	orange	yellow
>>> list_colors = colors.split("\t")
>>> list_colors
['red', 'green', 'blue', 'orange', 'yellow']
```

Once you have a string split into substrings stored in a list, you can process the substrings using the list processing strategies you have learned.

If you do not pass a delimiter to the `split` method, the default delimiter is used. The default delimiter is white space. Predict the output of the `split` operation on the `colors` string if no delimiter is specified, and then confirm your prediction in the console.

6.6.2   Reading data from a file

Quite often data is stored in a file in a tab-delimited or comma-separated values (CSV) format. If we are reading data from a file that is stored this way, then we can read each line as a string and split it into substrings to process the individual data elements. We will look at a comma-separated example, as it is easier to see commas, but the process is the same for any delimiter. When you are choosing to store data to a delimited file, it is important that the delimiter does not appear within the data, as it will cause the data to be split where it should not be split. For example, if you are using commas and storing numbers with commas in them (such as `1,000,000` for the number one million), then the number will be delimited at each comma and you will have the values `"1"`, `"000"`, and `"000"` as separate elements in your list.

In the following example, we have a file of community service hours that five students have completed. Many spreadsheet programs will save files in CSV format, so you can imagine that the data was entered into a spreadsheet as these hours were completed, and then saved to a CSV-formatted file. Each row in this file represents one student's hours. A sample file might look like this:

```
2,5,1.5,6,10,2,1,3.5
1,1,1,4.5,2,2,10,2,5,1,1
5,5,5,10,5
2,3,2,3,5,2,3,2,3,5
1,2,1.5
```

When we read data from a file, it is read as a string. We will read one line of the file from the console and split it, so we can see what the resulting list will look like.

```
>>> hours_file = open("hours.txt")
>>> first_line = hours_file.readline()
>>> first_line
'2,5,1.5,6,10,2,1,3.5\n'
>>> first_list = first_line.split(",")
>>> first_list
['2', '5', '1.5', '6', '10', '2', '1', '3.5\n']
>>> hours_file.close()
```

This is the sort of experiment that you might perform when you are writing a program, to help you fully understand the data that you are working with. Would you incorporate the code above into a program to read the hours records from the file and split them, or do you see anything that you might change? If you wanted to total or average the values, is the data in a format you can work with?

We might want to strip the line read from the file before we split it, to remove the newline character \n at the end. It will not make a difference in converting the strings in the list to floats, but it could affect any processing we do on the data in its format as a list of strings. If we want to perform any arithmetic on the data, we will need to convert each value to a floating-point value.

Listing 6.11 incorporates the code above into a loop that reads from the file until it reaches the end. This loop will work for the current file of five students, but it will also work for files with more or fewer student records. After it is read from the file and split, the record is passed to the function process_student_hours, which displays a small report for each line of the file. To keep the code short and focused, we assume the file exists, contains comma-delimited numeric data only, and is called "hours.txt".

```
1    """Read and process records of volunteer hours."""

2    def process_student_hours(hours):
3        """Display a report of the hours in the list."""
4        if len(hours) != 0:
5            total = 0
6            i = 0
7            # Loop over the list and accumulate a total.
```

```
8              while i < len(hours):
9                  total += float(hours[i])
10                 i += 1
11         # Compute an average and display the results.
12         average = total / len(hours)
13         print("Total hours worked: {}".format(total))
14         print("Average hours worked: {:.2f}\n".format(average))

15  def main():
16      """Read each comma-delimited line of the file and process."""
17      hours_file = open("hours.txt")
18      hours_data = hours_file.readline()
19      while (hours_data != ""):
20          hours_data = hours_data.strip()
21          if len(hours_data) != 0:
22              hours_list = hours_data.split(",")
23              process_student_hours(hours_list)
24          hours_data = hours_file.readline()
25      hours_file.close()

26  main()
```
Listing 6.11

In the `main` function, you see our standard file-processing loop which opens the file and reads the first line, then checks to see if we have read the end-of-file character before processing the line at the top of the loop. At the bottom of the loop, the next line is read. To process the line, we strip white space off both ends and split it into a list using the comma as a delimiter. We then send it to the `process_student_hours` function for processing.

The `process_student_hours` function takes the list of hours data (as a list of strings) as a parameter and checks to make sure there is data in the list before processing, to avoid a zero division error when computing the average. It then iterates over the list, converting each element to a float and adding it to an accumulator, `total`. When it is finished summing the values in the list, it takes the average and prints a brief report of the total and the average.

The output for the first record looks like this:

```
Total hours worked: 31.0
Average hours worked: 3.88
```

Python has another file-reading method called `readlines`. The `readlines` method will read an entire file at once, storing its contents into a list. Each line of the file will be one element in the list. This console session demonstrates reading our five-line volunteer hours file into a list using readlines:

```
>>> hours_file = open("hours.txt")
>>> hours_data = hours_file.readlines()
>>> hours_data
```

```
['2,5,1.5,6,10,2,1,3.5\n', '1,1,1,4.5,2,2,10,2,5,1,1\n',
'5,5,5,10,5\n', '2,3,2,3,5,2,3,2,3,5\n', '1,2,1.5\n']
>>> hours_file.close()
```

This allows us to read the file once and store it in a more-or-less raw format for later use, which is advantageous if we want to limit disk access to a brief period at the beginning of our program's execution or if we anticipate needing this raw form multiple times during program execution. However, the algorithms that we have learned for processing lists and files are quite similar, so it does not make our processing easier. Whether our data is read in one line at a time and processed, or read into an entire list and processed, we will still use an algorithm with a loop (to loop over the file or loop over the list) to process the data.

Try this

❖ Predict the output of each of the following statements and confirm in the console:
```
"a b c d e f g".split()
"a b c d e f g".split(",")
"12:02:31".split(":")
"http://www.domain.com/dir1/dir2/file.html".split("/")
```

❖ Convert the file used by Listing 6.11 to a tab-delimited file and change Listing 6.11 to process tab-delimited, rather than comma-delimited, data.

❖ Rewrite the `process_student_hours` function to find the largest and smallest numbers of hours worked and include them in the summary.

❖ Create a file which is composed of several paragraphs of text taken from a current news article. Write a program to open the file, read the first line, and split it without passing a delimiter as an argument to the `split` method. Predict what the resulting list will be. Does the result match your prediction?

6.7   Two-dimensional lists

We have seen lists of integers, strings, floats, and Booleans, but lists can also contain other lists. We will start by looking at an example. Suppose we are storing volunteer hours for 7 days of each week for 3 weeks. We might declare a list that has three elements (one for each week). Each element is a list of seven floating-point values (the number of hours volunteered on that day). The list might look like this:

```
>>> hours = [[0, 1.5, 0, 1, 0, 3, 0],
    [0, 2, 0, 1, 0, 2, 0],
    [0, 1, 0, 1, 0, 0, 3]]
```

The list `hours` has three elements. Those elements are separated by commas. We can ask the console to evaluate each of the elements in the list `hours` for us:

```
>>> hours[0]
[0, 1.5, 0, 1, 0, 3, 0]
>>> hours[1]
[0, 2, 0, 1, 0, 2, 0]
```

```
>>> hours[2]
[0, 1, 0, 1, 0, 0, 3]
```

This is hopefully not too surprising! We will want to access the individual elements within each list, however. If you consider that `hours[0]` is itself a list, then the syntax for accessing element `0` of that list makes sense: `hours[0][0]`.

A list that contains lists as its elements is often called a two-dimensional list because we think of the list as having rows and columns. We can picture a two-dimensional list as a table of data. Each element within the outer list is a row, and the second index indicates the column that the element belongs to. A graphic depiction of this, with indices, is often helpful. Figure 6-10 is a typical visualization of a two-dimensional list, showing the indices of each element.

		columns						
		0	1	2	3	4	5	6
	0	[0][0]	[0][1]	[0][2]	[0][3]	[0][4]	[0][5]	[0][6]
rows	1	[1][0]	[1][1]	[1][2]	[1][3]	[1][4]	[1][5]	[1][6]
	2	[2][0]	[2][1]	[2][2]	[2][3]	[2][4]	[2][5]	[2][6]

Figure 6-10 Two-dimensional list.

Find the patterns in the indices in Figure 6-10. If we want to visit every element in a row, we hold the first index steady while our second index steps through the values from 0 through row length minus one. (Look at the first row of the two-dimensional list as an example: the first index remains `0` while the second index increments from `0` through `6`.) If we want to visit every element in a column, we hold the second index steady while our first index steps through the values 0 through list length minus one. (Look at the first row of the two-dimensional list as an example: the second index remains `0` while the first index increments from `0` through `2`). Drawing pictures of your structure can be especially helpful when writing algorithms to process two-dimensional lists.

Listing 6.12 uses a nested loop to iterate over the list of volunteer hours one row at a time. The program prints the value at each element.

```
"""Create a weekly list of daily hours and display it."""

def main():
    """Declare the list of hours and print each element."""

    hours = [[0, 1.5, 0, 1, 0, 3, 0],
             [0, 2, 0, 1, 0, 2, 0],
             [0, 1, 0, 1, 0, 0, 3]]

    # Iterate over each row. Each row is one week.
    week = 0
    while week < len(hours):
```

```
10              day = 0
11              # Iterate over each column element.
12              # Each column element is one day of the week.
13              while day < len(hours[week]):
14                  print("Hours worked on week {}, day {} is {}."\
                          .format(week, day, hours[week][day]))
15                  day += 1
16          week += 1
```

```
17   main()
```
Listing 6.12

The outer loop syntax (lines 8, 9, and 16) should look very familiar to you. It is the same syntax you would use for iterating over a list of any data type.

```
8           week = 0
9           while week < len(hours):
16          week += 1
```

The inner loop syntax (lines 10, 13, and 15) should also look at least somewhat familiar.

```
10              day = 0
13              while day < len(hours[week]):
15                  day += 1
```

The first time we enter the body of the outer loop, this inner loop is iterating over the list `hours[0]`, which is `[0, 1.5, 0, 1, 0, 3, 0]`. The inner loop uses the stepper variable `day` to iterate over this list. On line 10, `day` is initialized to the value 0. It is incremented by 1 each time through the loop on line 15, and the inner loop stops when we reach the last element in the list `hours[0]`. The outer loop control variable then updates, and the inner loop begins iterating over the list `hours[1]`, which is `[0, 2, 0, 1, 0, 2, 0]`. This repeats for each row of the list `hours`.

Inside the loop we are printing the week number, which is our outer loop stepper `week`, the day number, which is our inner loop stepper `day`, and the value stored at that location in the list, `hours[week][day]`.

In Listing 6.12, we held the row value (the stepper `week`) steady while we iterated through each column value (the stepper `day`). Thus, we visited the elements in the list in the order shown in Figure 6-11.

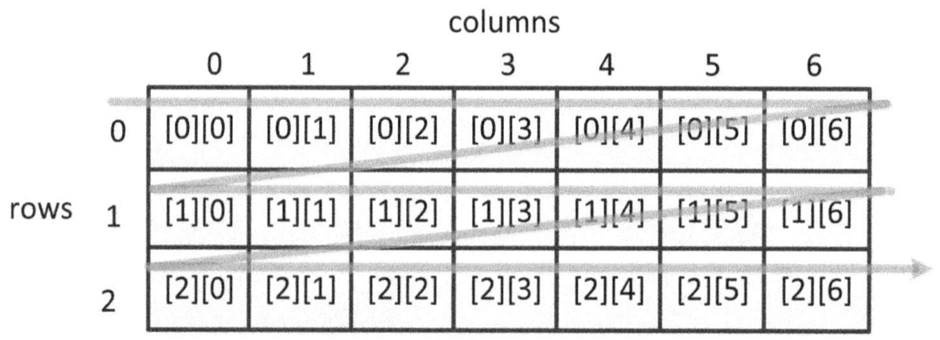

Figure 6-11 Row-major order for visiting list elements.

You can also write a loop to visit each element in the list in column-major order rather than row-major order. If we want to visit each element of a column first, then we visit the elements in the order shown in Figure 6-12.

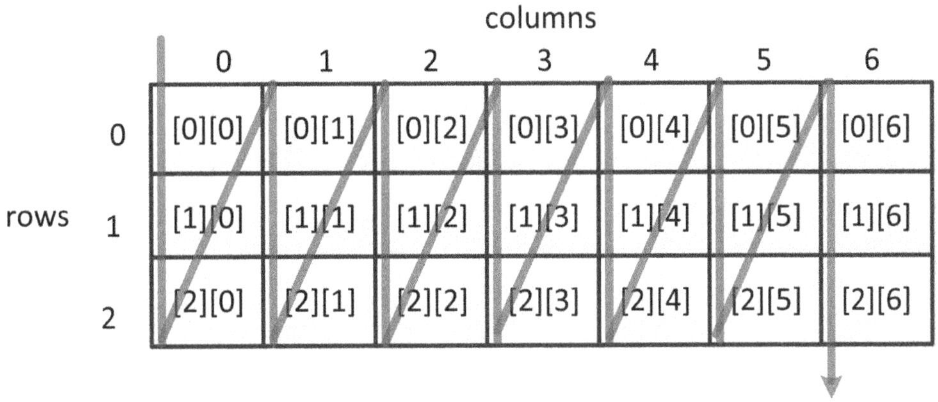

Figure 6-12   Column-major order for visiting list elements.

All elements will be visited in either order, but the pattern of which index is held steady while the other runs through all values changes. If we are going to iterate in column-major order, then the outer loop, which is the loop that holds steady while the inner loop runs, will be controlled by the variable that is stepping over the column indices. Listing 6.13 is a program that visits all the elements of the two-dimensional list in column-major order.

```
1      """Create a weekly list of daily hours and display it."""

2      def main():
3          """Declare the list of hours and print each element."""

4          hours = [[0, 1.5, 0, 1, 0, 3, 0],
5                   [0, 2, 0, 1, 0, 2, 0],
6                   [0, 1, 0, 1, 0, 0, 3]]

7          # Iterate over each column.
8          # Each column is one day of the week.
9          day = 0
10         while day < len(hours[0]):
11             week = 0
12             # Iterate over each row.
13             # Each row is a week.
14             while week < len(hours):
15                 print("Hours worked on day {} of week {} is {}."\
                       .format(day, week, hours[week][day]))
16                 week += 1
17             day += 1

18     main()
```
Listing 6.13

In Listing 6.13, the outer loop is the day of the week. While that variable, `day`, holds the value of 0, the inner loop iterates through the 3 weeks in the list, visiting `[0][0]`, `[1][0]`, and `[2][0]`. The outer loop control variable, `day`, then increments to 1 and the inner loop runs again, until we have visited all seven days and 3 weeks for each of the 7 days.

The outer loop uses the length of the first row as the loop entry condition, `day < len(hours[0])`, which means the variable `day` will take on the values 0 through 6. This will work only if all of the rows in the list are the same length.

It is possible to have lists that are nested further, for example, a list of lists of lists. A three-dimensional list can be visualized as a cube, adding depth to the width and length of a two-dimensional table.

Try this

❖ Given the following two-dimensional list structure:
```
letters = [["E", "T", "A", "O", "I"],
           ["N", "S", "R", "H", "L"]]
```
Give the indices of the following letters. Confirm your answers in the console.
"E" "O" "I"
"N" "S" "L"

❖ Desk check Listing 6.12, and then step through the code in the debugger to confirm your desk check.

❖ Desk check Listing 6.13, and then step through the code in the debugger to confirm your desk check.

❖ Create a three-dimensional list of weeks, days, and hours. You can make this relatively small, perhaps 5 hours over 3 days in 2 weeks, for example. Write a loop to visit each element in your three-dimensional list and print the value stored at the element. Draw a representation of your list to help you write the algorithm.

6.8   Parallel lists and records

The lists that we have looked at so far have all contained data of a uniform type, for example, a list of all strings or a list of all integers. There is a structure in many programming languages called an **array** which is an indexed collection, like a list, that can hold data of only one type, and there are many applications that can be solved by algorithms that process array data. It is therefore useful to understand how to design algorithms that use a single-type indexed collection structure.

However, there are many problems that have more complicated data that we would like to be able to store in a way that preserves the relationships in the data. For example, we might need to store information about a town's water usage that includes the name of the town, the number of residents, and the amount of water used in a month. Or we might need to store the name of an animal, the animal's weight, breed, and diet. We will look at two ways we can use lists to store more complex, mixed-type data like this: parallel lists and lists used as records.

6.8.1   Parallel lists

Parallel lists are two or more lists in which the elements of both lists are related by their index. For example, look at the following two list declarations in this IDLE console session:

```
>>> states = ["DE", "PA", "NJ", "GA", "CT", "MA", "MD"]
>>> years = [1787, 1787, 1787, 1788, 1788, 1788, 1788]
```

The list `states` is a list of state abbreviations for the first seven states to join the United States. The list `years` is the years that they joined. With parallel lists, the elements in the lists are related by index. The element at index 0 in each list is related. Therefore, Delaware (`"DE"`), at index 0 in `states`, joined the union in `1787`, at index 0 in `years`. Pennsylvania (`"PA"`) at index 1 in `states`, joined the union in `1787`, at index 1 in `years`.

Listing 6.14 is a program that iterates over our two lists and displays the related items together.

```
1    """Display state data stored in parallel lists."""

2    def main():
3        """Declare the lists and print related elements."""

4        states = ["DE", "PA", "NJ", "GA", "CT", "MA", "MD"]
5        years = [1787, 1787, 1787, 1788, 1788, 1788, 1788]

6        # Iterate over state and year data and display.
7        if len(states) == len(years):
8            i = 0
9            while i < len(states):
10                print("{} joined the union in {}."\
                        .format(states[i], years[i]))
11                i += 1
12   main()
```
Listing 6.14

On line 7 in Listing 6.14, we first check to confirm that the parallel lists are the same length, because we will be using the length of one list to control the loop that iterates over both. If the lists are different lengths, then iterating using the length of the longer list would lead to a list indexing error.

Lines 8 through 12 define the loop. We use a stepper variable to iterate through the indices of the `states` list, but we use the stepper to index into both lists when we print on line 10, so that we are printing the related values.

Parallel lists each contain data of a uniform type, but they relate data of different types. In this example, data of a string type and data of an integer type are related through being located at the same index in two parallel lists.

6.8.2   Using lists as records

Related data can be placed into a single list, even if it is of different data types. Returning to our states example, we could keep the state abbreviation and the year the state entered the union together in the same list. This console session demonstrates creating two lists, one to store the data for Delaware and one to store the data for Georgia:

```
>>> delaware = ["DE", 1787]
>>> georgia = ["GA", 1788]
```

This looks like a solution that will not work well for more than a few records of data. It is hard to imagine having a separate list variable for every state! However, if we remember that we can have a list of lists, then this becomes more useful. Our parallel lists of seven state abbreviations and entry dates from Listing 6.14 become the following two-dimensional list of state records:

```
states = [["DE", 1787], ["PA", 1787], ["NJ", 1787], ["GA", 1788],
    ["CT", 1788], ["MA", 1788], ["MD", 1788]]
```

It is important that the order of data in each record is the same. If we iterate through our list, then we are visiting one complete record at a time. For example, states[0] is the list ["DE", 1787], and states[1] is the list ["PA", 1787]. Using constants to store the indices of the different data elements makes it even easier to access the data in the records and makes the code much clearer to read. Listing 6.15 produces the same output as Listing 6.14 but using a nested list of records rather than parallel lists.

```
1    """Display state data stored in a list of records."""

2    NAME = 0
3    YEAR = 1

4    def main():
5        """Declare the list and print each record."""

6        states = [["DE", 1787], ["PA", 1787], ["NJ", 1787],
                    ["GA", 1788], ["CT", 1788], ["MA", 1788],
                    ["MD", 1788]]

7        # Iterate over state data and display.
8        i = 0
9        while i < len(states):
10           print("{} joined the union in {}."\
                    .format(states[i][NAME], states[i][YEAR]))
11           i += 1

12   main()
```
Listing 6.15

In Listing 6.15, we declare the list of state record data on line 6. We have the constants that we can use to index into each record, NAME and YEAR, initialized to 0 and 1, for the indices of the abbreviation and the year within each record. Once again, that must be consistent for all records.

On lines 8–11, we loop over the list of states and print the data that is stored in the current record, using states[i] to access the record, and then the second index, NAME or YEAR, to access the elements within the record. Both Listings 6.14 and 6.15 produce the following output:

```
DE joined the union in 1787.
PA joined the union in 1787.
NJ joined the union in 1787.
GA joined the union in 1788.
CT joined the union in 1788.
MA joined the union in 1788.
MD joined the union in 1788.
```

Try this

❖ Use parallel lists to represent state abbreviations and state names. Iterate through the lists and print the associated abbreviations and names.

❖ Create a list of records, where each record holds a state abbreviation and name. Iterate through the list and print the associated abbreviations and names. Use constants to index into the records.

6.9   Strings, revisited

You have seen strings before, of course, and you have learned some processing that can be done with string operators and methods, including the concatenation operator + and the `format`, `split`, and `strip` methods. Strings are a collection type that is like the list type in some ways, so we will cover some of the list operations that you have just learned that will also work with strings, in addition to a few new ones that can help with processing user input.

Strings are stored as an indexed collection of characters starting at index 0 and ending with the index at length −1. To reason about strings, it can be helpful to draw strings in the same way that we draw lists. Figure 6-13 is an illustration of the string `"Hello, world!"`.

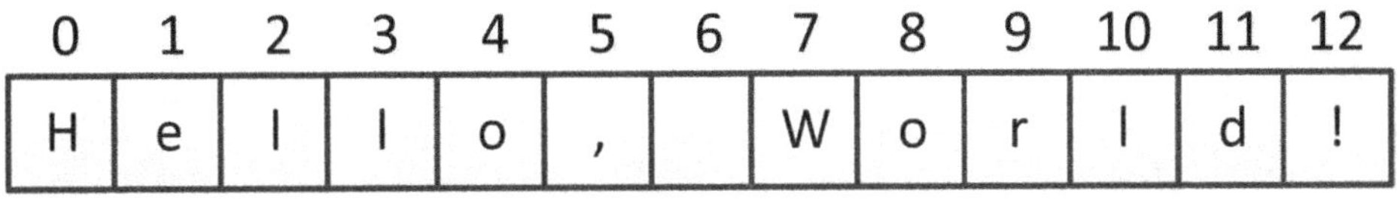

0	1	2	3	4	5	6	7	8	9	10	11	12
H	e	l	l	o	,		W	o	r	l	d	!

Figure 6-13   "Hello, world!" indexed.

As with lists, we can ask Python for the length of the string. We can use a subscripting syntax to index into a list and retrieve an individual character (using a single subscript), or to pull out a slice (using the same slicing notation we use with lists). The following IDLE console session shows the `len`, subscripting, and slicing operations:

```
>>> greeting = "Hello, world!"
>>> len(greeting)
13
>>> greeting[0]
'H'
```

```
>>> greeting[7:13]
'world!'
```

We can also ask Python if a character is contained in a string using the `in` operator, as in the console session below. This can be useful if you are searching for a substring within a string.

```
>>> greeting
'Hello, world!'
>>> "," in greeting
True
>>> "h" in greeting
False
```

You probably remember that uppercase and lowercase letters are not the same characters, and so `"h" in greeting` fails, even though the uppercase letter `"H"` is contained in the string `greeting`. There are two string methods that you can use, `upper` and `lower`, that will return a copy of the string that is all uppercase or all lowercase, respectively. This can make it easier to process user input that you are comparing to a value. For example, if you have asked the user to enter `"yes"` or `"no"` at a prompt, they could enter `"Yes"` or `"YES"` instead of `"yes"`, and you might not process these responses as being the same if you were using a straightforward comparison for equality. Listing 6.16 demonstrates the use of the `upper` method to process user input, but it could have also used `lower`.

```
1   """Process a user response of yes."""

2   def main():
3       """Ask the user to type yes."""

4       answer = input("Please enter yes: ")
5       upper_answer = answer.upper()
6       if upper_answer == "YES":
7           print("You entered yes!")

8   main()
```
Listing 6.16

In Listing 6.16, on line 4 the user inputs a value and it is stored in the variable answer. On line 5 it is converted to uppercase and stored in a new variable, upper_answer. This makes it possible to compare the user's answer to the uppercase string `"YES"`, regardless of whether they typed in uppercase, lowercase, or a combination.

One important difference between lists and strings is that lists are **mutable**, whereas strings are **immutable**. You might notice that these words are like the word "mutation," which can help you remember the meaning. A mutable data type is one that can be changed. When we sort a list, for example, the original list is changed. We must make a copy if we want to keep the original order and also have a sorted version. Strings are immutable, which means they cannot be changed. In Listing 6.16, on line 5 when we write `answer.upper()`, this method returns a copy of the string that is converted to uppercase. It has no effect on the original string. If we want `answer` to point to an uppercase version of the string, then we should write `answer = answer.upper()`.

Try this

❖ Rewrite Listing 6.16 using the `lower` method rather than the `upper` method and test it thoroughly. Are there other ways the user can type the word `"yes"` that are not processed as yes? How can this program be improved?

❖ Write a program that asks the user to enter a sentence. Use the `in` operator to determine if the sentence is a question (ending with a question mark), a declarative sentence (ending with a period), or an exclamation (ending with an exclamation point).

6.10   Problem-solving with lists

Suppose you have a video channel hosted by an Internet Service Provider (ISP). You have a loyal following and you enjoy making videos, but you do not have as much time as you used to have for the channel, now that you are studying computer science. (Perhaps you will start to make some programming videos!) You have several different categories of videos that you create, which you have tagged on your site. The dashboard provided by your ISP allows you to download a CSV file of statistics from your channel that will show you the following information: video name, tags, number of views, number of likes, number of comments, number of people who subscribed while watching the video. You have decided to write a program to read the information from the CSV file and find the categories that your viewers enjoy the most, so you can focus your attention on creating videos in those categories.

6.10.1   Define the problem

You are your own client, but there is a lot of ambiguity in your problem that you will have to clarify before you can begin to identify solutions. If you do not clearly define the problem, you might waste time investigating solution paths that do not solve the problem that you want to solve, or worse, not ever solving the problem.

For example, how will you define finding the categories that viewers enjoy the most? Is it finding the video category with the most views, the most likes, the most comments, or the most subscribe actions? Is it some formula that uses all of those data items? It is actually a very complicated question that you cannot answer without understanding more about your viewers' behavior. What you decide is that you want to keep your followers happy, so you will concentrate on the subscribe actions and comments, with the assumption that both actions indicate a strong wish to see more of the same sort of video. But perhaps when you have more time you will dive deeper into this problem.

Another thing that you should do is download the CSV file and look carefully at the data. The better you understand what the input to your program will look like, the more robust your program will be. In other words, it will be programmed to work with the variety of input that could be in the file or fail gracefully rather than crashing. You might pay particular attention to whether a zero is an empty column or the number zero, because one can be converted to an integer and the other cannot.

Other things might catch your attention as you look at the file. You see that the first five lines of the file look like this:

```
Late night food hacks,#food#lifehack#uplate,4052,25,0,0
Top ten worst escort missions,#gaming#topten#worst,10526,1047,38,5
Healthy gaming snacks,#food#healthy#gaming,200,3,0,0
DIY cosplay sword,#cosplay#DIY#con,8712,514,6,1
Worst MMO (RANT),#gaming#worst,15698,692,27,9
```

There is nothing very surprising there, but now you remember there are multiple tags for each video. You decide to rank your tags individually and not worry about tag combinations. You also decide that you will try to program this in a modular way, using functional decomposition, because this is a program that you might wish to change in the future. That will be easier if you have decomposed it into components that can easily be plugged in to different programs. (It is also less intimidating to program one small piece at a time, and easier to test.) You will use that criterion when selecting among solutions.

To further define the problem, you process chunks of your file by hand to develop the algorithm your program will use to compute the output. The first thing you do is make a list of tags, checking first to see if each tag is in your list before you add it to the end. After you have produced a list of tags, you add up the number of comments and subscribes for each tag. You come up with the following for the first five lines of the file:

Tag	Subscribes	Comments	Final Score
food	0+0=0	0+0=0	0+0=0
lifehack	0	0	0+0=0
uplate	0	0	0+0=0
gaming	5+0+9=14	38+0+27=65	14+65=79
topten	5	38	5+38=43
worst	5+9=14	38+27=65	14+65=79
healthy	0	0	0+0=0
cosplay	1	6	1+6=7
DIY	1	6	1+6=7
con	1	6	1+6=7

You decide that you will add the subscribes and comments scores and rank the tags, and have the program display the ranking for you. For the first five lines of the file, the tags "gaming" and "worst" tie for the highest rank, with 79 each.

After processing several chunks of the file by hand (which is extremely tedious—you are glad you have the skills to write a program to do this), you decide to begin thinking about solutions.

6.10.2   Identify and clearly express solutions

You start by thinking about how to decompose the problem into smaller pieces. What are the tasks that the program will need to accomplish? You know that you will be reading the file, and this seems like a good task to put into a function. You might have a function to count the subscribes for each tag and a function to count the comments for each tag. But then you wonder what sort of data will be passed into and returned from these functions, and you realize you have not given any thought yet to how the data from the file will be stored, or how the totals for the tags will be stored. You also realize that the way the data is stored is related to what functions you will write.

Your final product is your tag data, so you focus on that. You will store the file data in a way that helps you produce the tag data. But how will you store the tag data? It is not apparent how many tags there will be, and you want your program to be flexible, in case you add more tags in the future (such as "programming"), so you will need a dynamic structure that can add tags to itself as they are encountered in the data. A list is the perfect way to store your tags.

A tag does not stand alone—it has accumulators for the number of comments and subscribes that are associated with the tag. You know two ways that you can associate three pieces of data. You can store all of your tags in a list, with comments and subscribes as parallel lists, or you can store a tag, its number of comments, and its number of subscribes, as a record and store all of the records in the list. You draw pictures of these two solutions to help you think about the algorithms you will develop for your solutions. The parallel list solution is shown in Figure 6-14, and the list of records solution is shown in Figure 6-15.

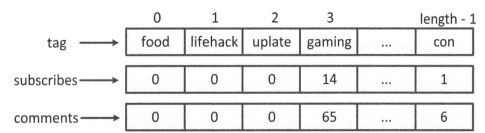

Figure 6-14   Parallel list.

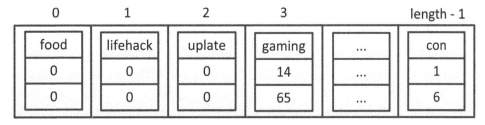

Figure 6-15   Nested list of records.

When you draw the records vertically within your nested list, you realize that the solutions are very similar. You will wait until you are evaluating your solutions to decide which one will be better based on the criteria you will use to judge.

You come up with a structure for your program that you draw as a structure chart, depicted in Figure 6-16. This is a little bit rough, as exactly what is passed to and from each function will depend upon the data structure you select.

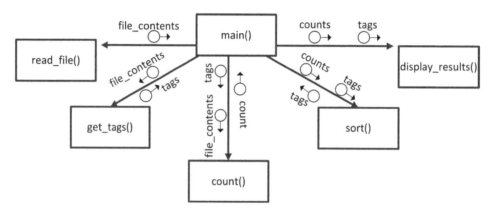

Figure 6-16 Structure chart.

6.10.3 Evaluate and select among those solutions

Although your decomposition is a little rough, you decide to evaluate the ideas you have had so far and select from among them. Your criteria for a good design are the following:

❖ It must be decomposed into components that could be reused if you decide to change your criteria for selecting the best tag.
❖ Each function must have a single, clearly defined task.
❖ Related data should be stored together.

Based on these criteria, you decide to try the nested list of records. That structure seems more cohesive than the parallel lists. You wonder about whether you should add another element to the record that is the overall score, and whether you should have a function that is responsible for computing the score. That would keep the part of your program that you are most likely to change in one function, which will make modifications easier.

6.10.4 Implement a solution

Because the focus of this chapter is lists, we will implement and evaluate one part of the solution that is related to lists. You can imagine that you decide to implement this program one small piece at a time and test the piece thoroughly before moving on. (Smart!) You write a function to use `readlines` to read each line of the file into a list and you write the `get_tags` function that will find all the tags in the `file_contents` list and create the new, nested `tags` data structure. Listing 6.17 is your partial solution.

```
1    """Program to analyze video channel data."""

2    def read_file():
3        """Return a list of the lines in the file."""
4        # to-do: take file name as parameter, confirm it exists
```

```
5        channel_file = open("channel_data.txt")
6        file_data = channel_file.readlines()
7        return file_data

8    def get_tags(file_contents):
9        """Find the tags in the file contents."""
10       TAGS_INDEX = 1
11       tags = []
12       i = 0
13       while i < len(file_contents):
14           # Separate each line in the file into pieces.
15           line = file_contents[i]
16           line_list = line.split(",")
17           # Pull the tags piece out of the line, then
18           # pull the tags out of that; remove blank first tag.
19           tags_string = line_list[TAGS_INDEX]
20           tags_list = tags_string.split("#")
21           tags_list = tags_list[1:]
22           # For each tag, if it's not already in tags, add it
23           for tag in tags_list:
24               if not tag in tags:
25                   tags.append(tag)
26           i += 1
27       return tags

28   def main():
29       """Get the tags from the file data."""
30       file_contents = read_file()
31       tags = get_tags(file_contents)
32       print(tags)

33   main()
```
Listing 6.17

The file `channel_data.txt` is the first five lines of the CSV file from the ISP, and the output from the program is the following list of tags:

```
['food',  'lifehack',  'uplate',  'gaming',  'topten',  'worst',
'healthy',  'cosplay',  'DIY',  'con']
```

To create records for each of the tags that include the tag and the two counts (comments and subscribes), you might iterate through this list and for each element in this list, create a new three-element list, for example, `["food", 0, 0]` for the first element, and append them into an outer list. (Or replace the tag in the list of tags with the three-element list.)

In the process of writing the code, you might have inserted several `print` statements to see exactly what the output of one stage looked like before further processing the results. For example, a `print` statement that prints the `file_contents` variable between lines 30 and 31 yields the following output:

```
['Late   night   food   hacks,#food#lifehack#uplate,4052,25,0,0\n',
'Top ten worst escort missions,#gaming#topten#worst,10526,1047,38,
5\n',  'Healthy  gaming  snacks,#food#healthy#gaming,200,3,0,0\n',
'DIY cosplay sword,#cosplay#DIY#con,8712,514,6,1\n',  'Worst MMO
(RANT),#gaming#worst,15698,692,27,9\n']
```

This is the data that is being passed to the `get_tags` function. You can see that it is a list of strings, where each string is a line from the file. Each line in the file is a list of comma-separated values, so on line 16, you split that by comma. If you insert a print statement of the variable `line_list` after line 16, you see the following output for the first line in the list:

```
['Late night food hacks',  '#food#lifehack#uplate',  '4052',  '25',
'0',  '0\n']
```

On line 19, you pull out the second element of this list into the variable `tags_string`. You can see that this variable is your tags, delimited by hashtag marks. You split that by the hashtag mark on line 20 into the variable `tags_list`. If you print `tags_list` after line 20, you see the following output for the first line in the list:

```
['',  'food',  'lifehack',  'uplate']
```

Because `tags_string` starts with a hashtag, there is an empty string at the beginning of the list. That is why you remove the empty string on line 21. You then iterate through the list and add tags to the list tags if they are not already there.

You repeat this process for every line in the list. You then return the list of tags from the function and print them in main.

6.10.5   Evaluate the result

Before you move on to implementing another piece of this program, you should thoroughly test this module. What sorts of test data should you use? It is a good idea to test typical cases as well as cases that are valid but not typical, and edge cases. For example, a new tag that is first in the list of tags, and a new tag that is last in the list of tags. Our small file sample shows different tags for each video, but suppose you accidentally included the same tag twice for the same video? Will that cause a problem with the algorithm? Suppose you included the # mark twice in a row by accident? Suppose you forgot a # mark? Suppose you have a video with no tags at all? How robust is this algorithm?

For each test case you develop, you must determine the output that is correct so that you can compare it to what the program produces. After you have thoroughly tested the code that is here, you can move on to the next part of the implementation. Soon you will have an answer to your video channel question!

6.11   Challenge accepted!

1. Create (by hand) a text file of grade data, with one grade per line. Write a program to read the grades into a list. Sort the grades and find the average (median), the average (mean), the highest and lowest grades in the list, and the range. Display the sorted grades, one per line, and the

statistics. The mean is the sum of the grades divided by the number of grades. The median is the middle grade, if there is an odd number of grades, otherwise it is the mean of the two middle grades. The range is the difference between the highest and lowest grades.

2. Create (by hand) a text file of rectangle data, with the length of a rectangle on one line and the width of the rectangle on the next line. Write a program to read the data and compute the area (*length × width*) of each rectangle and store the areas in a list. Display the areas, the highest area, the lowest area, and the average of all areas.

3. Create (by hand) a text file of names, with first name (or first and middle name) on one line, and last name (family name) on the next line. Write a program to read the data and create a list of names stored as strings in the format: last, first. (Or last, first middle.) Alphabetize the list and print it.

4. Rewrite the fortune-generating program from the Chapter 5 challenges. Write lists of options for each of the parts of the fortune. (e.g., the greetings list would be a list of any number of greetings that you could use to begin the fortune, such as ["This is your lucky year!", "Prepare for hard work and little reward.", "Your hard work is about to pay off."].) To generate the fortune, randomly select an item from each list. The random module has a choice function that will take a list as a parameter and will return a random item from the list. You can use this to generate the fortune from your lists.

5. Create a program with parallel lists of *x* and *y* coordinates. (You may hard-code them in.) Iterate through the list of coordinates and use them as the (*x*, *y*) location for dots that you make with the turtle. (Use turtle.dot(*diameter*), where *diameter* is the diameter of the dot.)

6. Enhance the last program to use three parallel lists. The third list should be a list of color words. You can use an optional second argument to turtle.dot which is the color of the dot (for example, turtle.dot(5, "red")).

7. Use parallel lists to store state abbreviations and state names. (You may hard-code them in.) Prompt the user for an abbreviation, then find and print the correct state name.

8. Solve the last problem using a nested list of records, where each record contains an abbreviation and a name.

9. Enhance the dot program with three parallel lists of *x* coordinates, *y* coordinates, and colors. Present a menu of the following options to the user: Add a dot, Remove a dot, List all dots, Plot all dots, Quit. Write functions to handle each option.

10. Create (by hand) a text file of (*x*, *y*) coordinates as comma-delimited values, with each (x, y) pair on a single line. Write a program to read the coordinates into two parallel lists. Print and plot the coordinates.

11. Create (by hand) a text file of movie information. Each line of the file should be a tab-delimited record that includes movie name, year, and a floating-point value indicating the star rating of the movie (from zero to five). Write a program to read the data from the file into three parallel lists. Display the names of all movies with a three-star rating or higher. As an alternate challenge, read the data into a list of records instead of using three parallel lists.

12. Create (by hand) text files of top headlines, movies, and songs from the decade surrounding your birth. Read these files into three parallel lists. Allow the user to enter their birth year, and if their year is in your lists, tell them the top headline, movie, and song from their birth year.

13. Create (by hand) a text file of customer information. Each record in the file should be a list of name, e-mail address, and whether or not the customer would like to be on a mailing list (yes or no). Make each record a list of comma-separated values. Write a program to read the data into two parallel lists, one for names and one for e-mail addresses, for all customers who answered

yes to the mailing list question. Do not include customers who answered no to the mailing list question in the lists. As an alternate challenge, read the data into a list of records instead of using two parallel lists.

14. Enhance the program in Listing 6.17 to create the list of records from the list of tags. The list of records should look like, for the example provided:
    ```
    [["food", 0, 0], ["lifehack", 0, 0], ["uplate", 0, 0], ["gaming",
    0, 0], ["topten", 0, 0], ["worst", 0, 0], ["healthy", 0, 0],
    ["cosplay", 0, 0], ["DIY", 0, 0], ["con", 0, 0]]
    ```
    Write the function `count` from the design. It should update the comment and subscribe counts for each tag, given the list of tag records and the original list of data from the file.

15. Rewrite the tic-tac-toe game from the Chapter 5 challenges using a list of lists to represent the board.

16. Rewrite the terrain quadrant problem from the Chapter 5 challenges by using a list of lists to store the terrain data. For example, the terrain from the Chapter 5 challenges could be represented as `[[0, 0, 1],[1, 1, 2], [2, 2, 2]]` where 0 represents forest, 1 represents rock, and 2 represents water. (You can choose any value or data type you wish to represent the different kinds of terrain.)

17. Write a program to obtain shape-drawing information from the user. The program should present the user with a menu of the following options: `Add circle`, `Add square`, `Add rectangle`, `Draw picture`, `Save picture`, `Load picture`, `Quit`. If the user chooses to add a shape, the program should obtain the information necessary to draw the shape (you can decide what that is, but (*x*, *y*) coordinate, size, and color are good options). Each shape should be saved as a record in a list of shapes. For example, a list might look like: `[["square", 0, 0, 25, "green"], ["circle", 100, 100, 50, "red"], ["circle", 0, 0, 75, "blue"], ["rectangle", -100, -100, 50, 100, "yellow"]]`. The program can save the list of shapes to a file and load a list of shapes from a file, draw the shapes using turtle graphics, or add to the list of shapes, according to user choice.

18. Create (by hand) a text file of file directory information. Each record of the tab-delimited file should include file name (e.g. `"shape_program"`), extension (e.g., `"py"`), size (e.g., `"1.5 KB"`), and last modified date (e.g., `"6/4/2018 1:05 PM"`). You can look at an actual directory for examples of what this data might realistically look like. Write a program to read the directory information into a list of records. Convert the file size information to a standard unit, such as KB, and store it as a float rather than a string. Present a menu of options to the user including: `List data`, `Find files by extension`, `Find files by size`, `Find files by date`, `Quit`. Allow the user to enter an extension (such as `"py"`), a size threshold (such as all files over 2 KB), or an exact date (such as `"3/25/2018"`), and list only those records that match their criteria.

Chapter 7

Supplementary chapter:
Number systems

7.1   What is a number base?

You have probably heard of the **binary** number system, and if somebody showed you a number that was composed entirely of zeros and ones, arranged in groups of three or four and without any commas, you might guess you were looking at a binary number. You might know that the binary number system is also called **base two**. And whether you have thought about it in this way or not, you have been engaged in numerical thinking using the **decimal** number system since you were very small and first learning to count. You probably know that the decimal number system is also called **base ten** (Figure 7-1).

But what exactly is a number base? Why do we use the binary number system in computer science, and why do we sometimes use **octal** (**base eight**) and **hexadecimal** (**base sixteen**)?

```
Binary          0111 1010 0010
Hexadecimal     7A2
Decimal         1954
```

Figure 7-1   Binary, hexadecimal, and decimal representations of the same quantity.

When you were learning to count, you had 10 digits to count with, although you may not have thought of zero as much of a digit. We do not generally start our counting with zero! If you had learned to count in base two, then you would have had only two digits—zero and one. And if you had learned to count in base sixteen, then you would have had 16 digits to count with. A number base is the number of digits you have available to count with. This always includes zero, so the highest digit you have is one less than the number base, like the digit nine in base ten, or one, in base two, or F, which represents 15, in base sixteen.

What happens when you run out of digits? You make larger numbers from the same digits using the place-value number system. In base ten, we have the ones place, the tens place, the hundreds place, the thousands place, and so on—with each position being the next power of 10, for an infinite number of positions. A digit in the ones place represents that number of ones. A digit in the tens place represents that number of tens, and a digit in the hundreds place represents that number of hundreds, and so on for all positions. For example, the number 2,109,583,647 has a seven in the ones place, representing seven ones. It has a four in the tens place, representing four tens, or 40. It has a six in the hundreds place, representing six hundreds, or six hundred. (You can continue this pattern to the two in the billions place.)

Although you already know all of this for base ten, there are patterns here that are the same for all number systems. One pattern is the meaning of each position in the place-value system. In base ten, the first three positions are the ones, tens, and hundreds. These are the first three powers of 10. Ten raised to the zero power is one. Ten raised to the first power is 10. Ten raised to the second power is 100.

In base two, the first three positions are the ones, twos, and fours. These are the first three powers of two. Two raised to the zero power is one. (Every number raised to the zero power is one.) Two raised to the first power is two. Two raised to the second power is four.

In base sixteen, the first three positions are the ones, sixteens, and two hundred and fifty-sixes. These are the first three powers of 16. This is the pattern for every number base. Each increasing position is the next power of the base.

Try this

* How many digits are available to count with in base eight (also called octal)? What are they?
* List the first five positions in base ten (e.g., the ones, the tens, the hundreds …).
* List the first five positions in base two.
* List the first five positions in base eight.
* Now that you have listed the first five positions in base two, do you notice an interesting relationship between base two and base eight and sixteen? How is base ten different?

7.2   Binary numbers

We will look first at binary numbers in more detail. In the base two number system, we have two digits to count with: zero and one. Those two digits have the same meaning that they have in the base ten number system. But once we have run out of digits (and we have, by the time we are finished counting one), we must move to the next position in the place value number system. That is the twos place. Figure 7-2 illustrates the first 11 positions in the base two number system using the number *110 1001 1110* as an example.

1024	512	256	128	64	32	16	8	4	2	1
1	1	0	1	0	0	1	1	1	1	0
2^{10}	2^9	2^8	2^7	2^6	2^5	2^4	2^3	2^2	2^1	2^0

Figure 7-2   Base two place value.

In base two, instead of having the ones place, the tens place, the hundreds place, and on in powers of 10, we have the ones place, the twos place, the fours place, and on in powers of two. Instead of having the digits zero through nine in each of the positions, we have the digits zero and one in each of the positions.

If we take a smaller number as an example, such as *11 1011*, then we have, reading from left to right, a one in the thirty-twos place, a one in the sixteens place, a one in the eights place, a zero in the fours place, a one in the twos place, and a one in the ones place. To be more succinct, we could say one 32, one 16, one eight, zero fours, one two, and one one. We could read our decimal numbers in a similar way. Instead of saying 157 as one hundred fifty-seven, we could say a one in the hundreds place, a five in the tens place, and a seven in the ones place, or, to be more succinct, one hundred, five tens, seven ones. It is not what we are accustomed to, but it is very clear and gives us more insight into our place-value number system.

Counting in each number system also follows the same predictable pattern. In base ten, when we run out of digits in one position, we reset the digit in that position to zero and add one to the next position. For example, once we reach nine in the ones place, we reset to zero and put a one in the tens place, giving us ten, or one ten and zero ones.

It is the same in base two. Once we have reached a one in the ones place, we reset that position to zero and put a one in the twos place, giving us *10*, or one two and zero ones. (That is the number two in base two.) The following table contains the first 15 numbers in base two and base ten.

Decimal	Binary	Decimal	Binary
0	0000	8	1000
1	0001	9	1001
2	0010	10	1010
3	0011	11	1011
4	0100	12	1100
5	0101	13	1101
6	0110	14	1110
7	0111	15	1111

Look at the patterns in the binary numbers. The number three is *0011*, and the number four is *0100*. That is equivalent to the transition from 99 to 100 in base ten. We have run out of digits in the first position, so we must reset the ones place to zero and add to the next position. But we have run out of digits in the next position as well, so we must reset to zero and add to the next position. The same kind of transition happens between *0111* and *1000*. It happens every time we are one away from the next power of the base.

Continue to analyze the table and answer the questions below to deepen your understanding of the binary number system.

Try this

❖ Using three positions, we can represent the numbers zero through eight in base two. Using four positions, we can represent the numbers zero through 15. What numbers can we represent with two positions? With five positions?

❖ Write out the next 16 binary numbers. You can check your answers using the Python `bin` function. The following console session illustrates the `bin` function:
```
>>> bin(14)
'0b1110'
```

❖ Do you see other interesting patterns in the binary numbers? What are they, and do they relate to a pattern in the decimal numbers?

❖ You might have seen the joke "There are 10 types of people in the world: those who understand binary, and those who don't." What assumption does the joke violate that makes it funny?

7.3   Hexadecimal numbers

The physical media that we use in computer science to represent data (e.g., hard drives (Figure 7-3), flash drives, DVD's, and RAM) are all composed of discrete (separate, distinct) components that can represent two states each. We can think of these two states as on and off, or 1 and 0. This makes the binary number system especially useful for modeling data. However, it is not easy for humans to read binary numbers. They are very long and repetitive. It is easier for humans to read decimal numbers, but it is not easy to convert between the decimal and binary number systems.

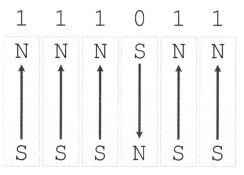

Figure 7-3   Magnetic bits.

Hexadecimal (base sixteen) and octal (base eight) are easier to read than binary, and binary is easily converted to base sixteen and base eight because they are powers of two. Hexadecimal is more widely used than octal, so we will discuss the hexadecimal number system and performing conversions between binary and hexadecimal.

You have probably seen hexadecimal numbers before, even if you did not know that is what you were looking at. The hexadecimal number base has 16 counting digits. Because we use only 10 digits, the letters A–F are used to represent the remaining digits in hexadecimal. The following table is an updated version of the table from the last section. It now shows the hexadecimal numbers in addition to the decimal and binary numbers from 1 to 15.

Decimal	Hexadecimal	Binary	Decimal	Hexadecimal	Binary
0	0	0000	8	8	1000
1	1	0001	9	9	1001
2	2	0010	10	A	1010

Decimal	Hexadecimal	Binary	Decimal	Hexadecimal	Binary
3	3	0011	11	B	1011
4	4	0100	12	C	1100
5	5	0101	13	D	1101
6	6	0110	14	E	1110
7	7	0111	15	F	1111

Hexadecimal numbers are very compact compared to the equivalent numbers in binary. As you can see, we can represent all of the values that require four binary positions in one hexadecimal digit. Consider the color orange that IDLE uses to highlight keywords, represented as a red, green, blue (RGB) triplet. In binary, the number is *1111 1111 0111 0111 0000 0000*. The much shorter version of the number in hexadecimal is FF 77 00.

Try this

❖ Once we have reached F in hexadecimal, we have used all the digits available for counting. What is the next number in hexadecimal after F, and what quantity does it represent?

❖ Add to your table of the next 16 binary numbers by including the next 16 hexadecimal numbers. What patterns do you see in the hexadecimal numbers? How do they relate to the patterns in binary and decimal numbers?

7.4   Conversions

We will first convert both binary and hexadecimal numbers to decimal, so that you can more easily understand the values of these numbers when you encounter them.

We will convert our binary number from an earlier example, *11 1011*. It will be easiest to convert it if we put the digits in a table showing the place-value position of each digit.

32	16	8	4	2	1
1	1	1	0	1	1

By referring to the table, you can see that we have ones in the thirty-twos position, the sixteens position, the eights position, the twos position and the ones position. We therefore have one 32, one 16, one eight, one two, and one one. To convert this number to decimal, we add those values. *32 + 16 + 8 + 2 + 1 = 59*. The number *11 1011* in binary is 59 in decimal.

We can convert from hexadecimal to decimal using a similar process. Here is a table of the first four powers of 16, and the hexadecimal number A30C.

4096	256	16	1
A	3	0	C

Referring to the table, you can see we have A 4096's, three 256's, zero 16's, and C ones. That probably feels like a very unnatural thing to read! We will convert the A and the C to base ten, giving us ten 4096s, three 256s, zero 16s and 12 ones. This is slightly more complex than converting from binary, because with binary, we could have only one or zero of each power of two. With hexadecimal, we can have as many as F (15) of each power of 16. (Just as in decimal, we can have as many as nine of each power of 10.) If we have ten 4096s, then that is $10 \times 4096 = 40960$. Three 256s is $3 \times 256 = 768$. And 12 ones is 12. If we add them together, then we have a decimal version of our hexadecimal number: $40960 + 768 + 12 = 41740$.

These conversion algorithms make sense when you relate them to the place-value number system, and so with practice, they will become easy to do. But converting to binary and hexadecimal from decimal is a little more difficult. We will not cover that process here because it is not important for you to learn a lot of number conversion algorithms—it is more important that you have a conceptual basis for considering problems related to number systems. We will, however, show how to convert between hexadecimal and binary, because it is very easy, and illustrates why we use hexadecimal.

We will take the hexadecimal number F50 as an example. To convert a hexadecimal number to a binary number, we simply convert each individual digit, in place, to its four-digit binary equivalent. In binary, F is *1111*, so those are the first four digits of our binary number. In binary, 5 is *0101*. Even though this number begins with a zero, we must include all four digits. So, our second four digits are *0101*. The final digit is 0, which is *0000* in binary. Therefore, F50 in hexadecimal is *1111 0101 0000* in binary. Figure 7-4 illustrates the conversion.

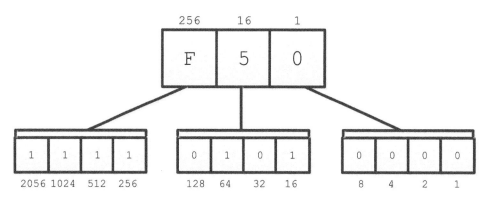

Figure 7-4   Conversion from hexadecimal to binary.

Converting from binary to hexadecimal is the process in reverse, although it is best if we begin from the right. We will take the binary number *10 1001 1110*. The right-most four digits are *1110*, which is E in hexadecimal. Our right-most hexadecimal digit is E, or E in the ones place. The next four digits are *1001*, which is 9 in hexadecimal. Our second digit is 9, or 9 in the sixteens place. And finally, we have *10*. We can pad this on the left with zeros if we want to, giving *0010*. That is 2 in hexadecimal. Therefore, *10 1001 1110* in binary is 29E in hexadecimal. Figure 7-5 illustrates the conversion.

This direct conversion of digits between binary and hexadecimal is quite easy to do, and the hexadecimal representation is more compact and easier to read than binary. That is why we often see the hexadecimal representation used in programming contexts.

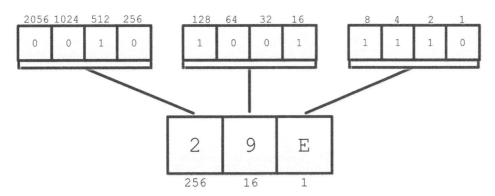

Figure 7-5   Conversion from binary to hexadecimal.

Try this

❖ Convert the following binary numbers to decimal and hexadecimal. You can check your answers using the `bin` and `hex` functions in Python.

```
10 0110 1001          1101 0001 0101
1000 0000 0001        1111 1111 1111
```

❖ Convert the following hexadecimal numbers to binary.

```
A03                   FFF
1FF                   111
```

❖ You can check your answers by typing the hexadecimal numbers into the IDLE console, preceded by `0x`, and then using the `bin` function on the result, as in this console session:

```
>>> 0x29E
670
>>>
bin(670)
'0b1010011110'
```

7.5   Seven-bit ASCII, 8-bit ASCII, Unicode: How many digits do we need?

Some standards for representing data, including some standards for representing text data (US-ASCII and the original Unicode), require that each unit of data be a fixed size. The US-ASCII representation of character data originally used seven bits for each character. That meant that a word could be stored using US-ASCII, and the word could then be retrieved by taking each group of seven bits, in order, and mapping it to the appropriate character. (e.g., the seven bits *100 0001* represent uppercase A.)

The original seven-bit US-ASCII represented only unaccented characters, and even when different groups started using eight bits for character mapping, it did not provide enough unique values to represent all accented characters in all languages. Unicode was a great improvement, doubling the size of a character representation to 16. The original goal was for Unicode to have enough values to represent every character in every language, but even a 16-bit representation is not enough! (Kuchling, Belopolsky, Brandl, & Melotti, n.d.).

In your future developing software, there will be situations in which you will have to know how much memory you need to reserve for data items. For example, most languages will offer you several different numeric encodings for integer and floating-point data that are different sizes. How will you know which one to choose, or if the encodings available are big enough or precise enough for your program's needs?

We will return to the problem of character mapping to illustrate. We can think of seven bits as a seven-digit (or seven-position) binary number. Each character must have a unique binary value. (In other words, we cannot assign A to *100 0001* and then also assign & to *100 0001*, or we would not know which character *100 0001* was meant to represent.) How many different values (or patterns) can we make with seven bits? We have the values from *000 0000* to *111 1111* available, or, in decimal, from 0 to 2^7-1 (127), which gives us a total of 128 values (because we can map 0 to a character). If we increase to eight bits, we double the number of values—instead of 2^7, or 128, we have 2^8, or 256. What about the 16 bits of the original Unicode encoding? That gives us 2^{16}, or 65,536, values.

It might make more intuitive sense if you think of a much smaller number, because you can easily enumerate (list out) all of the binary values. Suppose you are going to assign a binary number to each of the nine quadrants of a tic-tac-toe board. What is the smallest number of digits (or positions in the place-value system) that you need? If you start with one digit, you will count 0, 1, and run out before you are able to give a value to the third square. With one position you can uniquely map two squares, but you need to map nine squares. If you try to use two digits, then you can count 00, 01, 10, 11, and then you have run out by the fifth square. Two positions will map to four squares (Figure 7-6).

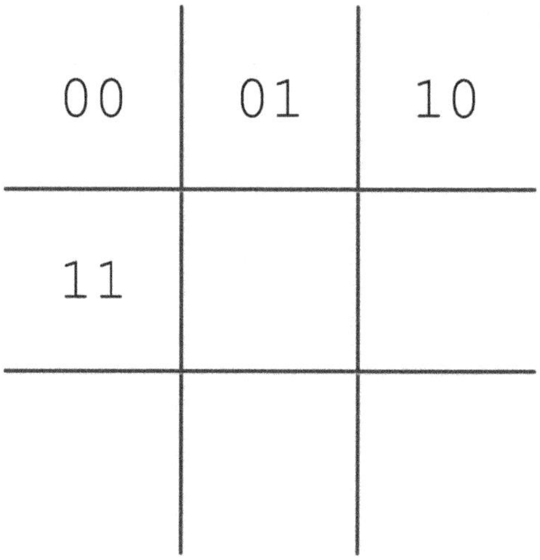

How about three positions? Then we have 000, 001, 010, 011, 100, 101, 110, and 111. So close, but still not enough! You ran out on the eighth square. You will therefore need four digits to represent the nine squares (Figure 7-7).

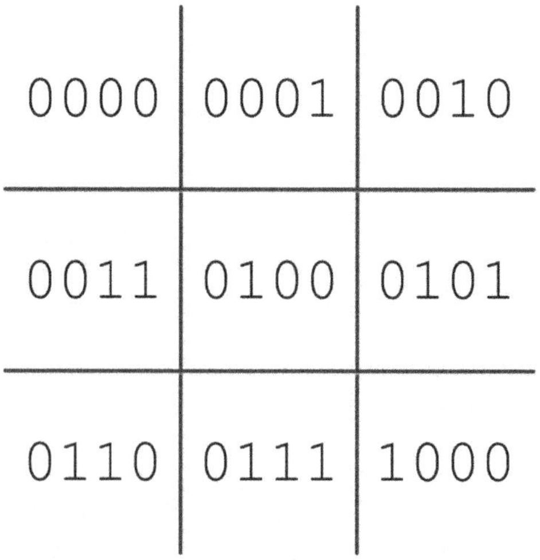

You might have noticed that the number of values you have in a given number of binary positions is two raised to the number of positions. We could represent 2^4, or 16, different values in four binary positions. (We have just enough unique sequences to play a more complicated version of tic-tac-toe with a four by four grid with our four-digit encoding.)

A modern Unicode encoding, UTF-8, allows for variable-length character encodings by using a few bits at the beginning of the character to indicate how many **bytes** (sequences of eight bits) will be used. This is more efficient than using 32 bits for each character, but the largest UTF-8 encoding is four bytes and allows for 21 bits of that to be encoded as a character. Twenty-one bits will give us 2^{21}, or 2,097,152, values, although only about half of these values are used in UTF-8 for various reasons.

Figure 7-6   Not enough digits.

Figure 7-7   Tic-tac-toe encoded.

Try this

❖ Draw a four by four tic-tac-toe board and write out the binary mapping for it, as in Figure 7-7.

❖ IPv4 uses 32 bits for Internet Protocol (IP) addresses. How many different IP addresses can be represented with 32 bits?

❖ IPv4 is not large enough to represent all of the IP addresses that modern society needs. IPv6 uses 128 bits for IP addresses. How many different IP addresses can be represented with 128 bits?

❖ If you needed to represent the 64 squares of a chessboard using binary numbers, how many bits (place-value positions) would you need?

❖ If you assigned a binary number to each of your college courses, how many bits would you need?

❖ Develop a secret language that you can use with a friend (or for a private journal) composed of some number of phrases. How many bits would you need to encode your phrases in binary? Here is a very small and simple example:

```
Meet me at the café                         0000
Meet me in front of our Python classroom    0001
At 9 am                                      0010
At 10 am                                     0011
...
At 5 pm                                      1010
```

Chapter 8

Supplementary chapter: Introduction to security-conscious coding

8.1   What you already know

Much of what you have already learned in this book applies to writing security-conscious code. Defining the problem, writing simple, readable code, writing functions so code can be reused, and thoroughly testing functions and programs, including edge cases, are all habits that apply to designing systems in a security-conscious way.

Successful problem-solving begins with defining the problem. We can extend this step to include security by including the answers to security questions in the program requirements. Security questions will focus on the outside users and systems that your program will interact with and the associated security vulnerabilities. You will want as much information as possible about the inputs to your system so that you can detect invalid and potentially malicious input, and you will want to know exactly how your system should respond in each case. You will also want to know about the values that your program will send to external systems (such as an operating system or database) so that you do not inadvertently compromise another system. Security questions will also include the vulnerabilities in the programming language that you are developing with.

Writing simple, readable code will make the code easier to test and less likely to fail. It is harder to show that complicated code works correctly. Your code should meet specifications in the clearest, simplest way.

You should write one function for each block of code that is repeated in different parts of your system. This means less code to write and test, which means less opportunity to write buggy code. (Bugs can lead to security vulnerabilities.) Security functionality, such as password checking and input validation, should be in a single function for each security task. The functions should be used whenever they are needed in the system. This way important security components of the system are not written by different programmers in different ways, multiplying the amount of critical security code that can have errors.

Finally, a well-defined problem should lead to well-specified test cases. You can use the security requirements from the problem definition to write test cases that will be used to test the security of your system. Some software development groups will use a team of experts to perform security testing, which gives an expert, external perspective. It is important that your system responds as gracefully as possible to bad inputs. This means that it should not crash, should not allow a malicious actor to gain access to your system, and should provide intuitive, easy-to-use functionality to your users.

Writing secure code is not easy. There is no simple set of rules to follow and no way to guarantee that your code cannot be exploited. However, we will talk about some general practices and tools that build on what you already know. You can use these as a starting point for future study of specific, vulnerable software development contexts, such as network, web, and systems development.

8.2   What do malicious actors do?

To understand what motivates the practices described in this chapter, we will talk briefly about some of the ways that bad actors exploit vulnerable software systems. Our focus is on secure coding practices only. This chapter does not cover equally important topics related to physical and human components of security or techniques beyond the scope of this book, such as encryption. We therefore will not describe the sorts of attacks related to these topics.

Malicious actors find ways to force a system to execute code that they want to execute, or they change the data that the system is processing. Deswani, Kern, and Kesavan (2007) present two categories of vulnerabilities that we will discuss here: memory corruption vulnerabilities and command injection vulnerabilities.

In this book, we have worked indirectly with the computer's memory by assigning values to variables and invoking functions. Behind the scenes, while the program is running, the Python interpreter is storing code, data, and administrative information in memory. (Administrative information might include the memory location of the next block of code that will execute.) If a program has a memory corruption vulnerability, it means that there is an error with the memory management that allows the data part of memory to leak into the code or administrative part. To exploit this kind of vulnerability, a hacker will enter data that is too large for the memory space allocated for it, allowing them to write into the other parts of memory. If they figure out how to write the correct value into the correct place, they can insert new data into memory, new code into memory, or force the program to execute code that it should not be executing. Examples of memory corruption vulnerabilities include stack and heap overrun errors, integer overflows, and format string vulnerabilities. When these are exploited they can result in a denial of service (DoS) attack, unauthorized access to sensitive information, or the spreading of malicious code to other machines on a network.

In a command injection vulnerability, the bad actor enters data that a program interprets as a command, rather than data. This can happen when the programmer allows data from an untrusted source to be passed to systems that process commands, such as SQL (database) servers or operating systems. The hacker will use an input source to enter a series of characters that can be processed as a command when passed to the command processor.

A very simple example of a command injection vulnerability can be found in versions of Python 2. In Python 2, the input statement evaluates what the user types at the prompt. (In Python 3, you might recall, the input statement returns a string representing what the user has entered, which is much safer.) Listing 8.1 is a very brief program that demonstrates this vulnerability.

```
1    """Demonstrate command injection vulnerability."""

2    # Note: This program is written in Python 2.7.
3    value = input("Please enter an integer: ")
4    print "You entered", value
```
Listing 8.1

It appears that the program is simply echoing what the user has typed. Here is an example of the program running with expected input:

```
Please enter an integer: 42
You entered 42
```

The value that the user has entered is automatically evaluated by the input statement (just as values that you type are evaluated in the IDLE console), which means that the variable `value` is associated with the integer 42 and not the string '42'. (You might have noticed that we did not attempt to cast the input to an integer in the program, as we do in Python 3.) Because the `input` statement will evaluate what the user enters, the user can actually write a small program (just as you can at the IDLE console). Here is an example of the program executing in which the user has executed the `dir` command and displayed the location of the program, which reveals the directory structure of the hard drive. Depending on the program that is running and the system it is running on, a determined hacker could do worse mischief.

```
Please enter an integer: dir(), __file__
You entered (['__builtins__', '__doc__', '__file__', '__name__',
'__package__'], 'D:/listing8-1.py')
```

Hacking requires detailed knowledge of the systems being exploited. To write security-conscious code, you will also need to have robust knowledge of the systems you are developing with as well as a well-developed understanding of the problem you are solving. In the following sections, we will focus on ways to validate input so it is less likely to cause the sort of attacks described here.

8.3   Know your data

In this book, we have stressed the steps of the problem-solving process. The first step is to define the problem. This includes developing a thorough understanding of the inputs to your system: the size of each data item, the type, and the allowable range of values. When discussing inputs, we have considered the problem that we are solving. For example, we might ask if numeric data is discrete (requiring an integer type) or continuous (requiring a floating-point type). We might ask if negative numbers and zero are allowed, and what the largest and smallest meaningful inputs are. We might ask the precision required for a floating-point value.

We have not always considered what inputs could potentially crash our system or allow the user to access data or parts of memory that they should not be allowed to access. For example, when asking the user for a file name, we have not worried that they might supply a file path that gives them access to part of the hard drive they should not be able to see. We have not been concerned that they might ask our program to open a file that is so large the program crashes while trying to read it. In our programs, we are usually acting as the user, and even if we had a mischievous friend test our code, there has not been much damage that they could do besides crash the program. In this book, we have often stated the assumption that the user would enter data of the correct type so that we could focus on the programming topic we were learning.

In security-conscious programming, you must ask new questions about your input and output, and not just the input and output between the program and outside entities (like the user and other applications), but also within the program (e.g., parameters to functions, and arguments passed to programming language functions such as print). The assumption that you should make is that all input is potentially malicious. When you consider input this way, you need to know more about it. What special characters are allowed that might also be part of commands, such as backslashes, pound signs, percents, and quotes? What is the longest possible string the system might receive from a user or other input source and what is the longest possible string you can accept? How should your system respond if it receives bad input?

Exactly what input and output should look like will depend on the problem you are solving and the systems you are solving it with. You will need to know what valid input and output looks like, and you will need to write code to validate the data that moves through your system.

8.4   Validating type with exception handling

We will begin with numeric data type validation. You may recall that if we attempt to convert a string that does not represent a number to a numeric type, Python will respond with a value error. You can see an example of this in this IDLE console session:

```
>>> int("one")
Traceback (most recent call last):
  File "<pyshell#1>", line 1, in <module>
    int("one")
ValueError: invalid literal for int() with base 10: 'one'
```

In Python, the type conversion functions are considered the best way to determine whether a string represents a number. But you do not want to write code that crashes if you are processing a string that cannot be converted to a number. You will therefore use a built-in mechanism in Python that will allow you to "catch" the value error exception so that it does not crash your program.

Listing 8.2 asks the user for an integer and attempts to convert the string that the user enters to an integer.

```
1    """Demonstrate exception handling with number conversion."""

2    def main():
3        """Obtain a value and check that it's an integer."""

4        # Obtain the input.
5        value = input("Please enter an integer: ")
6        # Cast to an integer or print an error message.
7        try:
```

```
8                value = int(value)
9        except ValueError as e:
10              print(e)
11              value = 0
12       else:
13              print("Value accepted!")
14       finally:
15              # Print the integer.
16              print("Your value is {:d}.".format(value))

17   main()
```
Listing 8.2

Listing 8.2 illustrates how an **exception handler** works in Python. An exception handler is a block of code that handles the situation in which an exception is raised. This block of code begins, on lines 7 and 8, with a `try` clause. We place the code in the `try` clause that might raise an exception. In this example, casting the user's input to an integer might raise a `ValueError` exception.

We can then specify the exception-handling code in one or more `except` clauses. On line 9 we are handling a `ValueError` by printing the error and setting the variable `value` to 0. This is an example of something that you might do so the program can continue from the point of the exception without crashing and is not necessarily the best way to handle bad input. (We will look at a better example in a moment.) If there is more than one kind of exception that might be raised, you can list multiple `except` clauses here. You can also have an `except` clause which is simply the keyword `except` followed by a colon. You might include an `except` clause like this after other `except` clauses to handle any exception not handled by a prior `except` clause, like an `else` in an `if` / `elif` / `else` block.

The `else` clause on lines 12 and 13 executes if none of the `except` clauses execute (in other words, if no exception was raised). The `finally` clause always executes last, regardless of which other clauses have executed.

Here is the output of the program running when the user enters an integer at the prompt, and the output of the program running when the user does not enter an integer at the prompt:

```
RESTART: D:/listing8-2.py
Please enter an integer: 42
Value accepted!
Your value is 42.
>>>
RESTART: D:/listing8-2.py
Please enter an integer: no
invalid literal for int() with base 10: 'no'
Your value is 0.
>>>
```

A better way to handle this situation might be to encapsulate the code in an input validation function. If you are obtaining integer input from the user or other input sources in multiple places in your program, then you can call one input validation function everywhere you are obtaining an integer.

This strategy puts the input validation code in one place, which allows you to thoroughly test one input validation function. Having one function minimizes the opportunity to build bugs into your system. Listing 8.3 is an example of an input validation function that checks for integer input being used in an input validation loop.

```
1    """Demonstrate exception handling with an input
2        validation function."""

3    def is_integer(value):
4        """Return True if value is an integer; False otherwise."""
5        success = True
6        try:
7            value = int(value)
8        except:
9            success = False
10       return success

11   def main():
12       """Obtain a value until the user enters an integer."""

13       # Obtain the input.
14       value = input("Please enter an integer: ")

15       # Continue asking for the value until the user
16       # enters an integer.
17       while not is_integer(value):
18           value = input("Please enter an integer: ")

19   main()
```
Listing 8.3

The function is_integer in Listing 8.3 begins by initializing a Boolean flag called success to True. It then uses a try clause to attempt to convert the parameter, value, to an integer. If this raises an exception, then the except clause will execute and set the flag to False. The flag is then returned. This code is simpler than Listing 8.3 because it is only checking to see if the parameter can be converted to an integer. It is not deciding what to do if the parameter is not an integer.

The main function prompts the user for an integer value and then uses an input validation loop to prompt for an integer again if the user did not enter an integer. It invokes the is_integer function with the user-entered value as an argument. The result of this function is used as the entry condition to the input validation loop. Remember that we want the loop entry condition for an input validation loop to describe bad input, because the loop will prompt the user to enter the input again. Therefore, the loop entry condition is not is_integer(value), which will be True when the user has entered something other than an integer.

Encapsulating the validation code in one place is a good idea for the reasons we already discussed, but also because it separates the validation from the response to invalid input. It is possible that different parts of the program will handle noninteger input in different ways. Code that has a single, clearly defined function is easier to read and test.

Try this

❖ Various kinds of errors can be raised if you attempt to index into a list with a bad index (out of range or noninteger). Write a brief program with a hard-coded list that allows the user to enter an index. Print the value at that index from the list. Wrap the code in an exception handler to guard against bad indices. As an alternative, write a separate version of the program with a check to test that the index is within range before indexing into the list. Do this in a way that will still work if the list size changes.

❖ Listing 4.21 obtains a voltage and a resistance from the user, and then performs a division. If the user enters 0 for the resistance, Python will throw a `ZeroDivisionError`. Modify Listing 4.21 by wrapping an exception handler around the division operation. As an alternative, write a separate version with a check to test that the value for resistance will not cause any errors before computing the division.

❖ Listing 4.21 also converts the two user inputs to floating-point values. Wrap this code in an exception handler so that it does not crash if the user enters a nonnumeric value.

8.5   Restricting input size with files

One of the general categories of software vulnerabilities that can be exploited is overflows that lead to memory corruption vulnerabilities. To take advantage of these vulnerabilities, the hacker enters data that is too large, and the vulnerable code writes the data into memory where it does not belong. Many of these vulnerabilities occur when the programmer works directly with memory and makes a mistake in allocating it. If you search on the Internet for memory corruption vulnerabilities in Python, you will find websites with lists of very specific vulnerabilities in different versions of Python and Python libraries. These vulnerabilities occur with structures and functions that we have not discussed in this book. (If you are curious, an example that affected Python versions 3.3–3.5 can be found on the Python bug tracker page, here: https://bugs.python.org/issue25021)

Our goal here is to talk about general strategies for avoiding writing vulnerabilities into your own code; however, and not specific Python vulnerabilities. In general, you should be careful about the size of input and the range of values that you are obtaining from external sources (such as the user). In this book, we have discussed constructing a complete description of values that are related to the problem being solved. In many programming contexts, however, we allow the user to enter values that are related to the solution process. These values might be used to index into lists, to allocate blocks of memory, to determine how much to read to or write from a file, or to determine how many times a loop will execute. It is important that we define the valid range of values for these control values from external sources as well.

Memory corruption vulnerabilities can occur if your program uses an unexpected value, obtained from an external source, to index into a structure such as a list. For example, suppose you ask the user to choose a value stored in a list by giving the index, and the user enters a negative number or a number that is larger than the index of the last value. If you use the user-entered number to index into the list without first checking that it is a valid index, it could crash your program. Python will throw an exception when you try to index past the boundaries of the list; however, some Python libraries use code written in C that might have vulnerabilities that can be exploited. It is a good habit to think about and prevent this sort of error, because it can lead to an exploitable vulnerability. (And even if it does not lead to an exploitable vulnerability, a crashing program is not a good thing!)

Python is unique in that integers are restricted in size only by the amount of memory available. That does not mean that your program is safe from an integer overflow, because an external source can still ask your program to process a value that is too large for memory, or a value used in a computation that results in a value too large for memory. For example, if you write a little program that will compute exponents for your user, and your user asks you to compute two billion raised to the two billionth power, this will likely hang your system. You need to consider not only the input that is entered but also the size of the results of computations on that input.

You should also be careful about allowing an external source to specify how much data is written to or read from a file, or how many times a loop will execute. It is sometimes necessary to obtain control information from external sources (such as the user), and this might not be part of the original problem definition process. As you develop your program, it is an important practice to specify the valid ranges and values for all data that your system will process.

We have discussed range checking in this book, but we have not discussed how to limit the size of an input provided by the user (or other source). One way that you can limit the size of a value that the user provides in Python is by using the `read` function when reading from a file and passing an argument that limits the number of bytes that can be read.

The `read` method will read an entire text file into one string variable. You can then split the value in the variable on the newline character if you want to have a list of strings, each representing a single line from the file. This is equivalent to using the `readlines` file method. The advantage to the `read` method is that you can restrict the number of bytes that the `read` method will read.

```
 1   """Demonstrate restricting input size."""
 2   def main():
 3       """Open, read, and print the file."""

 4       # Open and read 100 bytes of the file.
 5       long_file = open("too_long.txt")
 6       data = long_file.read(100)
 7       long_file.close()

 8       # Split the data into separate lines.
 9       file_lines = data.split("\n")

10       # Display the file contents.
11       for line in file_lines:
12           print(line)

13   main()
```
Listing 8.4

In Listing 8.4, a file that is prohibitively long is opened and read using the `read` method with the parameter `100`, which restricts the amount of data read from the file to 100 bytes. This number was arbitrarily chosen for this example to illustrate that you can control the amount of data you read from the file. You would determine the actual amount of data that you are going to read based on an analysis of the input size during the problem definition. Restricting the amount of input read limits the opportunity for a hacker to overflow your input variable, but you must be careful not to limit valid data.

After the first 100 bytes of the file are read into the string variable `data`, the file is closed and the string is split using the newline character `"\n"` and stored in the list `file_lines`. This is so we can process each line of the file separately, although that may not be necessary for every application. Lines 11 and 12 then iterate over the list and print each line to the console.

Try this

❖ Modify Listing 8.4 to read fewer bytes from the file (such as 5 or 10) and print each character to the console on a single line.

❖ Use your modified listing to answer the following questions:
  ✦ What characters are included in the character count when you restrict the byte size of the input?
  ✦ Are newline characters counted?
  ✦ Is other white space counted?
  ✦ Are nonprinting characters counted?
  ✦ How do bytes correspond to characters? (Is it one byte to one character?)
  ✦ What happens if you include characters in your file that are beyond those found in US-ASCII, such as the Arabic letter ص (Sad, U+0635) or the Greek letter λ (small lambda, U+03BB). (You can write non-US-ASCII characters into a file by using the Unicode code point for the character, like this: `"\u0635"`.)

8.6   Validating input with string functions and regular expressions

We have now discussed how to check the type and size of input, and we know how to validate a numeric range. These strategies will help us prevent certain overflow errors and system crashes. Without more strategies, however, we are still open to vulnerabilities related to string input, such as command injection vulnerabilities. Command injection vulnerabilities occur if a programmer allows string input to be passed to part of the program that processes commands without first checking that the string is free of command syntax. This can be very difficult to do because it requires anticipating all the different ways an attacker might target your system. A better strategy, if possible, is to check that the string falls within a well-defined range of expected values (that does not include any command syntax). For example, if you are asking for a name, then you can expect that the user might enter uppercase and lowercase letters, and possibly an apostrophe (for a name such as O'Brian) or a dash (for a hyphenated name such as Scott-Heron), but you do not expect characters such as a double quote, double dash, or backslash, which could all appear in command injection attempts.

8.6.1   Unicode

Unicode is a character encoding standard that facilitates globalization because it can represent most characters in most languages. It is more complicated than US-ASCII. Because it encodes so many characters and because of the complexity of its implementation, it poses some security problems. (Davis & Suignard, 2014). A detailed discussion of Unicode is beyond the scope of this book; however, a few key concepts will help clarify some Unicode-related security issues and safe Unicode string handling practices.

There are 1,114,112 different **code points** in Unicode. A code point is a number that maps to a specific character. For example, the code point for Latin Capital Letter A is U+0041, the same hexadecimal representation that the character has in US-ASCII. In fact, the Unicode code points match all the US-ASCII characters, making them compatible, but Unicode contains code points for many more characters. Instead of using one consistent 32-bit encoding to represent Unicode characters (as there was an 8-bit representation used for US-ASCII), there are several different and more efficient encodings. The different encodings encode the code points to different numbers of bits. For example, there are 8-bit, 16-bit, and 32-bit Unicode encodings that encode different sets of Unicode code points.

String data in Python is represented in Unicode, so when we are working with strings in Python, we are working with a Unicode representation of the string. Davis and Suignard (2014), in their technical report of Unicode security considerations, describe many of the technical issues that can occur when using Unicode. Some of these are handled at a low level that will not be a concern for programmers using built-in Unicode libraries, but others are worth discussing as they relate to input validation.

In your programming career so far, you may have had an error that resulted when you accidentally substituted similar-looking characters in a variable or function name. For example, look at the following Python console session:

```
>>> googol = 10**100
>>> googo1
Traceback (most recent call last):
    File "<pyshell#18>", line 1, in <module>
        googo1
NameError: name 'googo1' is not defined
```

It might look as though the name `googol` certainly was defined, but the second expression at the prompt is `googo1`, in which the number one has been substituted for the lowercase L. An uppercase i can also be mistaken for these two **glyphs** (the representation of a character on the screen), depending on the font.

The very large number of characters available in Unicode means that there are more characters that can be substituted for others. This is sometimes used to spoof a website, for example, and steer Internet traffic to a malicious site masquerading as a well-known site.

Another feature of Unicode is that more than one set of Unicode encodings can represent the same character. Davis and Suignard (2014) use the example of ä, which can be the code point for a (Latin Small Letter A) followed by the code point for an umlaut (Combining Diaeresis), or the code point for a umlaut (Latin Small Letter a with Diaeresis). This is illustrated in the following IDLE console session:

```
>>> "\u00E4"
'ä'
>>> "\u0061" + "\u0308"
'ä'
```

You might notice two things about this example. First, the letter ä can be represented by one code point or two code points. What size is the letter? Does this affect the length of a string? Because overflow errors can sometimes be exploited, we want to be careful with the assumptions we make about memory. One of these strings appears to be twice as long as the other, even though they both represent just one character. Second, you might wonder if we have a string containing one version of ä in it, and we are checking to see if that character is found in the string, do we need to check for both versions?

The `in` operator can be used to test for a character in a string. We will check to see if U+00E4 is in the string composed of U+0061 followed by U+0308:

```
>>> test_str = "\u0061" + "\u0308"
>>> test_str
'ä'
>>> "\u00E4" in test_str
False
>>> "\u0061" + "\u0308" in test_str
True
```

Although the sequences look the same, one slips by our test because it is a different Unicode code point. What about the length? From the following IDLE console session, you can see that the two different versions of the ä string are different lengths:

```
>>> len(test_str)
2
>>> test_str_2 = "\u00E4"
>>> test_str_2
'ä'
>>> len(test_str_2)
1
```

Python has a `unicodedata` library that you can use to **normalize** Unicode strings, which will modify the string so that there is only one mapping for each character. This will remove ambiguities that arise from the same character being represented in different ways. You must pass a parameter to the normalization function which specifies the way that the strings will be normalized.

Listing 8.5 illustrates the normalization function.

```
1    """Demonstrate Unicode normalization."""
2    import unicodedata

3    def main():
4        # Create a string of different a umlauts.
5        umlaut_str = "\u0061" + "\u0308" + "\u00E4"
```

```
6        # Print the string, its length, and characters.
7        print("The string: {}\nIts length: {}"\
                .format(umlaut_str, len(umlaut_str)))
8        for char in umlaut_str:
9            print(ord(char))


10       # Normalize using NFC (normal form composed).
11       umlaut_str = unicodedata.normalize("NFC", umlaut_str)


12       # Print the string, its length, and characters.
13       print("The normalized string: {}\nIts length: {}"\
                .format(umlaut_str, len(umlaut_str)))
14       for char in umlaut_str:
15           print(ord(char))


16   main()
```
Listing 8.5

Here is the output from the program executing:

```
The string: ää
Its length: 3
97
776
228
The normalized string: ää
Its length: 2
228
228
```

On line 5, the program creates a string called `umlaut_str` which is composed of the two different versions of ä. It then displays information about the string: the string, its length, and the ordinal value of each of the characters. On line 11, the string is normalized using the `unicodedata.normalize` function. The argument `"NFC"`, for Normal Form Composed, is passed in as the form that will be used. The result is assigned back to `umlaut_str`. The same information is displayed about the new version of the string. You will notice that the string is now composed of two copies of the same ä character, and its length has changed to reflect that it now represents two, and not three, Unicode code points.

Unicode normalization can take care of some of the comparison issues that can arise from the large number of characters available in Unicode, but it does not turn characters that have glyphs with a similar appearance (such as lowercase L, uppercase i, and the number 1), called **homographs**, into the same character. There are some characters that can be used in command injection attacks that have homographs, such as the forward slash and quotes.

One other concern when working with Unicode is compatibility with the encoding being used by other systems that your program is interacting with, such as file systems, servers, and databases. The `open` command in Python, used for opening a file for reading or writing, has an optional encoding argument that allows you to specify the encoding that should be used when reading text from the file. Knowing what Unicode encoding your data needs to use should be part of your problem specification.

8.6.2   String methods

Once you have a normalized Unicode string, you may wish to confirm that it contains only the characters allowed by your problem specification. This practice is known as **whitelisting**, and it refers to specifying allowed characters. (As opposed to **blacklisting**, which specifies prohibited characters, and is a more difficult strategy to use successfully.)

You should first consider the available string methods built into Python. String methods will be efficiently written, well tested, and might be sufficient for validating that your input contains only the characters that it should. We will look at the following string methods, although there are other useful methods that you can find in the Python string documentation. Remember, too, that we can index into strings, which allows us to iterate over them to examine each character. We can also use the `in` operator to check if a specific character or substring is contained within a string.

- ❖ `casefold()`
  This method will return a version of the string that is the preferred lowercase form for performing string comparisons.
- ❖ `count(sub)`
  This method will return the number of occurrences of the argument *sub* within the string.
- ❖ `startswith(prefix)`, `endswith(suffix)`
  Return `True` if the string begins with the argument *prefix* or ends with the argument *suffix*.
- ❖ `isalpha()`
  Return `True` if the string is composed entirely of alphabetic characters. What is alphabetic is based on the Unicode category of the character.
- ❖ `isdecimal()`,`isdigit()`, `isnumeric()`
  These three methods return `True` if the string contains only numeric characters. Each function returns `True` for a specific subset of Unicode code points related to numeric values. Roughly speaking, all three will return `True` for the digits zero through nine, but `isdigit` will also return `True` for superscripts, and `isnumeric` will also return `True` for the fraction characters.
- ❖ `isalnum()`
  This method will return `True` if the string is composed of alphanumeric characters. This means that each of the characters would return `True` for `isalpha`, `isdecimal`, `isdigit`, or `isnumeric`.

Listing 8.6 is a program with a function called `check_name` that will check that the string passed to it consists only of letters and at most one apostrophe and one dash. (This function assumes, for simplicity's sake, that the problem analysis has specified that the names being entered will all fit this form. This is an unrealistic assumption.)

```
1    """Obtain and validate a name."""
2    import unicodedata

3    def check_name(name):
4        """Check that name consists of letters,
```

```
5                  apostrophes, and dashes, with no consecutive
6                  apostrophes and dashes."""
7          # Check if it's all letters.
8          result = name.isalpha()

9          # If not, check for dashes and apostrophes.
10         if not result:
11             apostrophes = ["\u0027", "\u0060", "\u00B4", \
                                "\u2018", "\u2019"]
12             dashes = ["\u002D", "\u2010", "\u2011", "\u2012", \
                            "\u2013", "\u2014", "\u2015", "\uFE58",\
                            "\uFE63", "\uFF0D"]
13             apostrophe_count = 0
14             dash_count = 0
15             other_count = 0
16             index = 0

17             # Check each letter until we reach an
18             # invalid letter or the end of the name.
19             while index < len(name) and other_count == 0:
20                 if not name[index].isalpha():
21                     if name[index] in apostrophes:
22                         apostrophe_count += 1
23                     elif name[index] in dashes:
24                         dash_count += 1
25                     else:
26                         other_count += 1
27                 index += 1
28         result = other_count == 0 and dash_count <= 1 \
                    and apostrophe_count <= 1

29     return result

30 def main():
31     name = input("Please enter a name: ")
32     name = unicodedata.normalize("NFC",name)
33     while not check_name(name):
34         name = input("Please enter a valid name: ")
35         name = unicodedata.normalize("NFC",name)

36 main()
```
Listing 8.6

Despite the unrealistic assumptions, Listing 8.6 is still somewhat complex and it allows through improbable names such as 'Smith- and S'-mith. But it does not allow through any string that contains more than one apostrophe, dash, or any other nonalphabetic characters. The function is efficient if most names that are entered contain no punctuation, as it tests first for a string composed entirely of alphabetic characters, using the string method `isalpha`. If this method returns `True`, then the rest of the function is bypassed and `True` is returned.

If the string contains characters other than letters, then the code from lines 10–28 executes. On lines 11 and 12, lists of Unicode characters that could be used for dashes and apostrophes are defined. These lists are not necessarily exhaustive, but they contain many of the characters that might commonly be used for an apostrophe or dash. These lists illustrate the complexity of working with Unicode, as we must consider homographs and commonly used characters when performing string comparisons.

Lines 19–27 check each character in the string one at a time, counting apostrophes, dashes, and other nonalphabetic characters. A nonalphabetic character will end the loop. (We could have written the loop entry condition to also fail if there is more than one apostrophe or more than one dash.) On line 28, the return flag `result` is set. If no more than one apostrophe and dash and no illegal characters were found, then the flag is set to `True`. Otherwise it is set to `False`. The flag is then returned.

The complexity of this imperfect whitelist check for allowed characters underscores why validation code should be encapsulated in a single, well-tested function that is used by all parts of the program that need to perform this check.

8.6.3 Regular expressions

Some input requirements are too complex to validate with the string methods available. When you are in this situation, you might use a **regular expression** to check that the input matches a specific pattern of characters. For example, a U.S. telephone number can be of the form open parenthesis, three digits, close parenthesis, three digits, dash, four digits (such as (555) 555-1212), with spaces allowed between the punctuation and the numbers, but not required. This might be tricky to check with string methods, but it can be checked by constructing a regular expression and using Python's `re` module to confirm that the input matches the specified pattern.

Regular expressions consist of patterns constructed using a regular expression mini language, and there are entire (very good) books about writing and using regular expressions. What we will present here is a very brief overview so that you have an understanding of when and how they are used. If you want to learn more about regular expressions in Python, consider reading A. M. Kuchling's Regular Expression HOWTO (https://docs.python.org/3.6/howto/regex.html).

Regular expressions are useful for matching a general pattern that a string must fit, allowing for variability within the pattern such as optional characters and varying numbers of specific classes of characters. They can be very inefficient, however, which is why you should use built-in string methods if possible.

You will specify a regular expression as a string, using the regular expression language, and then use functions in the `re` module to match the string you are validating against the regular expression. Listing 8.7 is an example of input validation using a regular expression. It validates that the string entered by the user is an area code of the form open parenthesis, three numbers, close parenthesis, with white space allowed, but not required, between the punctuation and the numbers.

```
1     """Validate input with a regular expression."""
2     import re

3     def check_area(area):
4         """Return a list of all valid area codes in area."""
5         valid_area = re.compile("\(\s*\d{3}\s*\)")
6         match_information = valid_area.match(area)
7         return match_information

8     def main():
9         """Obtain and validate an area code."""
10        area = input("Please enter an area code: ")
11        match_information = check_area(area)
12        print(match_information)

13    main()
```
Listing 8.7

The regular expression code can be found on line 5, enclosed in quotes and passed to the re.compile function of the regular expression module. We will dissect the regular expression in a moment, just to give you an idea of how one is constructed. The regular expression is used by first compiling the regular expression string, on line 5. Once we have a compiled regular expression (here we have assigned it to the variable valid_area), then we can use it to test strings. We use the method (dot) notation on the regular expression to do this on line 6, using the match method. This method will check if the beginning of the string fits the regular expression pattern and will return information about the part of the string (if any) that matches. We are printing that information in the main function, on line 12.

Before we discuss the regular expression string, we will run the program on four different test strings to see what information is returned.

```
Please enter an area code: (401)
<_sre.SRE_Match object; span=(0, 5), match='(401)'>

Please enter an area code: (     401)
<_sre.SRE_Match object; span=(0, 11), match='(     401)'>

Please enter an area code: 401
None

Please enter an area code: (1234)
None
```

The first two strings that we entered matched the regular expression. One was the area code string "(401)", and the other was the same area code but with six spaces between the open parenthesis and the number 4. The last two strings did not match the regular expression. The first was the area code without the parentheses, and the second contained four numbers instead of three.

You will notice that the match method returns `None` if there was no match to the regular expression, but it returns both the text that matched and the indices of the matching slice within the string if there was a match. There are methods for sorting through this information and extracting what you need.

We will now turn to the regular expression string itself. The regular expression language is its own mini language within Python and it takes time and practice to master. (The good news is that regular expression mini languages are very similar for most programming languages, so once you have mastered regular expressions in one language, you will easily be able to pick them up for others.) The examples here are intended only to give you a general idea of how regular expressions are used to match strings. The regular expression for matching an area code composed of an open parenthesis, followed by any amount of white space (including none), followed by exactly three digits, followed by any amount of white space and a closed parenthesis in the program was:

```
"\(\s*\d{3}\s*\)"
```

The regular expression is enclosed within quotes in Python, because it is a string. The enclosing quotation marks, therefore, are not part of the regular expression. This regular expression is giving descriptions, from left to right, of what must be found in the string in order for the string to be considered a match to the regular expression. The regular expression describes this:

❖ An open parenthesis	`\(`
❖ Any amount of white space (including none)	`\s*`
❖ Exactly three characters in the digit class	`\d{3}`
❖ Any amount of white space (including none)	`\s*`
❖ A close parenthesis	`\)`

The backslash that you see in each of these elements of the regular expression is an escape character, just as it is in a regular Python string. Because regular expressions have their own set of symbols which have special meanings, called **metacharacters**, some characters must be escaped if we want to match the literal character. If we do not escape a metacharacter, the character would be interpreted to have its metacharacter meaning within the regular expression. Parentheses in a regular expression are metacharacters that are used to group characters, and so we must escape them with the backslash, because we want the regular expression to match a literal open parenthesis, and then later a literal close parenthesis.

Backslashes are also used as the first character of some special classes of characters. We can see two of these in use here. The `\s` class represents white space. The `\d` class represents digits. Each of these is followed by a repetition modifier. The asterisk `*` indicates zero or more occurrences. We are allowing any amount of white space between the parentheses and the numbers. The curly braces allow us to specify a number (for example, three) or range of numbers (e.g., three to five) of repetitions. Here we are specifying three, meaning the regular expression will match exactly three digits. If we wanted to specify a range, we would separate the start and end values with commas.

We demonstrate a few simpler regular expressions in Listing 8.8.

```python
1    """Demonstrate some simple regular expressions."""
2    import re

3    def main():
```

```
 4        """Match some simple regular expressions."""
 5        # Match zero-any number of digits.
 6        digits = input("Enter a value with any number of digits: ")
 7        any_number_digits = re.compile("\d*")
 8        match_information = any_number_digits.match(digits)
 9        print(match_information)

10        # Match the strings Yes yes or YES.
11        yes = input("Enter yes: ")
12        any_yes = re.compile("Yes|yes|YES")
13        match_information = any_yes.match(yes)
14        print(match_information)

15        # Match one or more alphabetic characters.
16        word = input("Enter any word: ")
17        any_word = re.compile("[a-zA-z]+")
18        match_information = any_word.match(word)
19        print(match_information)

20   main()
```
Listing 8.8

Can you guess what these regular expressions might match, based on the comments and the regular expression strings? The first one \d* is composed of a special character class and a repetition modifier that you have already seen. This regular expression will match any number of consecutive digits, including no digits.

The second regular expression contains an operator you have not seen, |. This bar means *or*, so this regular expression will match the literal sequence of characters Yes or the literal sequence of characters yes or the literal sequence of characters YES. (Note that it is more efficient to use a string comparison to perform a match like this, rather than a regular expression.)

The third regular expression contains a character class that is not predefined with a special sequence, so we are defining it using the square brackets. This class will match any (Latin) alphabetic character. The plus sign + is a repetition modifier that means one or more times, so this will match a string of letters of length one or more.

8.6.4   Summary

As a rule, you must consider all input to your program to be potentially malicious. Strings account for a large proportion of the input that you will receive from interacting with users, and strings present many challenges because we use strings within programs to allow access to sensitive data and to form commands to subsystems. The topics and strategies presented here should be considered a very general introduction to the practices that you will use to develop security-conscious applications. This is a very challenging aspect of programming, but if you apply the problem-solving strategies that you have learned and practiced in this book, you will develop a robust approach to even these difficult problems.

Try this

❖ The Unicode Consortium (https://www.unicode.org/) has code charts on their website. Find some interesting Unicode characters and type them into the IDLE console using "\u" followed by the hexadecimal code. For example, "\u2656". Can you find symbols that could be used to spoof other symbols? For example, can you find symbols to spoof numbers or letters that you might see in a website address?

❖ Modify Listing 8.5 to construct some other strings that will change length when normalized. (Hint: Look at characters with "combining" in the name.)

❖ Look back at some of the program listings in this book that take string inputs and think about what characters would be allowed in the input. (This is a good exercise for discussion with friends or classmates.) Look for examples of similar data in real-world situations. Would you be able to check for the valid characters using string methods?

❖ Research a string method that is not discussed here by visiting the Python library documentation (https://docs.python.org/3.3/library/stdtypes.html#string-methods). Practice with the method in a program. How could it be used to validate input?

❖ Modify (or add to) Listing 8.8 to check for specific strings other than the yes strings (e.g., you could check for the user entering your name), to check for one or more digits (rather than zero or more), and to check for one or more characters followed by one or more digits.

Chapter 9

Supplementary chapter: Recursion

9.1   Recursive problems

Some problems lend themselves naturally to a recursive solution. A recursive solution is one that is defined in terms of one or more previous solutions. The trick is that eventually at least one of the previous versions of the problem must have a simple answer and may not be recursively defined (otherwise, we would never reach a solution).

Suppose you want to add together the number of courses that you and 99 of your classmates are taking this semester. When we solve a problem recursively, we find a pattern that is partial solution + rest of solution, where the "rest of solution" is partial solution + rest of solution, which is partial solution + rest of solution, and so on, until you reach a simple case that has a simple answer. If you want to add up the number of courses that you and 99 of your classmates are taking, the partial solution is to add the number of courses that you are taking to what the rest of the class is taking. The "rest of solution" is to pass the problem of how many courses the rest of the class is taking along to the next classmate. That classmate will do exactly what you did: add the number of courses that they are taking to what the rest of the class is taking, and then pass the problem of how many courses the rest of the class is taking to the next classmate. This continues until the simple case, which is the 99th classmate, who has nobody else to pass the problem along to. From that student's perspective, what the rest of the class is taking is what they are taking, and they can give that simple answer to the 98th classmate, who will sum it to their value, and pass the results back up until you have an answer to what the rest of the class is taking that you can add to your value, and the problem is solved. Each person did something relatively simple, adding the number of courses they are taking to the number of courses the rest of the class is taking (Figure 9-1).

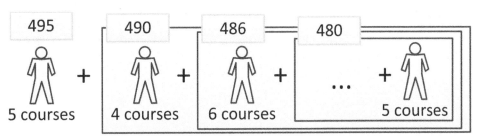

Figure 9-1   Adding courses for 100 classmates.

Another problem that can be solved recursively is the drawing of a fractal. We could describe the drawing of a fractal branch as drawing a stem, and then drawing two smaller branches at angles to the left and right of the original stem. Each of those branches would be drawn in the same way: draw a stem, and then draw two smaller branches at angles to the left and right of the original stem. This process repeats until we reach the version of the problem with a simple answer, such as a stem too small to draw, so we draw a leaf (Figure 9-2).

We could solve both problems using a loop, but when we solve a programming problem recursively, we write a **recursive function**. A recursive function is a function that calls itself. A recursive function is generally structured with an if statement that checks if it is solving a simple case (called the **base case**), or if it is solving a **recursive case**, which means it will call itself with a reduced version of the problem. (Like summing the courses being taken by the rest of the class, or drawing a tree starting with a smaller stem.) Eventually, the problem reduces to the base case (the last student or the leaf) and the recursion ends.

For example, if we are solving the fractal-drawing problem, we write a function that takes as parameters an (x, y) location that is the start of the branch, the angle at which we will draw the branch, and the length of the branch. The function then checks to see if we have reached the base case, which might be a branch of length 5 or less, for example. If so, it will draw a leaf. If not, then we have a recursive case, and the function will draw the stem, and then call itself two more times with a reduced version of the prob-

Figure 9-2 A recursively drawn fractal tree.

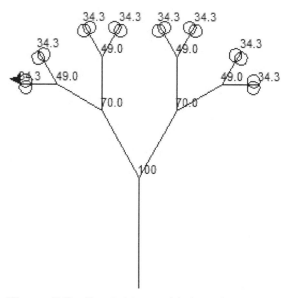

Figure 9-3 Fractal tree with lengths.

lem. Because we are checking for a branch length of 5 or less, reducing the problem means reducing the length of the branch so that eventually we reach the base case of a branch of length 5 or less. Figure 9-3 is a small recursively drawn tree with the branch lengths labeled. In the drawing in Figure 9-3, the base case was reached if length was less than or equal to 25. (This number was chosen so the drawing would not be too cluttered to read.)

Listing 9.1 is a Python turtle graphics program that draws a fractal tree. The base case is a branch of length 5 or less.

```
1    import turtle

2    def draw_branch(x, y, heading, length):
3        """Recursive function to draw one branch of a fractal tree."""
4        # Set up the drawing environment.
```

```
5        turtle.penup()
6        turtle.setpos(x, y)
7        turtle.setheading(heading)
8        turtle.pendown()
9        # Recursive case: draw the stem and two smaller branches.
10       if length > 5:
11           # Draw the stem.
12           turtle.forward(length)
13           # Draw branches 30 degrees to each side and reduce length.
14           x = turtle.xcor()
15           y = turtle.ycor()
16           draw_branch(x, y, heading-30, length*.7)
17           draw_branch(x, y, heading+30, length*.7)
18       # Base case: draw a leaf.
19       else:
20           turtle.right(90)
21           turtle.circle(length // 4)

22   def main():
23       """Draw a fractal tree with a starting length of 100."""
24       draw_branch(0,-200,90,100)

25   main()
```
Listing 9.1

We will focus on the structure of the recursive function draw_branch. It takes four parameters: The *x* and *y* coordinates, the heading, and the length of the stem it should draw. The length of the stem is 100 for the first call to draw_branch from main. The function first moves the turtle to the (*x*, *y*) coordinate and sets the heading. It then checks whether this is a base case or recursive case, on line 10. The base case is a value for length less than or equal to 5. Because 100 is greater than 5 and therefore not the base case, the code for the recursive case executes.

The block of code for the recursive case is found on lines 11–17. Line 12 draws the stem. The *x* and *y* coordinates of the turtle are then obtained from the turtle on lines 14 and 15. (You could also calculate the coordinates from the heading angle and the length of the stem, but it is simpler to ask the turtle where it is since it has already performed these calculations.)

Lines 16 and 17 are the recursive calls. Here we call draw_branch twice, passing in the end of the stem (the turtle's current (*x*, *y*) location), angles 30 degrees to either side of the stem's heading, and a branch length that is 70% of the current branch length.

Lines 19–21 are the base case, in which we have been passed a value for length that is 5 or less. In the base case, we draw a circle at the end of the stem, representing a leaf. You will notice that there are no recursive calls in the base case.

We will step through some of the program to see how it works, but we will use a base case of length <= 40, as this will greatly reduce the number of recursive calls and make the execution a little easier to follow. We will conduct a visual desk check using the drawing, as it will make following the recursion easier. You can see that the code itself is not very long or complicated. What is interesting in the desk check is the pattern of recursive calls.

The `draw_branch` function is first invoked from `main` on line 24. The parameters that are passed from `main` tell `draw_branch` to draw a branch with a heading of 90 degrees (straight up), and a length of 100.

Within the function, `draw_branch` uses an if statement to determine if this is a base case or a recursive case. Because the length is greater than 40 (the value we will use for this desk check), `draw_branch` determines that we have a recursive case. In the recursive case, `draw_branch` draws a stem of length 100. Figure 9-4 shows the first stem that is drawn.

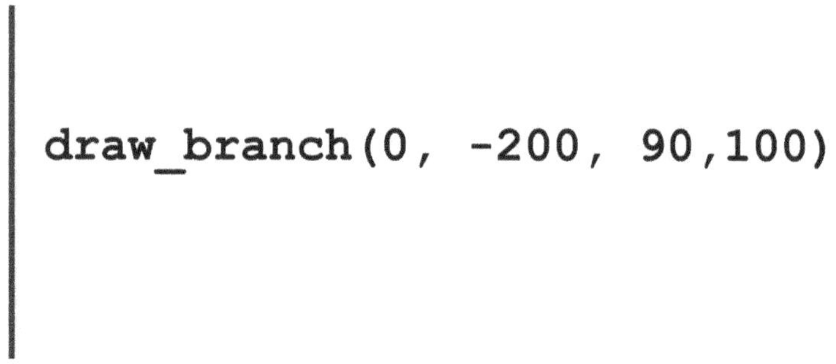

draw_branch(0, -200, 90,100)

Figure 9-4   First call to draw_branch.

The first recursive call to `draw_branch` is on line 16. In this call, `draw_branch` passes `heading-30` to the new invocation as the heading, and it reduces the length of the stem being drawn to 70% of the current stem length.

You can think of the `draw_branch` function as waiting to complete its work (there is still that second recursive call on line 17) while this new invocation of `draw_branch` begins execution. Within the new invocation of the function, `draw_branch` uses an if statement to determine if this is a base case or a recursive case. Because the length is greater than 40, `draw_branch` determines that we have a recursive case. In the recursive case, `draw_branch` draws a stem of length 70. Figure 9-5 shows the stem that is drawn from this second call.

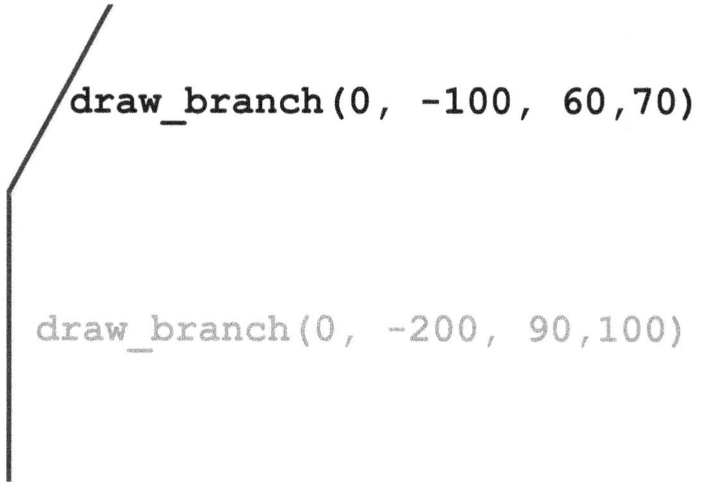

draw_branch(0, -100, 60,70)

draw_branch(0, -200, 90,100)

Figure 9-5   Second call to draw_branch.

There is now a recursive call to `draw_branch` on line 16. In this call (once again), `draw_branch` passes `heading-30` to the new invocation as the heading, and it reduces the length of the stem being drawn to 70% of the current stem length.

Now we have two invocations of draw_branch waiting to complete their work (which will resume with the second recursive calls on line 17) while yet another invocation of draw_branch begins execution. It is, once again, a recursive case, and so a stem is drawn and another recursive call is made. Figure 9-6 shows the fractal tree after three calls to draw_branch.

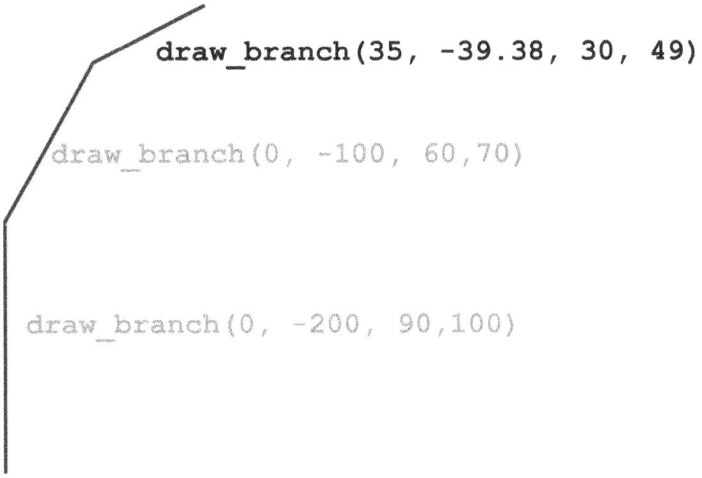

draw_branch(35, -39.38, 30, 49)

draw_branch(0, -100, 60,70)

draw_branch(0, -200, 90,100)

Figure 9-6   Third call to draw_branch.

Within this next call to draw_branch, the test for a recursive case, length > 40, fails. We have reached the base case of a stem that is not long enough to draw, and so draw_branch draws a leaf and then ends. We return from the call without making another recursive call. Base cases guarantee that the recursion eventually ends. (Or they do if the recursive function is written correctly.)

When we return from the third recursive call to draw_branch, we reach line 17 of the second recursive call, which is another call to draw_branch. Once again, the test for a recursive case, length > 40, fails. The function draws a leaf and returns to the end of the second recursive call to draw_branch. The second recursive call also returns, and we reach line 17 of the first recursive call. Figure 9-7 illustrates the two base case calls to draw_branch which result in the drawing of leaves.

On line 17 of the first recursive call, we make another recursive call to draw_branch. (This is our fifth recursive call to the function.) This call will mirror the second recursive call: it will draw a stem, and then make two recursive calls that are base case calls resulting in leaves, and then return. The right side of the tree is now complete, and control returns to line 17 of the first invocation of draw_branch. Now the left side of the tree will be drawn following the same recursive process. Figure 9-8 shows the set of calls for the completed right half of the tree.

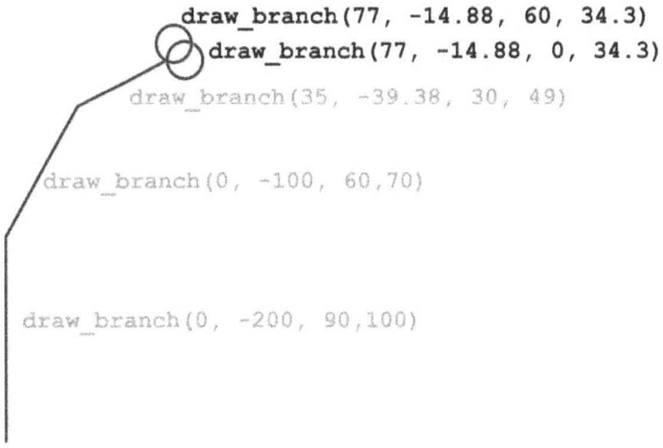

When you are solving a problem recursively, you need to find the pattern that is partial solution plus rest of solution, where "rest of solution" is partial solution plus rest of solution (where "rest of solution" is partial solution plus rest of solution ...). The pattern must reduce the problem each time so that it eventually reaches the base case that has a simple solution. Many problems that you see

draw_branch(77, -14.88, 60, 34.3)
draw_branch(77, -14.88, 0, 34.3)
draw_branch(35, -39.38, 30, 49)

draw_branch(0, -100, 60,70)

draw_branch(0, -200, 90,100)

Figure 9-7   Base case calls from lines 16 and 17.

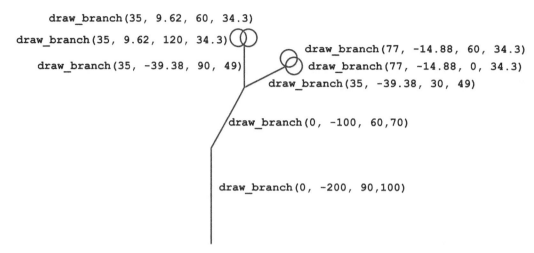

Figure 9-8   Recursive calls for half of the tree.

presented as introductory recursion problems also have an obvious looping solution. There are some similarities in the problem-solving approach. When solving a problem with both a loop and recursion, you must identify when you are done: either done looping or done making recursive calls. In a loop, we are done when the complement of our loop entry condition is true. In a recursive function, we are done recursing when we reach our base case. With both looping and recursion you must find a repetitive pattern. In a recursive solution, the pattern could roughly be described as stating how the solution to case n is obtained, assuming you already have the solution to case n−1.

Try this

❖ When we use a starting `length` of 100 and the test `length > 40`, we have recursive cases for `length` equal to 100, 70, and 49. How many times is `draw_branch` entered under these conditions? (Remember that it is invoked twice each time we enter the code to handle the recursive case, and it is invoked the final time when we reach the base case and nothing is drawn.)

❖ When we use a starting `length` of 100 and the test `length > 5`, we have recursive cases for `length` equal to 100, 70, 49, 34.3, 24.01, 16.807, 11.7649, 8.23543, and 5.764801. How many times is `draw_branch` entered under these conditions?

❖ Modify the fractal tree program in one or more of the following ways:
  ✦ Draw four branches for each recursive case, rather than two.
  ✦ Change the angles at which the branches are drawn.
  ✦ Change the value for the base case and observe the results.
  ✦ Add color to the tree and make the color lighter for each recursive call.

❖ Write a recursive function to draw a set of concentric circles. Pass in an (x, y) coordinate and the radius of the circle as parameters. Use a radius of 20 as your base case and invoke the function with a radius of 100. Reduce the radius of the circle each time you invoke the function from within itself.

❖ In the Chapter 4 challenges you were asked to draw a fractal composed of circles using a loop. Draw the same fractal recursively. The structure of the recursive function will be similar to the `draw_branch` function.

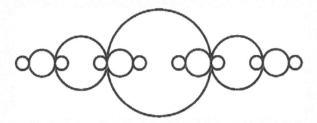

9.2   The call stack

Recursion is easier to understand if you know something about what Python is doing behind the scenes as your functions execute. We will use the fractal tree program as an example to explore how Python manages so many different calls to the same function.

Each time you invoke a function in a program, Python creates a **frame** on the **call stack**. The call stack is a data structure that Python maintains to manage functions and the data that is associated with them. A frame is a block of memory on the call stack that is dedicated to one invocation of one function. A **stack** is a particular kind of data structure that is last in, first out (LIFO), which means that the last data item into the stack is the first one to be removed. These operations of adding an item to a stack and removing an item from a stack are usually called **push** and **pop**. A list can behave as a stack in Python, as shown in this IDLE console session:

```
>>> stack = [1, 2, 3, 4, 5]
>>> stack.pop()
5
>>> stack
[1, 2, 3, 4]
>>> stack.pop()
4
>>> stack
[1, 2, 3]
```

Unfortunately, there is no push command for lists in Python. If you were to write your own push operation, it would work in the same way as `append`. All new activity in a stack happens at the end (thus, last in, first out).

In our stack example, the stack contains integers. The call stack contains more complicated information, which we refer to as frames. You can think of a frame as a record of information about the function call. When you invoke a function in Python, Python creates a frame for that function. The frame includes all of the variables in the function (parameter variables and local variables) as well as administrative information, such as where control will return to when the function is finished executing. So while the code for a function does not change, there is a separate frame on the call stack for every invocation of the function as the program is running. Every function invocation has its own copy of the function's local variables, for example. When a function is executing, its frame contains the local namespace and, more generally, it is the environment in which the code is executing. When a function finishes executing, its frame is popped from the stack and the frame below it, which is the one that called it, becomes the current execution environment.

In our fractal tree-drawing program, execution begins at function `main`, which has no local variables. The function then invokes `draw_branch`. Figure 9-9 is an illustration of the call stack while the first invocation of `draw_branch` is executing. Below the dashed line within the frame you can see some of the administrative information that Python keeps track of, such as the line number on which the function was invoked, and the "context," which is the function call that invoked the function. Above the dashed line are the local variables for the frame. You might also recognize this as the namespace for the function.

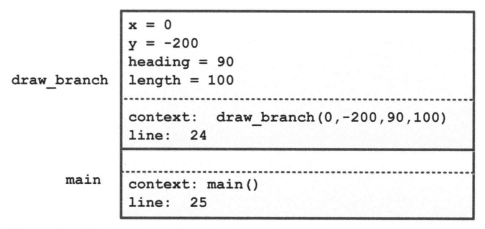

```
draw_branch    x = 0
               y = -200
               heading = 90
               length = 100
               - - - - - - - - - - - - - - - - - - - - - - - - - -
               context:   draw_branch(0,-200,90,100)
               line:   24

      main     - - - - - - - - - - - - - - - - - - - - - - - - - -
               context:  main()
               line:   25
```

Figure 9-9   The Python call stack after main invokes draw_branch.

The function `draw_branch` then recursively invokes `draw_branch`, which recursively invokes `draw_branch`, which recursively invokes `draw_branch` one more time before we reach the base case. Each time the function is invoked, a new frame is placed (or "pushed") on the call stack. Figure 9-10 shows the Python call stack after the series of calls to `draw_branch` which result in the right-most branches and leaf. Figure 9-11 shows the call stack after the base case is finished executing and its frame is popped from the call stack. The context information from the frame tells Python which line of code was executing when the function was called, and it is where control returns when the function is finished executing.

One thing you might notice is that a lot of information is stored every time a function is called. It takes time and space (in memory) to invoke a function, so there can be a significant overhead cost associated with a recursive solution. The code itself can look a lot clearer and can be easier to read and understand than a looping solution, particularly for the sorts of problems that are naturally recursive. But if the recursion is very deep (if there are many calls, therefore many frames on the call stack), there is a time cost and a danger of overflowing the call stack. In Python, you can import `sys` and type `sys.getrecursionlimit()` at the IDLE console to find out how many recursive calls are allowed before Python throws a `RecursionError`.

The function `draw_branch` does not return a value, but many recursive solutions depend on the call stack holding intermediate state information as functions are invoked and as they return. We will

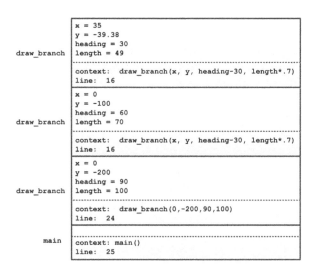

```
draw_branch   | x = 77.44
              | y = -14.88
              | heading = 0
              | length = 34.3
              |-------------------------------------------------
              | context:  draw_branch(x, y, heading-30, length*.7)
              | line:  16
draw_branch   | x = 35
              | y = -39.38
              | heading = 30
              | length = 49
              |-------------------------------------------------
              | context:  draw_branch(x, y, heading-30, length*.7)
              | line:  16
draw_branch   | x = 0
              | y = -100
              | heading = 60
              | length = 70
              |-------------------------------------------------
              | context:  draw_branch(x, y, heading-30, length*.7)
              | line:  16
draw_branch   | x = 0
              | y = -200
              | heading = 90
              | length = 100
              |-------------------------------------------------
              | context:  draw_branch(0,-200,90,100)
              | line:  24
       main   | context: main()
              | line:  25
```

```
draw_branch   | x = 35
              | y = -39.38
              | heading = 30
              | length = 49
              |-------------------------------------------------
              | context:  draw_branch(x, y, heading-30, length*.7)
              | line:  16
draw_branch   | x = 0
              | y = -100
              | heading = 60
              | length = 70
              |-------------------------------------------------
              | context:  draw_branch(x, y, heading-30, length*.7)
              | line:  16
draw_branch   | x = 0
              | y = -200
              | heading = 90
              | length = 100
              |-------------------------------------------------
              | context:  draw_branch(0,-200,90,100)
              | line:  24
       main   | context: main()
              | line:  25
```

Figure 9-10   Python call stack after four calls to draw_branch.

Figure 9-11   Python call stack after base case call to draw_branch is popped.

look at a summation problem, solved recursively, and examine how the call stack is used as part of the recursive solution. Listing 9.2 uses recursion to sum the integers from 1 to 100.

```
1    """Recursively sum the integers from 1 to 100."""

2    def sum_ints(num):
3        """Return the sum of the integers from 1 to num."""
4        if num == 1:
5            return 1
6        else:
7            return num + sum_ints(num-1)

8    def main():
9        """Compute the sum of integers from 1 to n two ways."""
10       n = 100
11       print("The recursively computed sum is {:d}." \
              .format(sum_ints(n)))
12       print("Gauss' formula tells us the sum is {:.0f}." \
              .format((n * (n+1) / 2)))

13   main()
```
Listing 9.2

Listing 9.2 sums the numbers from 1 to 100 two ways: using a recursive function called `sum_ints` and using the summation formula that is sometimes attributed to the mathematician Carl Friedrich Gauss. The function `sum_ints` solves the summation problem in the way described at the beginning of the chapter, when we imagined the problem of summing the number of courses being taken by you and 99 of your classmates. The base case is when we have one number left, the number 1. The sum of the numbers from 1 to 1 is 1. The recursive case adds the current number to the sum of all numbers that come before. That is the parameter `num` plus the recursive call, passing in `num-1`. This is equivalent to adding your courses to the courses of your 99 classmates and passing the problem of computing that to the 99th student (who adds their courses to the sum of the courses of the other 98, passing that problem to the 98th student, until eventually we are down to the last student, who represents the base case).

If you were to solve this problem with a loop, you would use an accumulator to store the sum. How is this solved recursively without an accumulator? Instead of thinking of the problem as one of repeatedly adding a value to a variable, think of it as one of expanding an expression until it can be solved. It is the call stack that is doing the expansion work, holding the pieces of the expression in the frames on the call stack until it is ready to evaluate the result. Suppose, rather than summing the numbers from 1 to 100, we sum the values from 1 to 5. The call stack, on the last call to `sum_ints`, will look like Figure 9-12.

Each frame on the call stack holds the context in which the next call was made. The context includes the piece of the summation expression that was created in that call.

For example, we begin with `return 5 + sum_ints(4)`. `sum_ints(4)` expands to `return 4 + sum_ints(3)`. `sum_ints(3)` expands to `return 3 + sum_ints(2)`. This expands to `return 2 + sum_ints(1)`. If we write it all out as one expression, it might look like:

`5 + sum_ints(4 + sum_ints(3 + sum_ints(2 + sum_ints(1))))`

It is when the calls return that the expression is assembled and evaluated. The last call, when `num` is equal to 1, is the base case, and the value 1 is returned on line 5. When the top frame is popped from the call stack, the expression `sum_ints(num-1)` evaluates to 1. This is embedded in the expression `return num + sum_ints(num-1)`, in the call frame in which `num` is equal to 2. That expression then evaluates to 2 + 1, or 3. When that frame is popped from the call stack, the expression `sum_ints(num-1)` evaluates to 3 in the previous invocation of `sum_ints`, and the expression `num + sum_ints(num-1)` evaluates to 3 + 3, or 6. The sum is accumulated through the return values as the expression is evaluated as frames are popped off the call stack, eventually resulting in the value 15.

When we design a recursive function, we should imagine (or trust) that our recursive call to the function will evaluate to the solution to the problem that we pose with the parameters we pass. We can therefore use the value that is returned as part of our solution for the parameters received. For example, if we are receiving

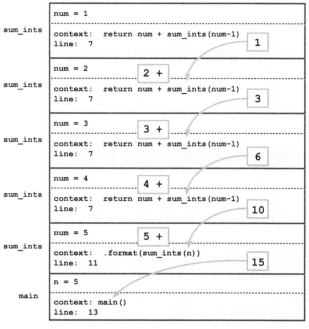

Figure 9-12   The Python call stack for the summing problem.

the parameter 5 to our `sum_ints` function, we should assume that `sum_ints(4)` will give us the sum of the integers from 1 to 4, and use that in our solution to the sum of the integers from 1 to 5 by adding `5 + sum_ints(4)`. If `sum_ints(4)` is doing its job, then `5 + sum_ints(4)` is also doing its job. Part of the trick here is ensuring that the base case is returning the correct result. The other is being able to see the problem in terms of an expanding expression of smaller versions of the same problem.

Try this

❖ Python has a module called inspect that will allow you to inspect the stack. Put `import inspect` at the top of a program with functions and then embed the call `print (inspect.stack())` as the first line of each function. Find the context and line number in the information that is displayed.
❖ The value n! (read that as "n factorial") is defined recursively as:
   ✦ If n is equal to 1, n! is 1.
   ✦ If n is greater than 1, n! is n * (n−1)!
   ✦ This problem is very similar to the summation problem solved in this section. Modify Listing 9.2 to compute a factorial rather than a sum.

9.3   Designing recursive solutions

We will design two recursive solutions to computational problems to illustrate the recursive problem-solving process and some of the different sorts of problems that can be solved recursively.

9.3.1   Solving a problem that is defined recursively

Listing 5.8 is a fraction-reducing problem with a function that uses Euclid's algorithm to find the greatest common divisor of two numbers. We will assume that both numbers are positive. (In a program, you can validate this before invoking a function that finds the greatest common divisor of a and b.) We can define the greatest common divisor of a and b recursively, as follows:

❖ Compute m = b % a.
❖ If m is equal to 0, then a is the greatest common divisor.
❖ Otherwise, the greatest common divisor of a and b is the greatest common divisor of m and a.

You will be able to find a proof in a number theory book that we will always reach a solution using this definition, so we can safely use this approach to design a recursive solution. If a problem has a recursive definition like this one, then it is relatively straightforward to design a recursive function to solve the problem. Our base case is the case in which *a* divides evenly into *b*. When we reach the base case, we return *a*. That is the greatest common divisor. Our recursive case occurs when a does not divide evenly into *b*. In that case, we must repeat the computation on a reduced version of the problem, which is to find the greatest common divisor of *m* (instead of *a*) and *a* (instead of *b*). Listing 9.3 is a recursive solution to the greatest common divisor problem.

```
1    """Find the greatest common divisor of two integers."""

2    def gcd(a, b):
3        """Compute and return the gcd of a and b
4           using Euclid's algorithm."""
5        remainder = b % a
6        if remainder == 0:
7            return a
8        else:
9            return gcd(remainder, a)

10   def main():
11       """Obtain two integers from the user and find the gcd."""
12       # Obtain two integers.
13       a = int(input("Please enter an integer: "))
14       b = int(input("Please enter another integer: "))

15       # Find the greatest common divisor.
16       greatest_divisor = gcd(abs(a), abs(b))
17       # Display the greatest common divisor.
18       print("The greatest common divisor of {} and {} is {}." \
                .format(a, b, greatest_divisor))

19   main()
```
Listing 9.3

In Listing 9.3, the recursive function gcd is found on lines 2–9. The base case, in which a divides evenly into b, is on lines 6 and 7. The recursive case, in which the problem is reduced and the function is called again, is on lines 8 and 9. Imagine the function is called with a value of 6 for a and 17 for b. On line 5, we compute the remainder of 17 % 6, which is 5. This is not 0, so we have the recursive case. Notice that this line of code is return gcd(remainder, a). We trust, when we write this code, that eventually gcd will compute the proper greatest common divisor and return it in a base case. So that is what we return from this recursive case—whatever ultimately gets returned from the base case when we reach it, some number of recursive calls deep. The second invocation of gcd has a value of 5 for a and 6 for b. When we compute 6 % 5, we obtain 1 for remainder. This is not 0, so the function is invoked again with 1 and 5. The remainder 5 % 1 is 0, so we finally reach the base case, and 1 is returned. This propagates up through the return statements on line 9 until it is returned from our initial call to the function and back to main. (The numbers 6 and 17 are relatively prime, which means they have no common divisor other than 1. It is a good idea to test the function on a relatively prime set of numbers and on numbers that have a greatest common divisor other than 1. What are some other good test cases?)

9.3.2   Solving a collection processing problem recursively

Collection objects, such as strings and lists, can be processed recursively. The base case is generally reached when you are down to a single element of the collection. Reducing a collection or list for the recursive case can be achieved through slicing, in which you use a smaller copy of the collection in each recursive call, or through indexing, in which you simply consider a smaller piece of the collection by moving an index. Because slicing uses memory and involves computation that is more involved than a simple increment, using an index is sometimes the preferable way to process a collection object.

Imagine that you have a string and you want to determine if the string is a palindrome. A palindrome is a string that reads the same forward and backward. Examples of palindromes include the following:

- ❖ Able was I, ere I saw Elba
- ❖ A man, a plan, a canal: Panama
- ❖ Wow

As you may remember, uppercase and lowercase letters are represented by different Unicode code points, and spaces, colons, and commas, of course, are also characters with values. If we want to check if these strings are palindromes, we would have to first reduce them to the same case and remove all nonalphabetic characters (giving us, e.g., "amanaplanacanalpanama" or "wow").

To write a recursive palindrome-detecting function, we should begin (as always) by defining the problem. To define the problem, it would be a good idea to look at different examples of palindromes. We have already noticed that punctuation, spacing, and capitalization do not interfere with human palindrome detection, but might make programmatic palindrome detection difficult. Our three palindrome examples happen to each contain an odd number of alphabetic characters. Is this typical? Checking over lists of palindromes (or imagining them), we find that "Anna" is a palindrome with an even number of alphabetic characters (proving they exist). We might also wish to confirm that we are looking only at alphabetic characters.

Once we understand that our palindrome detector will need to detect palindromes of both odd and even length, and that we will need to preprocess our string to remove punctuation and spacing and resolve all characters to the same case, then we might begin to think about solutions.

It is helpful, when thinking about collection processing tasks, to draw a picture that shows the collection with indices. Figure 9-13 is a representation of a palindrome string (after preprocessing) that has an even length, a palindrome string that has an odd length, and a string that is not a palindrome at all. Look the strings over and think about how you might determine if you have a palindrome.

To determine if you have a palindrome, you might consider the string from the outside in, compar-

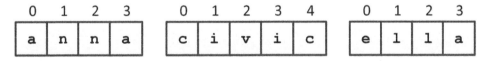

Figure 9-13   Two palindromes and a nonpalindrome string.

ing the first and last characters, and then the second and second-to-last characters, and so on, until you reach either the middle or middle two characters. Or you could determine the middle of the string and compare from the inside out. As we mentioned before, you can use indices, comparing, for example, with the middle string `"civic"`, the characters at indices 0 and 4, then 1 and 3, and then by default the character at index 2 matches itself, or you could reduce the string each time, comparing the first and last characters of `"civic"`, and then removing the first and last characters and comparing the first and last characters of `"ivi"`, and then again removing the first and last characters, and finally comparing `"v"`, which by default matches itself.

We will choose the more efficient solution, which does not involve changing the string itself, but rather the indices. We will also move from the outside in, as it also involves less computation because we do not need to find a middle point before we begin.

Having made those decisions based on the criteria of efficiency, we should think about how to solve this problem recursively. Before you look at the discussion and solution, think about the following questions:

- ❖ What is the base case, if we use indices to move from the outside in to the center of the string?
- ❖ Is the base case different for strings of odd and even length?
- ❖ What happens if we reach the base case?
- ❖ What happens if two characters do not match as in the first and last characters of "ella"?
- ❖ What parameters are passed to the recursive function?
- ❖ How do we reduce the problem each time?

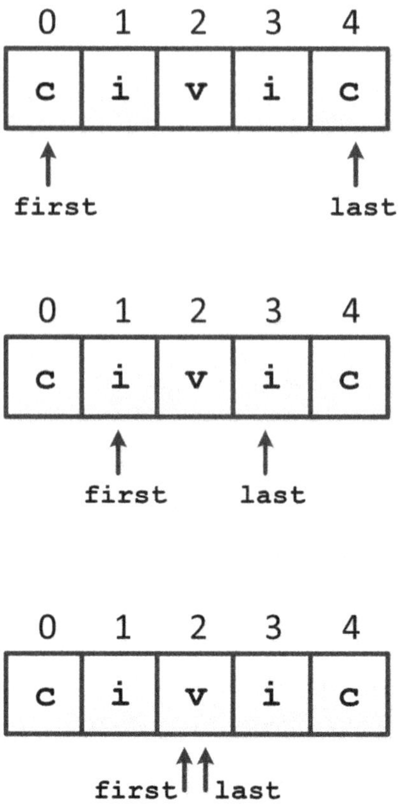

To develop the algorithm, it is helpful to draw the steps as a string is being processed. When you are writing the algorithm, you should do this for all of the different cases that the algorithm must process. To illustrate, we will do one example here, which is the odd-character-length palindrome string `"civic"`. Figure 9-14 shows the steps as this string is processed.

Figure 9-14 Processing an odd-length palindrome.

We are comparing two characters: those at the first and last positions. We must therefore maintain two indices into the list. In Figure 9-14, these are called `first` and `last`. If the characters at `first` and `last` are equal, then we increment `first` and decrement `last` and perform the comparison again. Reducing the problem, therefore, means incrementing our index that points to the first character and decrementing our index that points to the last character.

When `first` and `last` are equal (the indices, not the characters they reference), then we have reached the base case for an odd-length string. If we reach the base case, then we have a palindrome.

If we reach a comparison in which the characters at `first` and `last` do not match, then we do not have a palindrome and the algorithm is finished. This is also a base case.

Finally, if we are comparing an even-length string, then we might reach the point at which `last` is less than `first`. This is also a base case in which we have a palindrome. Listing 9.4 is a recursive solution to the palindrome-detection problem in which we reduce the problem by changing index values.

```
1    """Detect a palindrome recursively."""

2    def is_palindrome(string, first, last):
3        """Return True if string is a palindrome."""
4        # Base case string is a palindrome.
```

```
 5            if first >= last:
 6                return True
 7            # Base case string is not a palindrome.
 8            elif string[first] != string[last]:
 9                return False
10            # Recursive case.
11            else:
12                return is_palindrome(string, first+1, last-1)

13    def main():
14        """Obtain a string and determine if it's a palindrome."""
15        # Obtain the string.
16        string = input("Please enter a string: ")

17        # Determine if it's a palindrome and report.
18        if is_palindrome(string, 0, len(string)-1):
19            print("That is a palindrome!")
20        else:
21            print("That is not a palindrome.")

22    main()
```
Listing 9.4

Listing 9.4 does no preprocessing on the string the user enters, so if the user does not enter a string that is in the same case and without punctuation and spacing, then our palindrome detector will not work. We did not include any preprocessing so that we could focus on the recursive function `is_palindrome`. This function takes three parameters: the string that we are examining, and the indices `first` and `last`, which you should recognize from our planning diagram.

We first test for the two base cases. The test `first >= last` will take care of both odd and even base cases in which `string` is a palindrome. If we have an odd-length string, then the indices will be the same when we reach the middle of the string (as in our example string `"civic"`). If we have an even-length string, then our last comparison will be two characters next to each other (such as the two n's in the string `"anna"`), which will be our last recursive case, and then we will increment `first` and decrement `last`, and in the next invocation of the function, `first` will be larger than `last`. (If this is not clear, you should draw a planning diagram as in Figure 9-14 to satisfy yourself that this will be the case with an even-length string.)

We then test for the base case in which we do not have a palindrome. If the characters in `string` at indices `first` and `last` do not match, then `string` is not a palindrome, and we can return `False` from our function.

The final case is the recursive case. If we reach this else, then it means we are not at the middle of the string (or past it) and the characters at `first` and `last` match, so we must continue checking. We therefore reduce the problem by incrementing `first` and decrementing `last`, and we call the function again. Notice, again, that we return whatever the result of this function is, because eventually we will reach a base case that will return either `True` or `False`, and we want this to propagate up and out of the call chain and back to `main`.

If we test this program on palindromes of even and odd length, and nonpalindromes of even and odd length (as long as we enter them properly, as the program does no preprocessing), and a palindrome of length 1, then we find the program works.

Try this

❖ Write a recursive function to determine if a number is prime. A number is prime if it is divisible only by 1 and itself. You can determine if a number n is prime by dividing all numbers from 2 through $\sqrt{n}$ into n. If any of them divide evenly, then n is not prime. Note, also, that once you have determined that n is odd (not divisible by 2), you do not need to check if n is divisible by even numbers.

❖ Solve the palindrome problem by reducing the length of the string rather than changing the indices. Follow the same process to design the algorithm that we followed for the index-reducing solution.

❖ Write a recursive function to sum the numbers stored in a list.

References

Davis, M., & Suignard, M. (2014). *Unicode security considerations* (Unicode Technical Report No. 36). Retrieved from The Unicode Consortium website: http://www.unicode.org/reports/tr36/

Deswani, N., Kern, C., & Kesavan, A. (2007). *Foundations of security: What every programmer needs to know.* Berkeley, CA: Apress.

IEEE. (2008). *IEEE standard for floating-point arithmetic. (754–2008).* New York, NY: Institute of Electrical and Electronics Engineers.

Jones, E. M., & Glover, K. (1995). *The frustrations of Fra Mauro: Part I.* Retrieved from https://www.hq.nasa.gov/alsj/a13/a13.summary.html

Kuchling, A., Belopolsky, A., Brandle, G., & Melotti, E. (n.d.). *Unicode HOWTO.* Retrieved from https://docs.python.org/3/howto/unicode.html

Logo Foundation. (2015). *Logo history.* Retrieved from http://el.media.mit.edu/logo-foundation/what_is_logo/history.html

Index

CPSIA information can be obtained
at www.ICGtesting.com
Printed in the USA
BVHW09s0932020918
526196BV00009B/109/P